MAKING MAGIC: THE MARION MAHONY GRIFFIN STORY

Marion Mahony from New-York Historical Society. Magic of America collection. BV Griffin, Section 4: neg #71734.

Making Magic

The Marion Mahony Griffin Story

Glenda Korporaal

Making Magic: The Marion Mahony Griffin Story
Copyright © 2015 Glenda Korporaal

All rights are reserved. The material contained within this book is protected by copyright law, no part may be copied, reproduced, presented, stored, communicated or transmitted in any form by any means without prior written permission.

Published by Oranje Media. Sydney, Australia.

Typeset by BookPOD.
Cover design by Zoran Regan-Vieira.
Cover images: Marion Mahony Griffin with Frank Lloyd Wright (left) and Walter Burley Griffin (right). Below Marion's drawing of the View from the Summit of Mount Ainslie, National Archives of Australia. Marion's photo courtesy New-York Historical Society. Wright's photo courtesy Frank Lloyd Wright Trust.

A Catalogue-in-Publication is available from the National Library of Australia.

ISBN: 978-0-9924769-0-8 (paperback)

978-0-9924769-1-5 (e-book)

Contents

Prologue 1
Chapter 1. The Telegram 5
Chapter 2. The Fire 9
Chapter 3. Roaming Free 13
Chapter 4. Back to the City... 17
Chapter 5. The Architect 25
Chapter 6. The House and Studio of a Painter......................... 27
Chapter 7. Enter Frank 33
Chapter 8. Oak Park 41
Chapter 9. Our Little University 47
Chapter 10. Japanese Woodcuts 55
Chapter 11. Scandal 65
Chapter 12. Out on Her Own 73
Chapter 13. The Serpent's Wisdom... 83
Chapter 14. Madness When It Struck 91
Chapter 15. Proposals 95
Chapter 16. Fetching Up the Genii 103
Chapter 17. News from Australia 115
Chapter 18. Mason City 121
Chapter 19. The World Turned Upside Down 125
Chapter 20. Leaving Home... 131
Chapter 21. The Arrival 135
Chapter 22. Storm Clouds 139
Chapter 23. The Dogs of War 145
Chapter 24. Newman College... 153
Chapter 25. The Most Beautiful Café in the World 159
Chapter 26. The Case of Mr. Reeves.. 167

Chapter 27.	An Ancient Land	174
Chapter 28.	A Home of Their Own?	180
Chapter 29.	No Fences, No Boundaries	188
Chapter 30.	A Crystal Cave	194
Chapter 31.	Changes	198
Chapter 32.	A Community Develops	206
Chapter 33.	New Friends	210
Chapter 34.	Drawing Nature	218
Chapter 35.	1929	226
Chapter 36.	The Split	234
Chapter 37.	Fairies and Herons	240
Chapter 38.	A New Life	247
Chapter 39.	An Invitation from India	253
Chapter 40.	A New Land	257
Chapter 41.	Lucknow	263
Chapter 42.	Like an Indian, Mrs. Griffin Follows Her Man	273
Chapter 43.	The Exposition	279
Chapter 44.	His Eyes Never Left Mine	285
Chapter 45.	Going Home	289
Epilogue	Marion's Legacy	299
Endnotes		311
Bibliography		330
Acknowledgments		334
Index		339

Prologue

It was an increasing fascination with American architect Frank Lloyd Wright which brought my husband and me to Chicago in the summer of 2008.

But it was during the visit to Wright's home and studio in Oak Park that the full force of the Australian connection with Wright struck home. There, in a small studio a little like an old fashioned schoolroom with wooden desks, two people, who were to change Australian history, met. Walter Burley Griffin and Marion Mahony worked there almost side by side. Griffin's plan for Canberra, the capital city of Australia, changed Australian history. Like any Australian, I had heard of Griffin, but what about his wife? One of the first women architects in America. Who was she?

Having lived and worked as a journalist in both Canberra and Washington, DC, I was familiar with the issues of life in a planned capital city in both countries. The Griffins' role in designing the Australian capital, coming out of such a rich period of Chicago's history, and arriving in a new nation in its formative stages, kept drawing me into their story. Having been an Australian expatriate living in the United States for six years, I empathized with the ups and downs the Griffins faced as Americans living in Australia, operating between two developed Western societies so apparently similar, but with many cultural and historical differences.

In any study of "the Griffins," it is Walter who gets all the attention because of his acknowledged role as author of the plan for Canberra. But as I began to explore the couple's world, Marion became increasingly fascinating—her exact role maddeningly hard to pin down, made more difficult by her tendency to deliberately understate her own contribution. A closer look reveals an energetic, talented, creative, passionate woman whose role constantly changes. Her creativity is expressed in many forms—her architecture, her art and her writing—like a fierce light shining through a series of stained glass windows, filtered through different colors.

Reading a copy of *Drawing the Form of Nature*, the book about Marion's *Forest Portraits*, it is impossible not to fall in love with her striking, brilliant drawings of the Australian bush trees and be in awe of her detailed and passionate descriptions of my own country. A master wordsmith when she is at her best, and a sharp observer of the world around her, you can almost hear her heart beating as you read her words and take in her drawings.

Sitting in the Avery Library at Columbia University, I read through her correspondence to her architect friend William Purcell in the final years of her life. She so desperately wanted her "book" *The Magic of America* to be printed. It was not to be a book about architecture, but the story of the man she was so in love with and his vision for the world. But in trying to tell Walter's story, fragments of her own story emerge. As a writer, one longed to be able to sit down with Marion, help her order her thoughts and listen to her story and bring it together, go with her through her life.

Few people get the chance to view the stunning drawings she did of the plan for Canberra. But I was able to see them three times while they were lovingly displayed, laid out across several walls, as they were meant to be, in the National Archives of Australia in Canberra 2013. Each visit revealed some new delight of her masterful, intricate work, all conjured out of the Griffins' own imagination. Marion's artwork is not only masterful but somehow magical. Like the subtle, white paint strokes which she uses to provide glints of light in her drawings. Her brilliant artwork helped to make two men famous—first Frank Lloyd Wright and then her husband Walter Burley Griffin. It's now time that her own contribution is recognized.

Researching Marion's life was like going on a treasure hunt. She has left artistic jewels scattered around the world, hidden away in libraries and archives and private collections. She led a roving life with threads stretching from her family's ties with Abraham Lincoln and her own links with Frank Lloyd Wright, to Australia and India and back to America.

Her role as an expatriate for many years, and as a devoted wife, meant that the sum total of her most unusual life has never been pulled together into one story.

Making Magic seeks to tell Marion's story, the story of a remarkable, pioneering American woman who changed the history of my country.

Glenda Korporaal
Sydney, Australia, 2015.

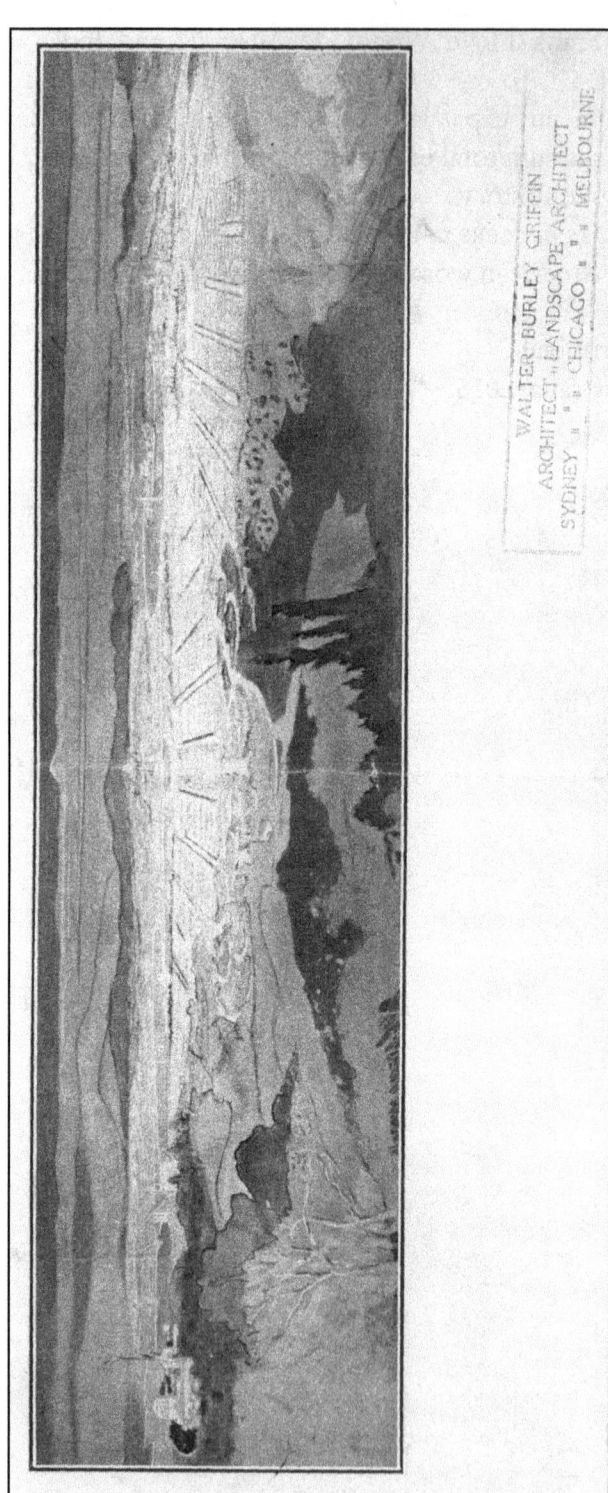

View from Summit of Mount Ainslie by Marion Mahony Griffin. 1911. Eric Nicholls collection. National Library of Australia.

ONE

THE TELEGRAM

Chicago: May 23, 1912. Marion Mahony was overjoyed when she heard the news. Her husband, Walter, had received a telegram from Australia. It was short, given its import.

> Your design awarded first premium.
> Minister for Home Affairs.[1]

The telegram had first come to their old office at the top of Steinway Hall in Chicago's Loop, and had taken a little time to reach them as they had recently moved to new offices at the top of the Monroe Building overlooking Lake Michigan. Their architectural practice was doing well, and their office in a new building had a far better view.

She was a woman in love with a handsome man five years her junior. She and Walter had been married less than a year. The marriage had been at her suggestion. Walter had been hurt in love once before and had no intention of forming a new romantic relationship with another woman. But Marion was a determined woman when she wanted to be. She had managed to convince him that he could not live with his parents forever, and it was time to wed. They had eloped, married in a courthouse in a small town in Indiana. And they now were one of the few husband and wife architectural teams in the world. Walter's plans, their plans, their entry in the competition to design the new capital city of Australia, thousands of miles away across the Pacific, had been awarded first prize.

Marion was a most unusual woman. A female architect in a man's world. Almost unheard of. The second woman ever to graduate with a degree from America's finest architectural school at Massachusetts Institute of Technology (MIT) in Boston, and the first woman in Illinois to pass the state's grueling architectural licensing exams. That made her the first woman in the United States to become a licensed architect. But Marion was always modest about her own achievements, and if she was aware of such milestones, she never paid them much heed. Now she was enjoying the acknowledgment from the world of her husband's great talents.

The work on the plan for the new Australian capital, as Walter admitted to someone later, was as much hers as his. Walter, Marion, and everyone in their office had worked hard on the plans in the cold months toward the end of 1911. They had packed the drawings into a long wooden box. On a cold night in December, they called a taxi to collect them. The taxi barely met the last train to make the last boat for Australia to meet the competition deadline at the end of January. Marion had been worried it wouldn't make it in time, but Walter had insisted that if the people of Australia really wanted a good plan for their new capital, they would be prepared to accept a late entry.

Their months of work on the drawings, all their years of collective experience in architecture, landscaping, city planning, and drawing, had come together into one magnificent idea, expressed in a collection of drawings superbly rendered by Marion and their loyal staff members. They had designed a new capital city for the world's newest democracy.

She looked at her husband expectantly as he studied the telegram. He was a man of careful words. "Ah, then," he said, "I shan't be able to see a better plan than mine."[2]

Marion agreed. She had no desire for any personal accolades but she knew the work they had produced was a masterpiece. She had developed her own unique style of drawing, inspired by the Japanese prints in the offices of her old employer, Frank Lloyd Wright, which she brought to her work on the plans for the Australian capital. Copies of the plans, painstakingly done by Marion in black ink on silk, were proudly on display in their new offices. They were the pinnacle of her skills as an artist as well as an architect.

She had been a loyal assistant of Wright's for almost 15 years, most of them in the studio next to his home in Oak Park, a middle-class suburb west of Chicago. Some said later she may have been a little in love with him. He had just published a portfolio of his work in Germany, but more than half of the actual drawings had come from her hand. Her work had helped make Wright famous in Europe as well as America, but he had betrayed his family and had ignored her.

Now she was making another man even more famous. Her beloved husband, with the help of her drawings, had won an international accolade, winning a competition against some of the leading architects of the world.

The plans, of course, did not have Marion's signature spidery monogram, MMG, hidden away in a corner among the bushes, as she occasionally did on the long scroll-like drawings she did for their architectural plans. But to anyone who knew her work, her mark was indelibly imprinted on them. Marion was at the peak of her career. She had summoned all her architectural and artistic skills to produce the stunning drawings that had been sent to Australia. Indeed, had she not pressured her new husband the year before, he would never have entered the competition.

The prize was worth more than $8,000. It was a handy sum of money for the newlyweds. It was money, they decided, they would put toward the home they planned to build together in the north of Chicago, not too far from where Marion grew up.

The telegram from Australia was maddeningly enigmatic. It did not say what would flow from Walter winning the prize. Surely the government of Australia would at least want to talk to the man who had designed their new capital city.

Walter sent an equally short cable in reply, eager to make contact with the government in Australia.

> Thanks for notifications. Honor appreciated.[3]

The news spread quickly. *The New York Times* wanted to speak to her husband as well as the local press. And there was a call from two Australian women living in Chicago who were eager to meet him and excited to learn that someone from the city had designed their country's new capital city.

The people of Chicago, Marion knew, were big dreamers. Its brilliant architects were experts at it. Only a few years ago, Daniel Burnham, one of the most famous architects in the city, had declared:

> Make no little plans, they have no magic to stir men's blood. ... Make big plans, aim high in hope and work, remembering that a noble, logical diagram once recorded will never die, but long after we are gone will be a living thing, asserting itself with ever growing insistence.[4]

Marion had spent hours imagining what the Australian capital city they had fashioned would look like, with the hills in the background and its own lake in the middle. She had drawn a stunning view of their dream city, their ideal city, as seen from a mountaintop, washed in purple, as if someone were looking down at the city in moonlight. It was the same time of the day that she had first seen Rome and Venice when she had visited some of the great cities in Europe years before with her favorite brother, Gerald.

Would she ever see this grand city she had imagined so many times? The Griffins had woven their own magic in the design for this new Australian capital, but what did this prize mean for them? What would the future hold?

Two

The Fire

The year of Marion Mahony's birth, 1871, was to be one that was forever seared into the pages of Chicago history.

When Marion was born, Chicago was already the third largest city in America, after New York and Philadelphia, with about 300,000 residents of varying fortune. Spread along the western banks of Lake Michigan, from north to south, it had become the great metropolis of the Midwest of America. It was first discovered 200 years before by Europeans coming down from the North. Canadian Louis Jolliett and French-born Jacques Marquette had explored the area in the 17th century, seeking to trade with the Indians. In a country rebuilding itself after the horrors of the Civil War, which had mercifully come to an end six years before, Chicago was one of the fastest growing cities in the Western world, a commercial center in the middle of vast fertile prairies, a city of trade and industry as America's citizens relentlessly pushed westward.

Marion's father, Jeremiah Mahony, known to his friends as Jere, had come to Chicago from Ireland with his family when he was a young boy, escaping the great potato famine and hoping for a better life. Three years before, on September 3, 1868, Jere had married Clara Perkins, a fellow teacher he had met in Chicago. The next year, in November 1869, they had their first child, a boy named Jerome. Their next child was a girl they called Marion who was born on February 14, in the last month of winter, just when Chicago citizens were looking forward to the spring. Clara named her daughter after her brother's wife, Marion, whose family had once been prosperous property owners in Chicago. Born in Tremont, in southern Illinois, Clara had become close to Marion Perkins after she had moved to Chicago to work as a teacher. They were both very strong women, hard workers, who shared the same Unitarian faith, with firm views on the importance of family, community and social justice.

The summer of 1871 brought a return of the drought that had gripped most of the great Mississippi Valley, which stretched from just below the Canadian border to the Gulf of Mexico. Only an inch of rain fell from July to October. By October, when Marion was eight months old, Chicago was a tinderbox, with dry autumn leaves scattered on the ground adding to the fuel waiting for a spark.

Baby Marion would have been asleep in her crib when the city's fire alarm rang at 9:30 p.m. on Sunday evening October 8, alerting citizens to the danger of yet another blaze. The day had been unbearably hot, with temperatures reaching 85 degrees, and the wind blowing from the south-southwest at around 20 miles an hour.

The fire began on the west side of the city and raged through the overcrowded immigrant neighborhoods. Some would say later that it was caused by a cow kicking over a lantern in a barn owned by Mrs. Catherine O'Leary. The flames were fueled by the strong winds.

There was much confusion. The city's firefighters were initially sent in the wrong direction, giving the fire time to grow. The fire crossed the southern branch of the Chicago River, engulfing the ships lining the river, the coal and timber yards, and then the city's wooden buildings and wooden planks along its streets. The flames tore through the central business district, burning the city hall, hotels, and department stores and raged northward. They jumped the main part of the river, burning the grand mansions of Michigan Avenue, heading toward the city's wealthier north side, "like a wild beast, intent on destroying ... the enemy."[1]

Jere and Clara grabbed their two young children. They put baby Marion in a clothes basket and fled the house, her brother Jerome, almost two, keeping up as best he could. The city's mayor called on surrounding areas for help, but the fire continued raging. The flames could be seen from 40 miles around. There was some relief late on Monday night when a light rain fell, easing the temperature. By early Tuesday, the fire was exhausted and burned itself out. But that was only the beginning of the problem. The city was in a daze, a smoldering rubble. The fire had destroyed an area four miles long and almost a mile wide. It was, as people would say later, the first peacetime destruction of an entire city.

When the smoke cleared, 125 bodies were recovered from the city's charred remains, but some said the death toll could have been as high as 300. Almost 20,000 buildings were destroyed and around 100,000 people, a third of the city's population, were left homeless. Most of the center of the city had been destroyed.

Jere hired a vehicle to take Clara around the burned-out areas. They saw people walking around the city in a daze, with what few belongings they had managed to retrieve from the debris. Clara saw one woman with glazed eyes walking around carrying a pan of milk. The Mahonys knew it was no place to bring up a young family.

They took their two young children northward, along Lake Michigan, to a place called Hubbard Woods, where they had friends involved in the Unitarian Church. Clara was a Unitarian, and Jere was a Catholic. They were, as he would say, "the only two logical positions to take."[2] When it came to religion, it was Clara's views that prevailed, and her church that provided the broader social connection for the family.

Marion was too young to remember the fire, but Chicago's tragedy was to prove a boon for her and her family. It provided the setting for a very different kind of life that shaped her soul. Hubbard Woods, as Marion would often recall later, was "the loveliest spot you could imagine."[3] Instead of growing up in a dirty, crowded city, she grew up in a vast natural playground, exploring the woods and forests, her territory bound by Lake Michigan on the east and rivers on the west. As she wrote later:

> Our home was at the head of a lovely ravine. A half-mile walk through the beautiful forest to the east took us to the shores of Lake Michigan with a bluff 50 feet high and a wide sandy beach, to the west, half a mile through scrub to the marvelous Skokie, head waters of the Chicago River, stretching for endless miles.[4]

A paradise on earth.

Marion's Family Ties

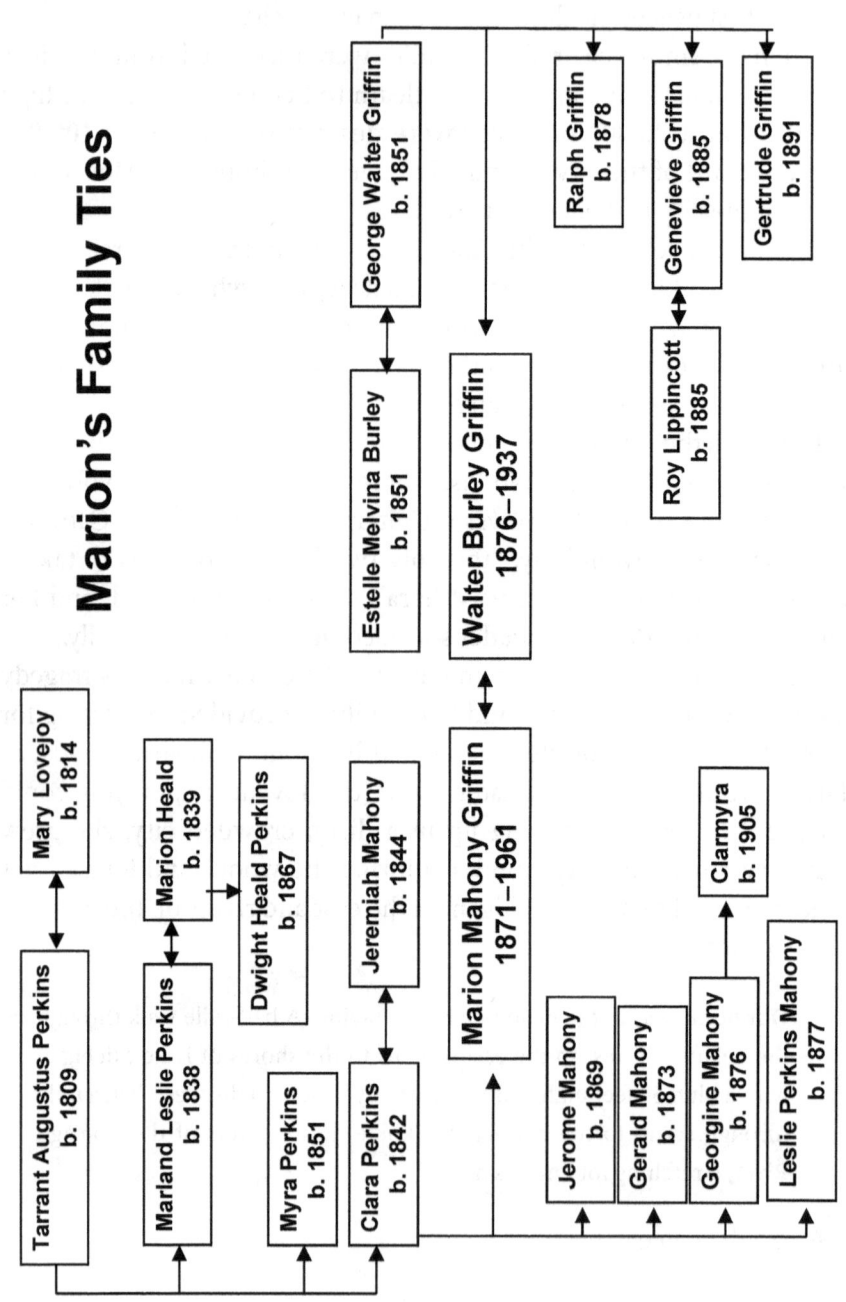

Three

Roaming Free

Hubbard Woods was away from the big city trying to rebuild from the fire, but it was close to the railway line going south to Chicago. The Mahonys' home was not too far from the railway station where Jere would catch the train to his work as a teacher in Chicago each day.

The family soon expanded. Marion and Jerome, and their younger siblings Gerald, Georgine, and Leslie, had the freedom to roam the countryside. Their parents encouraged them to be independent and never seemed to worry too much where they were. When the children got older, they hired an Irish nanny so that Clara could also work in Chicago.

Young Marion developed a fierce love of the outdoors and the natural environment. She hated being indoors. It made her ill, she would tell people. She loved to explore the woods and the rivers with her older cousin, Dwight Perkins, and her brothers. The children would think nothing of the one-mile walk to the one-room schoolhouse at Winnetka.

The Mahony family were known as "May-o-nee," not by the traditional Irish pronunciation "Mah-honee." The emphasis was changed when Jere's high school teacher in Chicago mispronounced it, as he battled to cope with the foreign names of the students whose families came from so many different European countries.

Marion became an astute observer of the natural world. She loved to watch the color of the leaves change with each new season. In the autumn, there were the "wild hickory nuts, black walnuts and butternuts and hazelnuts and the berries—raspberries, black berries, blue berries, June berries, wild grapes and crab apples."[1] In the winter, Jere and Clara would take their children walking through the woods to the lake and stand on top of the cliff, watching the waves pile up below them on the sand "battering and foaming up the bluff itself."[2] There would be ice hills and caverns and wintergreen berries. In the early spring, the children would gather purple flowers called hepaticas from under the snow. In the summer, the children loved to swim in the lake.

The Mahonys were a sociable family. On the weekends, the house was open to anyone who wanted to visit. Friends came from the city to enjoy the natural paradise. To the visitors, one thing was obvious—Jere Mahony's eldest daughter was a tomboy.

Next to the Mahony home was a giant tree whose branches did not start until above the roof of the two-story house. On the weekends, when the guests would come up from the city, Marion loved to show off. People would gather on the veranda and watch her climb, barefooted, like a monkey up the tree. The young boys from the city would try, but they could not reach the branches. Everyone would tease them because they couldn't do it, and Marion would take it all in with satisfaction. She loved to look down from her perch at the top of the tree. It was her own special bird's-eye view of the world.

Marion's cousin Dwight was like another member of their family. His father, Leslie, Clara's older brother, battled ill health from his time fighting in the Civil War for his hero, Abraham Lincoln. He eventually went home to be cared for by his parents, Marion's grandparents, at their home in Tremont. His father, Augustus Perkins, was a doctor and could give him the attention he needed while Leslie's wife, Marion, had to stay in Chicago working to support her son and her own family who had fallen on hard financial times after one of the city's many property busts. After the Mahonys moved to Hubbard Woods, Dwight and his mother spent time there, renting some rooms over the railway station. Clara was only too happy to have her nephew as part of the extended Mahony brood, helping her dear sister-in-law Marion whose once prosperous life had become very tough.

Younger Marion loved playing with the boys, but she adored her father. He was, Marion recalled proudly, "a poet, journalist and educator."[3] When he came home each night, she would climb onto his lap and listen to him recount the day's events. He was a principal of a junior school in Chicago and often wrote articles for the newspapers. To his young daughter, he was a writer of poetry and a weaver of dreams, a teller of tales who could have everyone spellbound.

Jere loved to talk. He had, as Marion described it, "the reputation of being the best slinger of the King's English in the city. ... He would sit quietly of an evening and then suddenly take the floor and the whole group would be aflame."[4]

He would often write poems, which Marion loved to hear him read. She particularly loved one poem, "The Legend of the Canyon," about a young Indian brave whose love had tragically died. Led by "the Great Good Spirit," the Indian went roaming, "towards the southland," searching for his love. The Spirit led him to the Colorado River, where the Indian saw "diamond drops [of water] speeding down a million rippling rills" and watched the "headlong rushing cascades feeding from liquid hoard of snow-clad hills." There he was comforted by "the voices of the river" and its echoing sounds in the canyon, which spoke "forever at the bidding of His word."[5]

Marion Mahony with Echo Simmons. M. J. Steffens Atelier, Chicago. Circa 1883–1891. New-York Historical Society. Magic of America collection. BV Griffin, Marion Mahony, section 4: neg#80943d.

Four

Back to the City

In the summer of 1881, a decade after they moved to Hubbard Woods, the family prepared for another weekend party.[1] Marion Mahony could not have been happier with her life. She was growing up in a carefree, natural environment, doing as she pleased. But that paradise was to be taken away from her.

Clara Mahony cleaned up the house, oiling the floors with rags that she put back in the attic. The rags must have smoldered in the top room, catching fire from the heat beating down on the roof. The wooden house caught fire in the middle of the night, and everyone ran outside watching it burn to the ground. The family had to pack up again and move back to Chicago. Back to the city, the crowds, the industrial grime. The city had already rebuilt itself at a frantic, chaotic pace and continued to grow.

It was a big shock for the feisty 10-year-old. However, Marion kept up her tomboy ways. Her new home had a pocket handkerchief backyard, and the streets were the only real place to play. Clara worried about her elder daughter. Her father was not well. Her younger sister, Myra, was living at home but she was often away from home in her job as a music teacher. Her aging mother could benefit from some assistance around the house. Marion, it was decided, would go to live with her aunt and grandparents for a while to help out.

Myra brought Marion to the Perkins' family home in Tremont. Marion's grandfather was very ill. She found her grandmother "stately" but soon struck up a strong friendship with her kindly aunt. Myra was 30—almost 10 years younger than Marion's mother. Myra rode her horse, Lucy, around the countryside giving music lessons. Marion went to the local school. She loved the evenings when Myra was home, and her aunt would teach her to play the piano. Living in a much smaller town than Chicago allowed Marion to enjoy the outdoors and continue her tomboy ways. She particularly loved sliding on the ice in winter, provoking the disapproval of her grandmother for wearing out her shoes. Spending time with her grandparents gave Marion a chance to learn more about her family background.

They had been adventurers in their early days. Tarrant Augustus Perkins and Mary Lovejoy were married in New Hampshire in 1835, and like so many young people of their time, they decided to venture west and make a new life. Three decades before, in 1803, President Thomas Jefferson had doubled the size of the territory under the United States administration with the Louisiana Purchase from the French government. Almost overnight, a wide sweep of territory from Canada, west of the states of Wisconsin and Illinois and down to the Gulf of Mexico, became part of the United States, opening up vast new lands for exploration and settlement.

The newly wed Perkins reached Illinois on a canal boat with an odd assortment of fellow adventurers and others who had set out for the West, not quite knowing what they would find when they got there.

As Marion's mother wrote later:

> What a strange combination of circumstances it was ... that brought together that little colony from New England, England, the South, Canada and the West Indies and planted them in Tazewell County, Illinois. In the canal boat that carried its precious load of venturesome dreamers were the young doctor, Augustus Perkins, and his bride, Mary, the English scholar, the Kentucky Colonel, the dashing young teacher Colonel James with his wife and beautiful daughter and young son, Quaker Wilson and his wife, Doctor's brother and wife, a German tinner, two sea captains with families, a banker and, in a short time members of father's and mother's families and other interesting people. On that boat was also a young peasant girl quiet and watchful who on the boat's stopping ran to the wharf and was going to get off when the captain told her this was Ashton. "Ashton," she said, "I thought it was Corpus Christi and here it is this damned place."[2]

Ashton was in the north of the state. The party traveled south to Chicago, where they found what they felt was a sordid little settlement in a muddy swamp. They kept traveling south to the Illinois River Valley, settling in Tremont, a small town 60 miles north of Springfield, a growing city which was soon to become the Illinois state capital. When they arrived, they could see "great prairies of waving grass, far from any river, sea-coast or mountains to charm the eye or to give promise of a great city rising out of that ocean of grass."[3]

The town of Tremont had become the seat of Tazewell County the year after the Perkins were married.[4] The city built a striking courthouse in the town square soon after they arrived. The Perkins built their home on a hill overlooking the square, surrounded by a garden and maple trees. Augustus became a respected doctor in the town. He traveled the area on horseback, delivering most of the babies for miles around and boasted that he had never lost a child. At a time when death in childbirth was all too common, it was a proud record indeed. Their first son, Marland Leslie Perkins, had arrived in 1838. Marion's mother, Clara, was born in 1842, and Myra, the youngest, arrived in 1851.

One of the highlights of Augustus's life, and that of most of the men in Tremont, was the visits by the traveling judge and lawyers who would come when the court was in session. The men gathered in the tavern and talked into the night. The best storyteller was a lawyer with little formal education, a tall dark man with a beard called Abraham Lincoln. Lincoln and Augustus were both born in 1809. Both had moved to Illinois from the east, Perkins from New Hampshire and Lincoln from Kentucky via Indiana. The Perkins were hospitable people with many of the townspeople gathering in their home every Sunday after church. Lincoln was a frequent visitor.

One Sunday morning, he knocked on the door of their house to find only Clara at home looking after Myra. He took them both to church with him and brought them home, very few words passing between them. To Clara, he was a tall man with a beard, but her older brother Leslie wanted to become a lawyer like Lincoln. Both father and son watched Lincoln's rise in politics with pride and admiration and shared his passionate ideals.

Leslie went to study law in Chicago, where he met his future wife, Marion Heald, at church. Lincoln provided one of the references he needed to set up a practice in the city. The Perkins were proud when Lincoln was elected president in 1860, but soon after he was sworn in, the Civil War broke out and both Augustus and his son went off to war. Clara had studied to become a teacher and soon she, too, wanted to move to Chicago like her brother. She applied to be assigned to one of the city's public schools and moved to Chicago where she met Jere Mahony.

Marion was arriving in Tremont 20 years after her grandfather had gone away to Virginia to help in the Civil War as a brigade surgeon. Her uncle Leslie had never recovered from the injuries he had suffered during the war and had already passed away. Now Augustus, too, was ailing fast. Marion was just settling into her new life when her grandfather passed away, and she was sent back home to her family in Chicago.

When she arrived home, Marion was probably still too young to see how her father was changing. It was well-known that he would take a mixture of laudanum and alcohol on occasions for pain relief. Sometime in the summer of 1882, Jere passed away. He was 39 and Marion was only 11. Marion would always tell people he died of a heart attack, but others believed it was suicide. In those days, it was common for people to take laudanum, and Jere may have made a mistake with the dosage. Maybe it was an accident, or maybe the strain of dealing with the unruly Mahony brood was too much for him. Whatever the reason, his death meant that Clara was now a widow with five children to bring up on her own. Her youngest, Leslie, was only four years old. The charming Irishman who had been so much a part of Marion's life had left her without any explanation at all.

Clara was a resilient woman; she had to be. Like so many other women of Chicago at the time, including her widowed sister-in-law Marion Perkins, she now had to fend for her family as best she could. But the tough times of Chicago also brought forth some feisty women with a strong social conscience. One of those was Mrs. Ella Flagg Young, the principal of the school the Mahony children attended.

One day, not long after Jere had died, there was a knock at the door of the Mahony home. Mrs. Young had a box in her hands. Clara invited her in and set the box down on the big mahogany dining table.

"It feels as if it were filled with gold," Clara said.[5]

Marion watched in anticipation as her mother opened it. It was filled with money, which had been collected by the teachers at the school. Marion swelled with pride. The gift, she believed, only served to show how much her father was loved by all.

Mrs. Young was influential within the Chicago school system and helped Clara study for the Chicago School Board Examination to become a primary school principal. This would give her more income than her job as a teacher. Clara passed and was given charge of the Komensky School in a working-class district south of the city, populated by migrants from Bohemia in central Europe. Many of her students arrived speaking no English. As Marion recalled later, her mother carried on her dual responsibilities as chief breadwinner and head of the household with no indication of the burden involved.

Soon after, Grandmother Perkins and Aunt Myra moved to Chicago to live with the Mahony family and help look after the children. There were now eight people living in the home. Marion found herself in a very matriarchal household, full of strong-minded women. She thrived on the female company. Her kindly aunt provided her with an intellectual companionship that she did not have with many other people of her age and their piano lessons resumed.

The expanded Mahony household was a busy one. Aunt Myra gave piano lessons to the local children. Clara worked all week at her school and earned extra money by giving art lessons on Saturday afternoons.

In the evenings, Aunt Myra played the piano. There would be songs and poetry readings, with Jere's lyrical Irish spirit living on in the household. As people would say later, Clara's home was not a dwelling but a community. Marion loved it, but the chaos of the Mahony household sometimes became too much for some other members of the family.

One day, Marion was at home playing the piano, when her younger brother, Gerald, asked her to stop. She refused. Marion had long black hair tied in braids down her back. Furious, Gerald lifted her up by her braids and pulled her across the room. He dragged the screaming Marion to the front door to throw her outside. Opening the door, they faced a young girl who had arrived, a prospective student ready for a lesson. The horrified girl fled, never to be seen again.[6]

Clara coped well with her circumstances but, at times, the tension of being a single mother to a brood of five strong-minded children showed, particularly when it came to Marion. In the winter, Marion would think nothing of hitching her sled to a passing wagon to get a ride, like the boys did. One day, she was playing hopscotch outside with the neighborhood children when her mother called her in. Clara had decided that Marion was too much of a tomboy. She felt it was time Marion developed some ladylike ways. She told Marion she was getting too big to play in the streets and needed to grow up. Marion was surprised at first, and then angry.

She fumed inside. "My soul was filled with astonishment and rage," she recalled later.[7] She was determined that growing up would not mean she had to change her ways. She would play hopscotch and climb trees even when she was a grown woman. No one would stop her.

But there were always the summers, which gave the Mahony children the chance to escape to Hubbard Woods. There were some vacant homes in the area that had been built near their old house, awaiting sale. They would spend the long summer holidays exploring the places where they had grown up, happily sleeping on the floor of an empty house. But each year they came, there were fewer vacant houses, and Marion was sad to see how the area was becoming more developed.

She fervently wished the family could move back to Hubbard Woods again. The move to Chicago only served to sharpen her awareness of the beauty of the natural environment and of the plants and trees around them. It was in the outdoors, roaming free, where she always felt the happiest.

The summers also gave Marion a chance to catch up with one of her friends from Hubbard Woods, Echo Simmons. Marion and Echo had become great friends, keeping up their ties even when Marion was back in Chicago. Living in the city, Marion was still painfully shy. If she saw someone she knew coming down the street, she would often walk around the corner to avoid them out of sheer awkwardness. But she would be overjoyed when Echo would make the long trip from Hubbard Woods to their home in Chicago to see her, sometimes walking the 20 miles on her own.

The girls would discuss the works of Herbert Spencer and Charles Darwin. They eagerly absorbed Darwin's Theory of Evolution, which was challenging the views of many in the established churches of the day, bolstered by fellow thinkers such as Spencer who developed the concept of the "survival of the fittest." Instead of the belief that God had created man in His own image, here were radical new ideas about the evolution of the human species. The Unitarian Church, which her family was involved with, emphasized a strong sense of community and a deep appreciation of nature. But, as she grew up, Marion's readings expanded her thinking, adding a new intellectual dimension to her understanding of the world.

Marion worked hard at school and thought about what she would do with her life. Although her parents had been teachers and they had many friends who were teachers, Marion, as usual, had other ideas. As she reflected later, "I guess I never was a conformist."[8]

Dwight H. Perkins. *The Forest Preserves of Cook County*. 1921. Pg 87. Richard J. Daley Library. University of Illinois at Chicago.

Five

The Architect

It has never been recorded what prompted Marion to become an architect, but it was probably the inspiration from Dwight Perkins.

He was sent out to work at an early age by his widowed mother. He was only 12 when he got a job helping deliver the payroll at the Union Stockyards, the giant meat slaughtering complex in a rough part of town not too far from his home.[1] But his mother soon realized it was a dangerous job, and he found a job in an architectural firm in the city. Chicago was becoming a magnet for architects. It had quickly rebuilt itself after the fire and then, in the 1880s, when Marion returned to live in the city, it began to rebuild itself again as its engineers learned how to build higher structures on the soggy soil. The buildings were so tall that people called them skyscrapers. As one observer recalled: "In 1880 ... a new generation of architects was about to begin rebuilding again in the recently restored downtown area, creating in a little over a decade the world's first vertical city."[2]

Dwight believed architecture was a noble career, which would allow him to help the less fortunate people of the city, people he had seen firsthand living near the Union Stockyards.[3] He wanted to build schools with plenty of places for children to play and suburbs with lots of parks. Supporting her son and her own parents, who had also fallen on hard financial times, Dwight's mother was always short of money. But she retained her connections with some of the wealthier people in the city who had known her family when it had seen better days. Some of her friends urged Dwight to get formal qualifications in architecture. The

University of Illinois had been offering architectural degrees since 1868, but Dwight's supporters all urged him to go to MIT in Boston.

Founded in 1865, it was the first school of architecture in the country. Its teachings were based on the classical French school of architecture, École des Beaux-Arts. MIT, he was told, (or the "Boston Tech" as it was informally described) was the best in the country. One of his mother's friends, a wealthy widow, offered to lend him the money for his studies. His mother's cousin, another wealthy widow, Mary Jane Wilmarth, taught him the French he needed to qualify.

Marion was 17 when Dwight returned from his studies in Boston in 1888. Things were changing at the university. The MIT was now accepting women students in its architectural faculty. The first woman to graduate from its two-year program, Anne Graham Rockfellow, had finished the year before, and there was talk of other women applying for the course. The Perkins and Mahony families were close, and it was clear that Dwight's passion for architecture, at a time when there was an abundance of new building work going on in Chicago, made a profound impression on Marion. She loved drawing and having a mother who taught art had helped hone her own artistic skills. If cousin Dwight could go to MIT and be an architect, then so could she.

Marion did not have the money to go to MIT either, but her family was friendly with the wealthy Wilmarths through their ties with Marion Perkins. Marion Mahony was friendly with Mrs. Wilmarth's youngest daughter, Anna, who was two years younger than her. In 1885, Anna's father died, leaving his family with considerable wealth including extensive land holdings in Chicago. Mary Wilmarth became increasingly active in social causes in the city, including the establishment of Hull House, a settlement house in the slums founded by Jane Addams to help the poor people of the city. Inspired by her mother's commitment to social work, young Anna generously offered to help her friend Marion go to MIT with the money from her inheritance. And Mrs. Wilmarth coached her in French for her entry examination, just as she had done for Marion's cousin Dwight.[4]

In the fall of 1890, Marion Mahony was off to Boston. She knew she could never repay her dear friend Anna. All she could do was become the best architect she possibly could.

Six

The House and Studio of a Painter

Marion had lived in Tremont with her aunt and grandparents, but going to Boston was the first time she had lived away from family. To her surprise, she found that, as the only person at the university from the Midwest, she was regarded as an oddity. But she soon got to know people.

Two weeks after she arrived, one young woman remarked to her, "I don't see that you are so different from other folk." Marion laughed. Had the woman expected her to arrive with feathers in her hair, like an Indian? The girl laughed back, admitting that probably was what she had expected.[1]

Marion cut a striking figure around Boston. All eyes would turn on the tall woman with long black hair when she got on the streetcar carrying her big drafting board and T-square. She threw herself into her new life. Determined to improve her drawing skills, she also sought out extra lessons from a couple in Boston. Her mother had been a passionate teacher of art, but now that Marion was studying to be an architect, she wanted to take her artistic skills to another level.

MIT's architecture faculty was founded on strict Beaux-Arts principles. Students were told to think of a building as a work of art and an object of artistic design. Marion scored well in her subjects of Mechanical Drawing, Shades and Shadows, Pen and Ink, Trigonometry, and Perspective and Stereotomy.[2] But her Midwestern sensibilities rebelled against the classical architectural style taught at MIT. It was very different from the type of architecture in Chicago, where more modern functional buildings were being erected. She narrowly failed her second-year design course at her first attempt but managed to continue.

There were few women on the campus in any field, but those who were there formed close bonds. As she grew up, Marion lost her childhood shyness. She made friends with some of them, enjoying the company of smart young women like herself who had made it to the Tech. Harriett Gallup, who studied biochemistry, and Sarah Hall, who studied physics, were in her year. She also became friendly with another younger woman, Marion Lincoln Lewis, who studied architecture two years behind her. The two of them would discuss various philosophies including Immanuel Kant's *Critique of Pure Reason*.

Marion took advantage of many extracurricular activities on the campus. She joined the French class, where she was the only woman, and was delighted to learn there were many outlets for her love of acting. She was involved in many plays. In her final year, she played the lead role of La Comtesse in *L'Amour de L'Art*. In another play, she took great delight in dressing up as a man. As she told her friends later, with considerable amusement, when she graduated she was voted "the handsomest man in my class."[3]

For her final year, she had to do a thesis. But she rebelled against what was expected of her. As she saw it, she was expected to go to the library and copy out the design of some grand classical-style building. There had only been one woman before her who graduated with a four-year architectural degree from MIT—Sophia Hayden. She had designed a grand building in the Beaux-Arts style for her thesis. Why couldn't Marion?

The head of design, Professor Constant-Désiré Despradelle, had recently arrived from Paris. Marion learned much from him but disagreed with his direction on her thesis. She only wanted to design houses, not buildings like everyone else. Designing houses appealed to her artistic skills, her love of nature and the outdoors, and her sense of family and community. Unlike others who were there to become architects, she was not interested in the complex engineering challenges of buildings.

Professor Despradelle did not know what to make of this independent-minded young woman from Chicago. The word had gotten around about the fate of Sophia Hayden. Despite the fact that there were plenty of architectural firms in Boston, Hayden was unable to find a job as an architect after her graduation and had to work as a teacher. In 1891, she entered a competition to design the Women's Building for the World's Columbian Exposition, which was to take place in Chicago in 1893.

She designed a three-story white Italian Renaissance-style building with arches and columned terraces. She only received $1,000 for her design, one-tenth of what the male architects had received for their winning designs for buildings for the Exposition, but she had eagerly accepted the prize. But she became upset when she found out her elegant classical building was going to be cluttered with an assortment of ornaments and furniture supplied by the leading women of the city, led by rich socialite Bertha Palmer. Hayden appealed to the architect of the fair, Daniel Burnham, for support. The diplomatic Burnham urged her to seek a compromise with Mrs. Palmer but Hayden refused, bursting into tears and collapsing. She was taken to the hospital in an ambulance and was said to have had a "severe breakdown with a violent attack of high nervous excitement of the brain."[4] The incident only served to reinforce the view of many at the time that women were not emotionally capable of working in the architectural profession.

Many of the young men in Marion's course did not know what to make of her either. She was clearly a bright student with a sharp mind and a strong personality. At one point, a cartoon of Marion circulated among the class. It showed her as a tall figure walking down the street with her toes turned out. Her long black hair was straight down her back, a band of cloth tied around her head, which was surrounded by a halo. She looked like an Indian. There were brass bands on both sides of the street, "blowing their heads off."[5] She was walking, as Professor Despradelle had quipped, toward the "temple of fame." Marion knew about the cartoon, and the sharp comments about her ambition and her Western background by some of the young men at the Tech, but she was not worried. She had grown up with boys and took it all in stride.

She was fond of her head of department, Mr. Chamberlain, one of the few people who she felt understood her and realized the struggle going on inside her. As she wrote later, he understood her "natural bent was toward independence," and the difficulty, the sheer "difficulty of suppressing revolution in a woman."[6]

But Marion's thesis proved a real problem for her. She was determined to do things her way. In the end, a compromise was reached. It would be a house, but it would be a house with a studio attached. As she explained in her thesis, *The House and Studio of a Painter*, the building was being designed for an artist who was "very fashionable." He was a public man who entertained elegantly dressed ladies and gentlemen in his grand two-story house on a corner block.

There was a courtyard between the house and the studio. The studio was attached to the house by a long corridor along the courtyard, with a door in the middle where clients could enter to go to the studio. The studio was a large building with floor-to-ceiling glass at the front, which allowed light to flood inside. There was a private studio for the artist to paint portraits of the fashionable ladies and gentlemen who came to sit for him. There was another room for his assistants and a space to store his canvasses.[7]

When it was done, Marion handed in her thesis with some trepidation. She was relieved to learn that not only had she passed, but also the professor had actually praised her design.

Marion and her girlfriends at MIT had formed a group called the Robins and they promised to stay in touch. With spring approaching, Marion couldn't wait to get back home to Chicago.

It was a time when many architectural firms would not accept women as draftsmen, and women architects were rare. But Marion, of course, had Dwight to smooth the way. He had his own architectural firm. After he had returned from Boston, he had gotten a job with one of the most prominent firms in the city, Burnham and Root. The firm had won the contract to oversee the construction of the 1893 World's Columbian Exposition, which was to be held in Jackson Park, south of the city. After his partner, John Root, died unexpectedly, Daniel Burnham stepped up to handle the task. It was a massive project, so he promoted Dwight, who was in his mid-20s, to handle the rest of his practice.

The fair consumed Chicago. The opening was a grand occasion, attended by President Grover Cleveland, who arrived in a carriage, greeted by a crowd of 200,000 people. The great pianist from Poland,

Ignacy Jan Paderewski, played on a Steinway piano at the ceremony. Journalist Richard Harding Davis declared that the fair was "the greatest event in the history of the country since the Civil War."[8] Chicago's can-do spirit was on show.

Six months later, by the time its turnstiles were closed, more than 27 million people had come to see the fair, in a country with a population of 65 million. It boosted the pride of a city that had literally rebuilt itself out of the ashes and was becoming the second most important metropolis in the country.

Once the fair was over, Daniel Burnham resumed control of his firm, but the end of the fair saw Chicago caught up in the Depression. Dwight decided to go out on his own, and Burnham set him up with a plum assignment—a commission to design a new office building in downtown Chicago. On the ground floor would be a concert hall and a sales office for the Steinway piano company, which wanted to expand its business in the increasingly affluent city.

Soon after Marion returned, the city was gripped by the terrible strike of the workers at the Pullman railcar works south of the city. The dispute was only resolved after President Cleveland ordered the army to step in. While other people struggled to find employment, Marion worked in her cousin's architectural firm, helping with the drawings for Steinway Hall. As she wrote to her friends later:

> I felt right proud when I obtained a position as a draftsman one week after leaving the Tech, and prouder still to be earning the lordly sum of six dollars a week, my employer's estimate of the value of my service far exceeding my own.[9]

Men in Chicago, she wrote, had no problem hiring women. What she didn't mention, of course, was that her employer was her first cousin. At the time, Dwight worked in the Schiller Building in Chicago's Loop, the downtown area surrounded by the city's railway loop. It was one of the city's newest office buildings designed by the other leading architectural firm in Chicago, Adler and Sullivan. The staff in Perkins' office supported the inexperienced young woman architect. Marion was a hard worker and she learned fast.

> One year in the office of D.H. Perkins, getting out at that time the working drawings of Steinway Hall, with the whole drafting force lending me a hand to put me through my paces, gave me a sound foundation in that field.[10]

Back home, Marion continued getting extra drawing lessons, as she had done in Boston, determined to further improve her skills now that she was working as an architect. She also caught up with some of her old friends, including Anna Wilmarth, who was studying at the newly established University of Chicago. Marion joined a French group that put on plays to help the students practice the language, but her new career was her main passion.

Marion Mahony, Harriet Gallup, and Sarah Hall. The three girl graduates of 1894. MIT. Boston. New-York Historical Society. Magic of America collection. BV Griffin, Marion Mahony, section 4: neg #80943d.

Seven

Enter Frank

Sadly, Dwight's business fell on hard times after he had finished his work on the Steinway Hall building. The city was caught up in the national economic downturn. Dwight found new work hard to come by and that, with other financial problems he faced, meant he had to let his cousin go.

But Marion took the decision in stride. Her education at MIT improved her drawing skills and gave her qualifications many Chicago architects did not have. Her skills as a draftsman became known among her cousin's circle of friends, some of whom had also gone to MIT. She worked for several months for a few architects and increased her salary to $15 a week.[1] Toward the end of 1895, she found a job with an architect in her cousin's circle who also had an office in the Schiller Building. His name was Wright. Frank Lloyd Wright.

Wright was the nephew of the Reverend Jenkin Lloyd Jones who came to the city around 1882 to set up a Unitarian church in the south of Chicago. Wright had attended his church when he first moved to Chicago, meeting his future wife there soon after he arrived. Marion's aunt, Dwight's mother, was also an active member of his congregation.

Wright began studying engineering at the University of Wisconsin but was drawn to the bright lights of Chicago where so much exciting new building was taking place. He joined the leading firm of Adler and Sullivan, which designed the most prestigious new building in the city, the Chicago Auditorium.

Wright, whose father had left home when he was growing up, became close to Louis Sullivan whose original ideas on architecture were becoming well-known in the city. Sullivan studied architecture at MIT in Boston and spent time in Europe. He returned questioning why a new country like America persisted with the classical architecture of Europe. It was time for America to develop its own style of architecture, he argued. Wright was inspired by his vision.

Sullivan treated Wright like a son until they had a serious disagreement. Sullivan was furious when he found out that Wright was designing houses for clients in his spare time, something Sullivan had expressly forbidden. In 1893, just as Marion began to work on her thesis at MIT, Wright walked out of Adler and Sullivan and set up his own practice.

Wright knew Dwight through their family connections with the Reverend Jenkin Lloyd Jones and his Unitarian church. They were the same age and both had offices in the Schiller Building. Marion said later that the connection for her job had come through Mrs. Davis, a friend of the Mahony family who lived near Hubbard Woods, who was also involved in the Unitarian church. She accepted Wright's offer of a salary of $10 a week, less than she had been receiving before, consoling herself with the fact that she was given the title of "Superintendent of the Office Force."[2]

Wright clearly had no qualms about hiring Marion to do the job. She was his first professional employee. He had never finished his formal studies, and he knew that this sharp, hardworking woman had been trained in the best architectural school in the country. Having grown up with a strong-willed mother and two sisters, Wright was used to dealing with independently minded women.

Marion would have found Wright very different from anyone she had ever met. He had an air of confidence, if not a touch of arrogance, about him. He dressed stylishly, his hat jauntily placed on his head, wearing a cape which swung when he walked. He knew his dress style provoked comment but he didn't care. He was only four years older than Marion, but Wright was married with four children, three sons and a daughter, while Marion was still single and lived at home. Wright had married Catherine Tobin, a girl he met at his uncle's church, when he was only 22 and she was not quite 18. Children had quickly followed. When Marion joined his office, Wright was almost single-handedly supporting his own family, as well as his mother and his two sisters who now lived next door to him in Oak Park, a suburb west of the city. It was a powerful incentive for him to expand his practice.

Wright had a drive and a conviction about his own ideas that was very attractive. Marion soon became drawn into his world. She had been an available architect when Wright needed some extra help but, as she would find, they also shared many similar views, apart from their Unitarian faith and their family's support for Abraham Lincoln and his ideals. They both had a strong passion for designing houses. Both had an aversion to the classical architecture of Europe and an interest in a style of architecture that was more suited to the Midwestern American environment, one more connected with nature.

When Marion arrived, Wright had had his own practice for almost two years and his striking house designs were already attracting attention. She was hired to help him with his first major building, the Francis Apartments, which was under construction. Maybe Wright felt Marion's experience working on Steinway Hall would have been valuable for the project. On the drawing boards, when she arrived, was the design of a house for an Austrian-born businessman, Isidore Heller. It was Wright's first work in the fashionable area of Hyde Park, south of the central business district. The design was later seen as one of the turning points in Wright's career, his move toward a more horizontal, geometric style which would later be called the Prairie School of Architecture.

Wright had a passion for Japanese art. It started with his first employer in Chicago, Joseph Silsbee, and was further fueled by the Japanese art and architecture on display at the World's Fair. This and the lessons learned from Louis Sullivan were inspiring him to create a new form of architecture. Three stories tall, the Heller House had flat roofs on the second and third floors, with overhanging eaves and windows grouped in horizontal bands. Wright commissioned German-born sculptor Richard Bock to help with some of the ornamentation. Marion was drawn into Wright's dynamic world. Unlike Sullivan, Wright had no objection to his staff doing work on their own time. Marion designed a vacation house for her family in Hubbard Woods, a long narrow oblong shape with an octagonal room on either side.

Next door to Wright's office was the office of another architect friend from Wisconsin, Robert Spencer. Wright had one of Spencer's house drawings pinned up on the wall of his office. Wright himself was never a great drawer and putting one of Spencer's drawings on his wall may have been an acknowledgment of his own shortcomings as an artist. But by this time, it was evident that drawing was one of Marion's great strengths.

Working in Wright's office, she found herself in a different role from her drafting work for Dwight. As she explained later:

> In entering my second office I was graduated from pure drafting to experience and began to function, in my first stage of design, in a realm fairly natural to me, that of the art of the painter. ... We were, to be sure, practicing as architects but were really functioning as artists, as painters.[3]

Marion's comments were probably more applicable to herself than Wright, but they showed her changing role as he relied on her highly refined artistic skills to show his plans in their best light to his clients.

In the summer of 1896, Marion made her first trip to Europe. Traveling with her younger brother, Gerald, they visited some of the great cities. Marion particularly loved Rome and Venice, which they first saw in moonlight. As an architect, she could appreciate their beauty. When they arrived back in New York Harbor on September 1, the entry form requested people to put down their profession. Marion described herself as an "architect."[4] It was a title that only a few women in the world at the time could truthfully claim.

Dwight's Steinway Hall opened in the same year. It was an 11-story office building with a big loft at the top that let the sun stream in. In a city with long, dark winters, it was a perfect place for architectural work. Dwight had deliberately designed it that way and decided to move his firm into the 11th floor of the building, giving him access to the loft. There was plenty of space, and he invited others to join him there to help pay the rent and share the secretarial services. Robert Spencer, who had known Dwight when they were both at MIT, was one of the first to take up his offer of space. And soon he brought over his friend, Wright, who brought his assistant, Marion.

The young architects shared a common drafting room in the loft, their workrooms separated by screens. They were like-minded people inspired by the new style of architecture developing in the Midwest, and they formed close bonds. Marion became part of a tight-knit group of colleagues, friends, and associates who were increasingly making their mark on the city's architecture.

Working in an environment which had been created by her cousin, both physically and socially, meant Marion was particularly welcome. Another young woman trying to get work in architecture at the time, an outsider to the group, might have struggled. But again, Marion's links with Dwight, whose family also had links and similar views to Wright's family, made it all that much easier. They were soon joined by others who were attracted to the exciting atmosphere on the top of Steinway Hall. There was Myron Hunt, who had been studying at MIT when Marion was there, the brothers Irving and Allen Pond, Birch Burdette Long, and Henry Webster Tomlinson.

Wright was to later describe the collegiate atmosphere in the Steinway Hall loft:

> I had met Robert Spencer, Myron Hunt and Dwight Perkins. Dwight had a loft in his new Steinway Hall building—too large for him. So we formed a group—outer office in common—workrooms screened apart in the loft of Steinway Hall. These young men, newcomers in architecture practice like myself, were my first associates in the so-called profession of architecture.[5]

Together these young architects formed a new voice in the Chicago architectural scene, inspired by the teachings of Louis Sullivan. Daniel Burnham had chosen classical Renaissance style architecture for the designs of the main buildings of the World's Fair of 1893. But Louis Sullivan, the most prominent architect in Chicago, apart from Burnham, had different views about architecture. He strongly rejected the classical style and produced a striking design for the giant Transportation

Building at the fair—a huge, square-like building with concentric arches for the entranceway with a massive golden door.

Wright, Perkins, and their colleagues were part of a growing band of architects in the city who supported Sullivan's rebellion against the conventional admiration for classical architecture in America. They were receptive to Sullivan's calls for them to develop a new American architecture, one not built on ornament but on designs where the form of the building would follow its very function. Marion found she was not alone in her natural distaste for the classical style of architecture she had been taught at Boston Tech. Maybe it was in their veins. Marion, Dwight, Wright, and the others shared a common love for the Midwestern landscape and its flat prairies, which was fundamental to their approach to work and life. The top of Steinway Hall became an incubator for what would become known as the Chicago School of Architecture, or in some quarters, the Prairie School of Architecture.

They also shared the new passion for things Japanese. The fair had featured a wooden Japanese temple on an island and displays of Japanese art. They had all visited the fair, some many times. They had loved the clean, simple lines of the drawings and the temple's setting within the natural environment. The opening up of Japan by US Commodore Perry in the 1850s had seen a flood of Japanese artwork to the West. Across the Atlantic, a group of young painters based in France, which would become known as the Impressionists, had also been inspired by the clean lines and the strong forces of nature in Japanese art. The group included Dutch-born painter Vincent Van Gogh, who in 1887 painted *The Bridge in the Rain (after Hiroshige)* based on a woodcut by the Japanese artist Utagawa Hiroshige.

Japanese art was inspired by nature at a time when the architects of Chicago could see the ugliest examples of the industrial age in their own city. Collecting Japanese prints became fashionable amongst these architects, just as it had been in the artistic circles of Europe, particularly Paris.

In October 1897, Marion, Wright, Dwight, his wife Lucy, and others from Steinway Hall were part of a group that met at Jane Addams' Hull House to form the Chicago Arts and Crafts Society. The Arts and Crafts movement had sprung up in England as a reaction to the horrors of the industrial age. It ushered in a new era of crafts made by hand, using motifs from the natural world including plants and flowers, which inspired these young architects.

Their approach to art and architecture came amid an atmosphere of broader passion for social reform in Chicago in the circles of the Mahonys, the Perkins, the Reverend Lloyd Jones, and their friends. Jane Addams had become a prominent social activist in the city. She had visited London in 1888 and became interested in the idea of settlement houses, community centers in the slums to help the poor. Determined to do the same in Chicago, she was allowed to take over a house that had been built by Charles Hull, in the south of the city, near the poorest and most overcrowded section of the city where many of the immigrants lived. Addams had founded her center in 1889 with a friend, Ellen Starr, and support from some of the city's most active women, including Mrs. Wilmarth. Hull House was not just a center for helping the poor but the focus of a broader circle of social activism and debate.

A few months after the Hull House meeting, in January 1898, 27-year-old Marion found herself in a room with 11 others in Chicago's City Hall, sitting a grueling three-day exam. It was the first licensing examination for architects in the history of the profession in America. The Illinois General Assembly had passed a law the year before, insisting that all architects be licensed. Wright was granted an exemption as he was already running an established practice, but others had to go through the demanding process. Marion received one of the highest grades and became the first woman anywhere in the United States to become a licensed architect. If she paid much heed to these historical milestones, she never said so.

Frank Lloyd Wright family home and studio. Oak Park, Chicago. Photographs by Vin Plant 2011.

Top: entrance to the studio showing pillars with storks.

Bottom: street view of entrance to studio. (Entrance to house is around the corner.)

Eight

Oak Park

Wright's business took off, and his family expanded, making it difficult to work at home in the evenings. He saw business opportunities among the good citizens of Oak Park and decided to build a studio next to his home.

How much Marion's own thesis, her vision for *The House and Studio of a Painter*, influenced what happened next is unknown.[1] But, around the time Marion worked for Wright in Steinway Hall, Wright designed the elegant studio to be attached to his house. Marion worked with him closely on the project.

Just as Marion had envisaged in her thesis, the studio addition could take advantage of the fact that it was on a corner block, allowing different entrances for the family and Wright's architectural clients. The studio itself had a number of rooms, including a drafting room, a little like a schoolroom, with a second-story balcony above it. At the other end was an octagonal room Wright called a library. It was a private room where he could take clients to show them his plans for their new homes. It had a skylight and high windows, which let light into the room, as if it was sent from heaven.

Marion wanted to ensure the entrance to the studio was different to that of the house and make a statement to clients about the modern, creative architects who would be working inside. She designed a loggia entrance to the studio with four columns along the front. She decided each column should be decorated with two tall birds on each side. She found pictures of the storks she wanted to have on the columns, "wise birds" she called them. Above them, on each column, would be a tree of knowledge and an open book. She gave her designs to sculptor Richard Bock and the result made a stylish entrance to the studio.

When the studio was finished, Marion and Wright left Steinway Hall and moved to the more genteel world of Oak Park. Five years after she wrote her thesis, Marion was actually working in *The House and Studio of an Architect*, which she had helped to design.

Marion developed her own flexible way of working with Wright. The astute Wright knew Marion was a reliable and hardworking assistant. In Marion he knew he had access to one of the finest architectural drawers in the country—someone who could turn his ideas for the new architecture of America into beautiful, magical drawings that impressed his clients. They began a new professional life together, alongside his own increasingly chaotic family life.

Marion was drawn into the community that grew around Wright's Oak Park studio. The drafting room, where the architects and draftsmen worked, was much smaller than the loft at Steinway Hall, and with the house right next to the studio, Wright's work and his family life were inevitably interwoven. His children loved to come into the studio to see their father. They particularly delighted in throwing down paper aeroplanes from the balcony to the architects working below.

Marion became firm friends with Wright's wife Kitty, as she was known. Their families were both part of the Unitarian Church movement in Chicago and Kitty had been part of the same congregation at All Souls Church south of Chicago as Marion's aunt.

Sometime around 1900, when Marion and Kitty were both 29, Wright took a photograph in his home of the two women. He loved photography, and with his typically confident view of his own skills, he believed no one could take a picture as well as he could. The World's Fair of 1893 had opened people's eyes to many new things, including the possibility that ordinary people could take their own photographs without having to go to a studio. Wright was always eager to embrace the new, and the camera gave him another form of expression.

The black-and-white photograph shows an unusual closeness between the two women. Kitty, the uneducated mother of his five children, wears a white gown. She leans against a table covered by a patterned cloth and looks directly ahead at the camera with clear, determined eyes. Marion stands behind her and to her right, wearing a dark, high-necked gown with long sleeves. She shows the right side of her face and looks directly at Kitty. Their faces are only a few inches away from each other's. Marion's right arm stretches across Kitty's body, her hand resting on Kitty's knee.

Exactly what was Wright thinking as he posed the two women for the photo? Marion appears as the overtly strong character of the two, the more dominant, in a somewhat protective pose to that of the seated Kitty. Is Marion protecting Kitty or is the photo a reflection of the closeness between the two women in Wright's life? Kitty was very much the traditional wife and mother but, in Marion, Wright was seeing a woman who was well educated and a highly competent member of his own profession. Was he now seeing that women could have two sides to their lives—motherhood and a profession? And who knows what he said to Marion about posing? Marion knew she was not a conventionally beautiful woman. After this photo, almost every photo of her was taken with only the side of her face to the camera, in profile.

Marion developed an unusual working relationship with Wright. She had her own desk in a corner of the studio, but she was not always there, coming and going as the work required. She did not have a telephone at her home. If there was a project where she was needed, someone would be sent to her house and tell her to come in.[2] She would take the streetcar west to Oak Park. Her initial role as superintendent of the office changed after the move to the Oak Park studio. If someone had asked Marion how she would describe herself, it probably would have been as an artist—an artist whose creativity expressed itself in drawing and design. In the 1900 Federal Census, her profession was recorded as an artist.

As Wright's business grew, he added more staff. Others with special skills would be called on when needed. There was a floating population of people with different skills—architects, draftsmen, sculptors, designers—who would come in and out of the studio, depending on the work. When word got around Wright's studio that Marion was set to come in, the small contingent knew they could look forward to an interesting time. Her arrival brought a dash of color to the studio. They were familiar with her tall, wiry frame, her love of bright, unusual clothes, and her penchant for having a bright turban wrapped around her head with her long dark hair flowing down her back. And there was always the possibility of some lively verbal sparring with the boss.

Barry Byrne, a young architect, joined the studio in 1902. He was taken with Marion, 12 years his senior. He later described her as:

> ... a thin, angular, shallow person with a beak of a nose. ... So homely that she looked almost distinguished. She had a fragile frame and walked as though she was falling forward. She was a good actress, talkative, and when around Wright, there was a real sparkle.[3]

Byrne looked forward to her coming into the office.

> Her mordant humor attracted me as a fellow Celt, and I can well remember welcoming her advent (she came irregularly) because it promised an amusing day. Her dialogues with Frank Lloyd Wright, who, as we all know, is no indifferent opponent in repartee, made such days particularly notable.[4]

Marion was one of the few people in Wright's studio who would take him on. Sparks could fly between them, or some verbal jousting at least. Her conversations with Wright ranged from art and architecture to Victor Hugo, the Bible, plays, and Sir Walter Scott.[5] Both of them had formidable intellects and were well-equipped to argue their case. What Wright lacked in formal education, he made up for with his sharpness and self-confidence.

She regarded herself as Wright's intellectual equal. She had a degree from the top architectural university in the country and was a fully licensed architect in the state of Illinois. Wright had never finished his degree and never sat the long exams that Marion had to earn her license. Always assured of his abilities, Wright had managed to get by without either. But Wright had the charm and ability to strike up powerful relations with wealthy clients, while Marion was happy to remain in the background, working with the team in his office.

Wright used his conversations with Marion to help sharpen his ideas. In 1901, she helped him with his major speech to the Arts and Craft Society at Hull House, titled "Art and Craft of the Machine."[6] The speech represented his view of the debate between the virtues of the machine and the Arts and Crafts movement. The industrial machine, he argued, was not an evil inflicted on mankind. While he acknowledged that machinery had its negatives, he believed that it could also be incredibly useful in the service of society. Sculptor Richard Bock remembered later that Marion was "a brilliant intellectual and a match for Wright in debate. She served as a source of practice and training for his lecturing."[7]

Walter Burley Griffin, a shy, handsome local lad with big dreams, was playing an increasing role in Wright's studio. He had completed a degree in architecture from the University of Illinois and had then worked at Steinway Hall, first with Dwight and then some of the others, before joining Wright's office in 1901. He knew the area well as his family had lived in Oak Park. He was a quiet young man, with an almost cherubic face. His degree had given him a strong grounding in the engineering and technical side of architecture. He was also a passionate follower of Louis Sullivan's ideals. He was fond of recounting how he had heard Sullivan address the annual meeting of the Architectural League of America in June 1900, where he urged young American architects to develop their own style of architecture. They should not, Sullivan insisted, take their mental nourishment from the architecture produced by "the withered breast of Despotism." Their architecture, he said, should be the architecture of democracy.[8]

Marion would have found Walter a pleasant and thoughtful colleague but, when it came to the Oak Park studio, Wright was the dominating personality who commanded her attention.

Marion Mahony and Catherine Tobin Wright. Oak Park, Chicago. Circa 1900. Photographer Frank Lloyd Wright. Courtesy Frank Lloyd Wright Trust.

Nine

Our Little University

In 1902, Marion stood outside a church in Chicago with a family friend, the 60-year-old Unitarian minister Reverend James Vila Blake, and elders from her church. They looked at a conventional church built in traditional Gothic architecture that the elders had wanted them to see. Blake was irritated.

"Why have you brought us here?" he asked. "I couldn't preach a sermon in a place such as this."[1]

Blake had taken a risk, giving Marion, a woman half his age, the commission to build his new church. He had been a minister at the Unitarian Church in Chicago, but he and his followers had a more liberal version of the church's teachings. He had broken away from his church and moved to Evanston, a middle-class suburb north of Chicago, a little closer in to the city than Hubbard Woods. He had gathered around him a group of like-minded supporters, including Clara Mahony and her friends, who wanted to build a church for him in the area. Blake knew of Marion's architectural skills and convinced his congregation to give her the project. This would be her first independent commission as an architect.

Delighted at the challenge, Marion had sketched out her design, confident that Blake and the elders would share her view about the need to have a more modern building for their church, one which broke with the conventional Gothic architecture and its inevitable steeples. She designed an octagonal building with a sunken parlor, a larger version of the octagonal room in Wright's Oak Park studio, which could be used as a meeting room.

Behind the octagonal building, there was a taller, two-story rectangular auditorium with a peak roof for the church itself. The entrance to the church was on the left side of the building. There was a long passageway which went past the parlor, to the auditorium behind. The focus, from the front, was on the striking octagonal building, with its stained glass windows letting in colored light from all directions. On the wall above the parlor, there was a round window, allowing light to flood into the church behind it where the congregation would gather to worship. The unchurch-like, modern design was too much for the board overseeing the project.

Marion tried to compromise, taking in the suggestions of the board members, but they kept pushing her. Finally, she would compromise no more, telling Blake that the board members' suggestions would mean a total destruction of the beauty of the building she had designed.

Now they stood in front of the traditional Gothic church in the city. Blake hated it, as Marion knew he would. He wanted something that reflected his liberal views. As he and Marion headed home together, he questioned her.

"Did you notice the height of this wall?" he asked.

"Yes," she said. "That is the dimension they were requiring of me."

"Do you mean they wanted you to duplicate that building?"

"Yes."[2]

From then on, Blake stood by Marion and told the board members they had to accept her plans. Finally, in 1903, Marion's simple, elegant All Souls Church was finished. It was a more conventional-looking church building than she had originally designed, with a tall gabled roof, like a steep triangle. But the interior showed Marion's fine eye for detail and her passion for stained glass windows, with stained glass skylights over the entrance area and the altar at the back. On the wall behind the altar, Marion had painted a mural of Christ and some of his disciples. The light from the stained glass windows streamed in from above, illuminating the Christ figure and the altar. Toward the back of the church, on each of the columns on either side of the entrance to the altar area, she placed a square planter box for flowers and vines, supported by two long, thin pieces of wood, her way of bringing the natural world into the church.

As Marion wrote to a friend later, "This was my first job and the foundation of my life's work."[3] Marion felt it was not just a building but a spiritual exercise. Encouraged by Blake, Marion believed that spirituality should continue to be a driving force behind her work. And her God was one very much in tune with the natural world, like the Spirit which guided the young Indian brave to seek solace for his loss in the tumbling rivers of Colorado.

The Reverend Blake, who had always been fond of Marion, was happy with it. When he wrote his book, *Discoveries*, in 1904, he dedicated a poem to her. Working with Marion had given him a greater insight into her forthright character. She would, he told her, have a hard time if she married a man who was not honest. Marion agreed.

There was plenty of work coming into the Oak Park studio. Wright's striking new style of architecture became known among some well-connected people, particularly those who saw themselves as very modern. A wealthy socialite, Susan Lawrence Dana, lived in the state capital of Springfield and approached Wright while Marion designed her church. The 40-year-old Dana had an Italianate mansion in the city's fashionable Aristocracy Hill area. Widowed two years before, she now wanted it completely remodeled to give her a stunning new house to entertain the important people of the city in.

Wright embraced the project, proposing a massive redevelopment of the building with a strong Japanese-influenced style. His renovation produced a house with 35 different rooms flowing into each other, over several different levels, with a staggering 450 stained glass windows. Many of the art glass windows were designed with the theme of the plant sumac depicted in geometric forms. The colors used in the house were typical of the Prairie School of Architecture—natural earth tones of brown, pale yellow, orange, and cream, with exposed darker-brown wooden beams. Wright not only designed the house but also insisted that his studio design all the fittings, as well as the furniture and the curtains, making the whole building part of an integrated concept. It was a major project involving most of the people at the Oak Park studio, taking two years to build.

The building had Japanese-style, low, horizontal roofs with wide, overhanging eaves, upturned at the end, and long ribbons of stained glass windows. Marion helped to design an internal fountain for the house. Called *Moon Children*, it featured a group of children in a circle around a central water urn, its water flowing down into a small pond below. The sculpture itself was done by Richard Bock, who had made the sculptures for the entrance to the Oak Park studio, while another craftsman, George Niedecken, painted a mural on the dining room wall.

The Dana House was a collective creative effort. Exactly how much work she did on the house has not been documented but it is likely Marion was involved in more than just designing the fountain. She was part of a team, working with some of the most talented craftsmen in the city. She drew a perspective drawing of the house, with her typical fine lines and hanging vines, viewed from street level, giving it a very imposing look. But she loved to work on the interiors of the houses, drawing on her artistic skills. One of the draftsmen in the Oak Park office recalled that Marion's work in the studio involved "doing designs for furniture, leaded glass, lighting fixtures and glass mosaics."[4] Given her interest in stained glass windows, she was probably involved in other interior design aspects of the Dana House, particularly the many stained glass windows.

Maybe it was the artist in Marion and her love of color that particularly drew her to designing stained glass windows. It was a time when colored glass designs were becoming popular with the rise of the Arts and Crafts movement. In New York, Tiffany's striking and colorful stained glass windows and craft work were attracting attention. Wright's designs were inspired by the American landscape, particularly the prairie lands of the Midwest. He loved the golds and greens of the fields and developed stylized chevron designs evolved from the shape of a staff of wheat.

Marion's stained glass window designs featured small squares, chevrons, and stylized plant forms inspired by the wheat and grasses of the prairie. She often designed bands of stained glass windows for the top story of Wright's houses, which all came together in a pattern.

Marion explained later the reasoning behind her enthusiasm for stained glass and how it should be used:

> It is hard to describe the lovely effects which can be obtained by a proper use of colored glass. ... The subdivision of the glass in windows and doors often goes a long way towards giving a home that feeling of domesticity which is necessary if it is to meet its requirements. These points will affect and hold all the occupants, especially the children whose whole attitude towards life is bound to be deeply affected by the home atmosphere. ... If we study the natural character of the material [glass] is easily broken in straight lines. We should not, therefore, make attempts to paint pictures with colored glass but should use geometric motives [sic] or purely decorative forms.[5]

Marion was happy with her loose working arrangement in the creative environment of Oak Park where she could come and go depending on the work. She worked occasionally as a teacher and did not feel the need to set up her own architectural practice. Given the attitude of the day toward women in architecture, it may have been very difficult for her to set up her own practice if the idea ever did cross her mind.

Wright dominated the office, and his personality and his new ideas attracted both clients and creative people around him. Over time, more people joined the studio as his business grew. Wright often called his studio "our little university." A university of which he was very much the professor in charge. Wright became known for his jaunty appearance, powerful personality, and personal style. Wright's son John later noted how those in the studio were followers of his father in more ways than one.

> His brilliant and attractive personality exercised a curious charm on those who knew him. ... William Drummond, Francis Barry Byrne, Walter Burley Griffin, Albert McArthur, Marion Mahony and Isabel Roberts and George Willis were the draftsmen. Five men and two women. They wore flowing ties and smocks suitable to the realm. The men wore their hair like Papa. ... They worshipped Papa! Papa liked them.[6]

Wright would occasionally sit at Marion's desk and work on a drawing. He had no formal training and used rulers and triangles, while Marion could draw freehand if needed. On one occasion, Wright's work ruined the drawing.

As Byrne recalled later, one outspoken member of the staff loudly proclaimed that Marion Mahony was Wright's superior as a draftsman. "As a matter of fact she was," Byrne felt. "Wright took the statement of her superiority equably," he noted.[7] But Wright was still highly sensitive about any of his staff overshadowing him.

Wright would often hold competitions between the staff for parts of houses such as murals, fireplaces, windows, mosaics, furniture, and even complete interiors. It developed a competitive spirit in the office and was a clever way for him to harvest the ideas of the bright men and women in his studio.[8] He often stored away their designs and ideas in a notebook, bringing them out later to use in a new project. Marion would often win these competitions, but Wright, who had a confidence bordering on arrogance, made sure he got the credit for everything that came out of his office. The staff soon learned to be careful about what they said. Any reference to "Miss Mahony's design" would receive a sharp reprimand from Wright.

Marion was also asked by Wright to work on some designs for low cost houses. True to her form, she wanted to break away from the conventional box-like house shape. She designed T-shaped houses with the living rooms spread across the front of the block and the kitchen quarters at the back. The bedrooms upstairs were set back, allowing the living rooms below to have a double height and more light. They may have been small houses, but her design gave them the spacious feel of a much more expensive design.[9]

Walter Burley Griffin had a very different role in the office. He managed the business and many dealings with clients and regarded himself as Wright's right-hand man. He was a man very much devoted to his work. Personally, he could have been seen as an eligible bachelor. Still living at home with his parents, he was a handsome, respectable, sweet-natured man in his mid-20s with a good degree in architecture and sound professional prospects.

Unbeknownst to most people, even those in the studio, the woman who had caught Walter's eye was Wright's younger sister, Maginel, who lived with her mother and sister in a house next to the Wrights' house and studio. A talented artist, she had gone to high school in Oak Park with Walter's younger brother Ralph. She would often come to the studio to work on her drawings. Sometime around 1903, Walter summoned up the courage to reveal his true feelings and proposed to her. Maginel was shocked and embarrassed, quickly rejecting him. Soon after, she and her mother went to Europe for a three-month holiday. Not long after her return, she married another man.

Other relationships developed around the studio. One of Kitty Wright's acquaintances was a neighbor, Mrs. Cheney, who was in her early 30s. They were both members of the Nineteenth Century Women's Club with another Oak Park resident, Grace Hemingway, the mother of writer Ernest Hemingway. Mrs. Cheney's husband, Edwin, was the president of the Wagner Electric Manufacturing Company. Around 1903, the Cheneys approached Wright to design a house for them. The house became more than a project for Wright, who spent a lot of time with Mrs. Cheney. Work began on the house in the middle of 1904, just as the Dana House in Springfield was opened with a string of parties.

Marion had a very active life outside the Oak Park studio. The Mahony household was always busy. Marion continued her passion for acting. She and her friends loved to perform plays. Monday evenings were set aside for rehearsals at the Mahony home by the church drama group. Reverend Blake would oversee the productions, which included many of Shakespeare's works. Marion was the most enthusiastic actress of her family and over the years played the parts of Portia, Beatrice, Olivia, and Cordelia.[10] There were musical evenings and poetry reading nights with Blake often reading his poems, just as Jere Mahony had done for the household when he was alive.

The Mahonys had a wide circle of friends who gathered every Christmas Eve. They included Mrs. Flagg Young, the former principal of the Mahonys' school, who became the first woman superintendent of Chicago Schools, the Wilmarths, and the Perkins. Dwight had by then married Lucy, a talented artist from Boston, and they had a daughter named Eleanor. Marion's dear friend, Anna Wilmarth, had married James Westfall Thompson, a university lecturer, in 1897, and they had a son called Wilmarth.

Marion's mother recalled the happy scenes in a note Marion kept.

Anna said she would hurry to cross the continent, if necessary, to be on time for that evening, [bringing] her eldest son Wilmarth who had been a guest from babyhood to a business man. ... The only rule made was no presents, and friends kindly observed it. ... At first we used to sit at a table for twenty-seven. Our chicken pie was a big dish pan covered with a crust and filled with toys for the tiny ones. I shall never forget how little Eleanor [Perkins] kicked and clapped her hands when, from a hole in the middle of the crust, a jumping jack stuck his head out. The tree was always a beauty with its frost and tinsel, the room gay with lights, berries and evergreens and happy faces. For a few years several children of our eighth grade we would treat to ice-cream up stairs, then, at the proper moment, ... they would come marching down the stairs to Aunt Myra's music and stand around the piano singing Christmas carols (breathtaking, the music, for Mother's school was in Chicago's Bohemian district). Sometimes a charade or a little play by the children themselves but, on account of the little ones, an early start home. After guests were gone we hung up our stockings and put a big basket in front of the fireplace for overflows.[11]

Interior of Marion Mahony designed Church of All Souls, Evanston, Illinois. 1903. Eric Nicholls collection. National Library of Australia.

Ten

Japanese Woodcuts

There was much excitement at the Oak Park studio at the beginning of 1905.

Wright and Kitty were going on their first overseas trip together. The Wrights had been invited by Ward Willits, a wealthy local client, to accompany him and his wife on a four-month trip to Japan. Wright had been inspired by Japanese art by his first employer, Joseph Silsbee, who collected Japanese prints. Then there was the 1893 World's Fair with its Japanese temple and art which attracted so much interest. Japanese art embodied many of the natural elements that Louis Sullivan and the new architects of Chicago were advocating, particularly the architects who had worked in Steinway Hall. As Marion wrote later, the "influence of the Japanese prints of the Columbian Exposition" had "waked up America to the beauty of the oriental arts."[1] Wright jumped at the chance to go to Japan and see it for himself.

Wright's mother, Anna, would take care of the family while they were away. Some felt it was unusual for Kitty to agree to be away from her brood for so long, but maybe she sensed some strains in her marriage and decided it would be wise to go with him.

Wright was always short of money, but this was not going to stop him from making the trip. He borrowed $5,000 from Walter to help pay for the journey. Walter was a trusting, idealistic young man who regarded himself as being in a partnership with Wright and was prepared to lend him some of his savings. Walter ran the studio while Wright was away.

When Wright came home, he was full of enthusiasm about Japan, its art, and its architecture. He had found the country even more exciting than he had imagined. He entertained everyone with stories of his nightly trips, in disguise, with a guide, roaming the backstreets of Kyoto, buying Japanese prints and woodcuts. He brought home more than 200 woodcuts, many by the artist Utagawa Hiroshige. He loved the carefully inked minimalist designs on the long thin scrolls, which featured stylized depictions of nature including birds and trees. He particularly liked Hiroshige's *Swallows and Cherry Blossoms*, which showed four birds flying in the top right-hand corner with a few slim tree branches in the bottom left.

Wright became an evangelist for Japanese art. He and Kitty held a Japanese social at their home, and he lent his collection to the Chicago Art Institute for an exhibition in March 1906. He lectured on Japanese art to groups, including architecture students at the University of Illinois.[2] Wright's new enthusiasm for things Japanese and the large collection of prints he had brought back with him had a strong effect on Marion. She loved the Japanese passion for nature and the simplicity of the designs in Japanese art. Inspired by what she saw before her, Marion's work took on a confident new style.

But the trip had other consequences for the group at Oak Park. Marion may have been swept up in Wright's enthusiasm for things Japanese, but Walter was more interested in getting his money back. When he got home, Wright had spent the money that Walter had lent him. Wright was notorious for borrowing money from people and not paying it back, if he could possibly avoid it. He admitted: "It was my misfortune ... that everybody was willing to trust me."[3]

Walter patiently waited for his money as he worked in the studio but, as the year went on, Wright showed no signs of repaying his debt, offering Walter some of his Japanese prints instead. Walter was furious, arguing that the woodcuts were not worth anything like what Wright had claimed they were. Rather than being grateful for the loan from Walter, Wright also complained about the way Walter had run the office while he was away. The head professor wanted to reassert his role at his little university.

Relations between Walter and Wright became increasingly tense. Walter realized that his perception of being in a partnership with Wright was an illusion held by him alone. He had not been looking to leave Oak Park, but it was time to think about making a change. Walter was passionate about landscape architecture and won an important commission to redesign the campus at Northern Illinois Normal School in DeKalb, a town west of Chicago. He was also working on plans for a city in Shanghai for a Chinese official he had met at the World's Fair in St Louis in 1904. Early in 1906, Walter learned that Dwight Perkins was moving out of his office in the Steinway Hall loft to take up a job as chief architect for the Chicago Board of Education. Walter jumped at the opportunity and moved into Perkins' old office in Steinway Hall, severing his ties with Wright.

If Marion was aware of the tensions between Walter and Wright, she probably did not know the full details. Walter was a low-key, private person and may well have kept the full extent of his animosity toward Wright to himself as he quietly planned a future on his own. And Marion was caught up in Wright's world, his new energy for his work, and his passion about Japanese art and architecture. She was more than happy to be part of Wright's dynamic orbit. If anything, Wright's little university had become even more interesting for her.

Marion was now clearly the best artistic and architectural drawer in his office, and she was used to his many moods and passions. But now her drawing skills were taking on a new dimension, inspired by the Japanese art she saw around her in the studio. And, unlike Walter, she was perfectly content to remain in a relationship which did not challenge Wright's ego. Soon there was an important new project for Wright's studio.

In June 1905, just after the Wrights had returned from Japan, the Unitarian church in Oak Park burned down. The elders of the church asked Wright to help rebuild it, but it was not an easy project. The congregation had a modest budget, and the land was on a rectangular site on the corner of a busy road, near several other churches.

Wright took a radical approach to the design. With limited funds, he believed that the new church should not try to compete with the existing churches nearby. He suggested that the new Unity Temple, as it would be called, not have a steeple, just as Marion had done with her first design for the All Souls Church in Evanston. He proposed a most unusual design—two tiered, box-like structures joined together by a central corridor. The taller structure, on the corner of the two streets, would have high windows to let the light into the church, while the smaller one would be a community center. The building was to be made of reinforced concrete, the cheapest and most fireproof building material around, with the roofs of reinforced concrete slabs. With the lessons of the Great Fire seared into their psyche, the architects of Chicago were increasingly interested in exploring the use of concrete, which was not only fireproof but also an economical building material.

The entrance to the building would be in the middle of the block, on the quieter side street. When people entered the central hall, they could turn left to the taller church section of the building or right into the room for the library and community center. The church section had windows, with art glass, around the second story, and a ceiling with amber-colored stained glass skylights. It would be a square-shaped auditorium with tiered seating looking toward the pulpit, different from the long rectangular interior of traditional churches. With the Unity Temple, people would go from the entrance hall of the building, through a series of turns, before finding themselves in a special, almost private room of worship, walking past the altar to their seats.

The design was radically different from a conventional church and shocked Wright's contact on the building committee. Only three years before, Marion had already had her own experience designing a church for her congregation. She would not have been surprised with the opposition Wright's early sketch plans received.

But Wright, as usual, was supremely confident in his design and was determined to get his way. It was getting close to Christmas 1905 when he had to present his proposals to the trustees of the church. He called on Marion to do the presentation drawing. The challenge was to make such an unusual concrete building look attractive. It was, as described later, "the most radical departure from traditional church architecture ever attempted."[4] Marion responded, drawing the building with fine ink lines, elaborate stained glass windows, and her trademark hanging vines and surrounding trees, which softened its twin box-like appearance. The trustees agreed to put the concept to a broad group of church leaders.

On a Wednesday evening at the end of January, 75 men from the church crowded into Wright's studio to inspect the plans. Wright had made a plaster model of the church and showed photographs of Marion's drawings on a screen. The combination of Marion's drawings and Wright's charm and powers of persuasion won the day. Once accepted, the congregation became excited about the modern new plan for their Unity Temple. In February 1906, the local paper, *Oak Leaves*, did a story on the church, with Marion producing two elegant new drawings for the article.

Marion's work on the Unity Temple showed the evolution of her more confident, distinctive drawing style. Those in the office could see it, even if her name was not on the drawings. Charles E. White, Jr, one of the architects in the office, wrote to his friends that "Marion Mahony has been doing great work (the Unity perspectives are hers)."[5] Writing to a friend later, he added, "I think she is one of the finest in the country in this class of rendering."

Marion and Wright admired the way Japanese artists used unusual perspectives for creative expression. She began drawing some of the houses on tall, rectangular canvasses, like Japanese scrolls, using perspectives from above or below, as she had seen with the Japanese drawings. Wright designed a house for Thomas Paul Hardy, the mayor of Racine, a town in Wisconsin on Lake Michigan. In June 1906 it was featured in the magazine *House Beautiful* in a story called "A House on a Bluff." The design was Wright's but the drawings were clearly Marion's. The article included a vertical drawing, a view of the house looking up from the lake. The house was a strong imposing structure at the top of the picture, with just a few simple lines depicting the cliff below. It was not a working architectural drawing, but a work of art, aimed at impressing the client and the outside world. Wright was an astute man and knew the importance of getting his radical designs widely publicized. Marion had just the skills to help him do it.

Sometime in 1906, Laura Bowsher, a friend of Isabel Roberts, who worked in the Oak Park studio, paid a visit. She commissioned Wright to design a home for her and her new husband, K.C. de Rhodes, in South Bend, Indiana. Marion did an elegant drawing of the house set in a forest of trees. Her drawing reflected her newfound inspiration from Hiroshige's woodcuts. There were the now familiar built-in planter boxes of vines, spilling over down the front of the house, connecting the building with the environment. She drew an elegant woman standing at the front door, toward the right of the drawing, as if to welcome guests. In the foreground, on the left, was a drawing of a bird on a tree, reminiscent of Hiroshige's bird and flower works. Marion's stylish inclusion of the natural elements helped to soften Wright's strong linear designs. When she finished, Marion did something new for her. She put her own initials on the drawing. She devised her own monogram, MLM. Marion Lucy Mahony. The interlinked M's looked like spider legs, nestled under the tree with the bird.

When he saw the final drawing, Wright was amused. He picked up a pen and on the lower right-hand side of the paper, he wrote, "Drawing by Mahony. After FLW and Hiroshige." Wright was not given to praise others much. The fact that he was at last prepared to acknowledge Marion on the drawings showed her increasing role in his studio and his appreciation of her evolving style. Her drawing of the house was also published in *House Beautiful* in 1906.

Barry Byrne noted that:

> The style of these drawings of Miss Mahony's was determined only in a general way by Mr. Wright, he having in mind, of course, the artistic character evident in Japanese prints. The picture compositions were initiated by Miss Mahony, who had unusually fine compositional and linear ability, with a drawing "touch" that met with Mr. Wright's highly critical approval.[6]

But, while Wright was full of praise for Marion about her more distinctive Japanese-inspired drawing style, his ego, of course, could brook no master in the studio other than himself. Behind her back, he was less congratulatory. While Marion *copied* Japanese prints, he would tell people later, he, Wright, was inspired by them.[7]

Toward the end of 1906, work in the studio increased. Wright planned to have a major exhibition of his work at the Chicago Architectural Club in April 1907. He turned to Marion to help with many of the 30 drawings of his houses, which would be used for the show. She produced a striking drawing of the Cheney House. It was a bird's-eye view, which could have been seen from someone sitting high up in a tree across the road, looking down into the house. It was another Japanese-style perspective, but it may also have been inspired by the view that Marion could see when she looked down at the world from the top of the tree near her home at Hubbard Woods as a young girl.

It was a busy time for Marion. The fire at the Oak Park church in 1905 added to Wright's passion for advocating the importance of fireproof housing and housing that was also affordable for the common man. In 1906, he designed a low-cost house for an estimated $5,000 made of concrete. Marion did the drawing and put her monogram, MLM, in the tree trunks of the lower right-hand side. Her drawing of the house was published in the *Ladies' Home Journal* in April 1907. Wright also designed a studio for the sculptor Richard Bock in 1906, in nearby River Forest. Marion drew the design with loving care for her occasional colleague. The two-story, flat-roofed building was festooned with Marion's trademark hollyhocks and trailing vines. There were trees behind it and one larger one off to the left-hand side in the foreground and flowers around its base.

Marion also did some architectural work for her family. She used funds from selling shares in her older brother's plantation in Mexico to build a house for her family in Rogers Park, north of Chicago.[8] A little later, her younger brother, Gerald, wanted her to design a house for him in Elkhart, Indiana, where he was working as an engineer. He bought a farmhouse on the banks of the St. Joe River, which he wanted to renovate. Gerald's landlady had suggested he use a local architect, but he was determined to have his sister do it for him. Marion went to Elkhart to work on the project.

She added a second story on the house, where she included a giant billiard room and a large studio. She put strips of stained glass windows along the walls, with geometric designs using vertical lines and chevrons, in yellows and greens and golds, similar to those in some of Wright's houses. She put a big brick fireplace in the middle of the living room.

When it was completed, Marion and her brother tested it out. "Though it was a hot day, we crept in under to build a fire and sat there hugging our knees and gloating over it."[9]

There was a barn on the property, which she moved closer to the riverbank so it could be used as a boathouse. She added a screened pavilion to the hayloft on top, allowing people to sit and look at the river. Her brother would later claim that she had "ruined him" with the cost, but Marion insisted they had a lot of fun together. Having created such a wonderful riverside house, Marion often came to stay with her brother. It was a magical place, a retreat from the chaos and industrial grime of Chicago.

In 1908, Marion designed a house for William Burke in Three Rivers, Michigan, on the recommendation of a former member of her congregation. The same year, she also entered into a competition held by the Chicago Architectural Club to design a concrete house, sponsored by the Universal Portland Cement Company. For her entry, Marion designed a large box-shaped building with overtones of the Unity Temple. It had a massive cantilevered slab of concrete over the top of the third floor, providing shelter for the penthouse, with a smaller slab below it over the entrance door. On either side of the entrance were three thin bands of vertical windows, integrating the floors. She didn't win, but her design was among those selected to be published in the book, *Plans for Concrete Residences*, for the company. [10]

Marion did the drawings for other projects in the Oak Park office, including a summer house at Lake Forest for Harold and Edith Rockefeller McCormick, who were members of two of America's wealthiest families. She did several drawings of Wright's proposed house including a bird's-eye view of the complex and another showing the residence from the lake, using fine dotted ink lines to show the reflection of the house in the water.

Marion's love of nature was also an integral part of her spiritual beliefs. There was an almost mystical element to the interest in nature by some of the fellow travelers in the Prairie School. Wright's own beliefs had roots in the thinking of his Welsh forefathers. His son John would write later:

> Like his ancestors the Druids, he [Wright] had a great veneration for Nature spirits, gnomes, undines, little creatures of the forests and rivers who lived under lily pads and in houses of moss sprayed by waterfalls. And Papa preserved his love for fairies in the midst of a prosaic world.[11]

It was a view Marion, with her Celtic background on her father's side, also shared. She knew about the fairies and the spirits, too. In her mind, they were part of the natural world, friendly forces helping God create nature.

Marion was good friends with Dwight's wife, Lucy, who had gone back to work to help her family's finances over a decade before, around the time that Dwight's practice had hit financial troubles. Lucy Fitch Perkins, as she was known, had become a successful book illustrator and was part of the circle of strong women in the extended Mahony and Perkins families. In 1908, Lucy was given a commission to do the illustrations for some new children's books and asked Marion to help. The two of them worked on the illustrations for the books, which were written by children's author Maud Summers.[12]

Marion and Lucy were both credited on the cover as the illustrators of the *Summers Readers*. But it was almost impossible to tell which one of them had done each drawing. Marion's name on the cover was second to Lucy's, but the books gave Marion far more public acknowledgment for her drawings than she was ever getting from her more important work helping to depict the houses in Wright's studio.

While the talented but egotistical Wright worked hard to publicize his own efforts and play down the contribution of those in his studio, Marion was happy with her low-key life and had no desire for fame. She may have been trained as an architect and an artist along with her male peers, but she had no desire to match them when it came to self-promotion and public recognition.

Frank Lloyd Wright 1905. Courtesy Frank Lloyd Wright Trust.

Eleven

Scandal

While Wright's practice was doing well, all was not well with his marriage. His relationship with Mrs. Cheney, Mamah as she was known, had turned into an affair. Kitty knew about it, but she was choosing to ignore it. It may not have been the first. Unbeknownst to most of those in the studio, Wright had already approached his wife for a divorce so he could be with Mrs. Cheney, but Kitty refused, asking him to wait a year.

Given the close relationship of Marion, Isabel Roberts, and Kitty, it would have been impossible for those in the studio to not have detected strains in the relationship. But Wright was known for his flamboyant ways, and in those days, men did not desert their wives and families for a passing affair. In February 1909, Wright traveled to the Bitterroot Valley in Montana where a group of university professors planned to build orchards as part of a summer colony. Marion did not go to Montana with him, but she helped to draw up a perspective of the project, its central clubhouse, and nearby cabins. A combination of Wright's descriptions of the site and her own imagination would have to suffice. Her drawings of the Como Orchards Summer Colony included a bird's-eye view of the site as it could have been seen from an imaginary hill—or maybe by a little girl looking down from a giant tree.[1]

Wright was also approached by a Chicago builder, Ingwald Moe, to design a house for him in Gary, Indiana. Marion was called on to draw the house. She drew the house in ink on light brown paper, coloring it with sepia washes. The building was highlighted with touches of opaque white gouache. The house was in a setting of trees, depicted again from the bird's-eye view. The use of the white paint was another technique she was using, adding light to a building in a natural way.[2]

Around the same time, Wright was contacted by a publisher in Berlin, Ernst Wasmuth, who asked him to put together a portfolio of his work for publication in Europe. Wright seized on the prospect, knowing that it was his big chance to get recognition in Europe, the recognition he believed he deserved. He decided he would go to Germany to work on the project.

There was a great rush in the studio as Wright prepared for his trip to Europe. He had to put together many of the designs he wanted to publish. The selected drawings would then have to be retraced to make them suitable for publication.

The core of the portfolio came from the drawings shown at the Chicago Architectural Club exhibition in 1907, many of which were done by Marion, including the Cheney House, Unity Temple, the Thomas Hardy House, and the K.C. de Rhodes House. While Marion may not have realized it at the time, more than half of the 70 or so plates used for the Wasmuth portfolio would be her drawings.[3] It was a tribute to the amount of work she had done in his studio and her artistic skills. Wright had taken to telling some of the other draftsmen in the office to copy her style, but their imitations were heavy-handed.

Wright declared that he intended to go to Europe for a considerable time. Not only did he want to make sure all his drawings were properly prepared for publication, he was eager to see more of the architecture of Europe. But, unlike his trip to Japan with Kitty in 1905, this time Wright would be traveling on his own.

It was a busy time at the studio. Wright was in the middle of building a house for Frederick C. Robie, a prosperous young bicycle manufacturer, in Chicago's Hyde Park neighborhood. The Robie House had dramatic living and dining areas combined into one flowing space. It also featured extensive rows of stained glass windows, which it is believed that Marion helped to design. Marion was also working with Wright on plans for a major project for a combined bank and hotel building in Mason City, Iowa, the state to the northwest of Illinois. Construction on the hotel was underway, under the supervision of Marion's Oak Park colleague William Drummond, but Marion was working on the drawings. Wright had also built a house for a Mason City doctor, George Stockman, and other leading businessmen in the city wanted him to design houses for them.

Wright continued to work on projects, aware of the need to generate funds for his trip and to support his family while he was away. He also sold some of his Japanese prints to raise more money. The time for Wright to leave for Europe was approaching, but new clients were still coming into the Oak Park studio. He received an approach from a wealthy businessman from Michigan who was becoming very famous, Henry Ford. Ford had set up the Ford Motor Company in 1903 and launched the people's car, the Model T, in 1908. It had the steering wheel on the left, instead of in the middle. The engine was enclosed, and it was cheap and easy to drive. Its price of only $825 put it within reach of ordinary Americans. It was only a year after its release, and the Model T Fords were becoming very popular. A few months before, in the summer of 1909, Wright had met with Childe H. Wills, Ford's chief designer, who had worked on the Model T, to discuss plans for a house for Wills in Detroit. Wills had sung Wright's praises to his boss, Henry Ford.

Wright was just about to leave and should not have entertained Ford's approach, but he was a big lover of cars and would have been eager to meet the man. Ford had bought 1,300 acres of land on the Rouge River in Michigan, near where he was born. He wanted to build a country house there for him and his wife, Clara. Both Wright and Ford had a lot in common, with their passion for machinery and their fascination with things new. Ford's arrival at the Oak Park studio must have created an impression among the others in the office, but Wright was clearly distracted. One worker later recalled his surprise at "Wright's inability to maintain his customary, self-confident manner."[4] It appears that the meeting ended with no specific agreement between the two.

Wright took Marion aside and asked if she would take over his practice while he was away.[5] She had been working with him for almost 15 years and knew his business well. But Marion remembered what had happened to Walter Burley Griffin a few years before. She knew how Wright was always short of money and about the bills that never got paid. She knew how one could never quite rely on his promises. And, this time, he was going to be away for a lot longer than on his trip to

Japan. Marion admired Wright and had often half-flirted with him. She had done well in his studio, but she knew his darker side. She had no hesitation in refusing him.

Wright tried several other architects. Finally, he found someone who would take on his business—Hermann von Holst.[6] Von Holst's lack of firsthand experience with Wright may have been one of the reasons he was prepared to take on the job. Three years younger than Marion, von Holst was born in Germany to a German father and an American mother. The family moved to America when Hermann's father was appointed head of the history department at the University of Chicago. Von Holst studied architecture at that university and completed the architecture program at MIT in 1896, two years after Marion. He worked for various firms before going out on his own in 1905. He was an active member of the Chicago Architectural Club, spending a year as its president in 1907, and a charter member of the Cliff Dwellers Club, which was formed in the same year by some of Chicago's leading artists, architects, authors, and their patrons. He had just moved into offices in Steinway Hall when he was approached by Wright. On September 22, 1909, Wright and von Holst signed an agreement for "Von," as his friends called him, to take over Wright's outstanding work. The next day, Wright left Chicago by train for New York and sailed across the Atlantic to Europe.

Von Holst knew of Marion's key role in the Oak Park studio and approached her to help him with the business. As von Holst told people later, "I engaged Miss Mahoney [sic] to work in my office as I could not carry on Wright's work without her help."[7] Marion accepted the position on the condition that she had "full authority and final decision on all matters of design and construction." Busy with his own practice, and knowing full well that Marion was a hard worker and one of the finest architectural drawers in the city, von Holst readily agreed.

Marion moved into von Holst's offices in Steinway Hall. With Wright gone, work at the Oak Park studio wound down. She was back working in the building that her cousin Dwight had designed, a project she had been involved in as a young architect. But this time she was working on the ninth floor and not the top floor with the loft. She was pleased with her arrangement with von Holst and quickly got to work. She continued working on drawings for the Park Inn Hotel in Mason City[8], while William

Drummond, who was making regular trips to Mason City to oversee its construction, moved into Dwight's old office space on the 11th floor.

Back at Steinway Hall, Marion was also back in touch with some of the leading architects of the city. Her old colleague from the Oak Park studio, Walter Burley Griffin, worked on the top floor along with Robert Spencer and now William Drummond. Walter's practice, it seemed, had done well since he left Wright's studio more than three years before.

Marion brought together a team of about six draftsmen for the work. Some came from von Holst's office and some had worked with her at Oak Park. Her little studio within a studio was beginning to hum and things seemed to be going along smoothly. But Wright had another trick up his sleeve.

Seven weeks after Wright had left for Europe, the tight-knit circle around the Oak Park house and studio, and indeed most of Chicago, received some shocking news. Wright had not just gone to Europe to see Herr Wasmuth about publishing his portfolio, but he was there with Mrs. Cheney. Mamah had abandoned her husband and two children and run away to Europe with Wright. They were living there together.

The front page of the *Chicago Tribune* on November 7, 1909, alerted the world to the scandal.

> Leave Families: Elope to Europe.
>
> Architect Frank Lloyd Wright and Mrs. Edwin H. Cheney of Oak Park Startle Friends; Abandoned Wife Loyal; Spouse a Victim of a Vampire, She Says, and Will Return When He Can; Other's Husband Silent.[9]

Oak Park, the quiet suburb that Wright himself had dubbed Saints' Rest, was scandalized. Marion rang Kitty and learned the worst. The poor woman was distraught, hounded by reporters, day and night. The children were having trouble at school, and she had closed the kindergarten she operated from her home. The newspapers were full of the story. They wrote of the "two abandoned homes where children play at the hearth sides," "strange infatuations" and a "fly-by-night journey through Germany."[10] Some reporters even climbed the tree next to the house to peer into the Wrights' bedroom window. Marion went to Oak Park to comfort Kitty.

But, as she arrived in Oak Park, Marion would have seen a city with other preoccupations. The neat, upper middle-class suburb was normally as quiet as the city was noisy. But in November 1909, it was abuzz with an air of excitement, its shops decorated with bright green and yellow colors, and the weather was unseasonably warm. The Oak Park branch of the Nineteenth Century Women's Club was about to play host to the annual convention of the Illinois Federation of Women's Clubs. There was a lot to discuss.[11]

The Illinois general assembly had passed a law restricting the hours women could work in factories and shops to 10 hours a day, but the big employers were mounting a legal challenge against it. And then there was the long campaign to give women the vote. If women could vote, as Marion had heard so often, the factory owners would not be able to treat women and children workers so harshly, there would be parks set aside for children to play, and the big companies would not be able to pollute the city's air and waters. It didn't have to be like that. It was regularly pointed out by those advocating for the vote for women that in Australia, a new country thousands of miles away across the Pacific, the progressive, socially minded government had granted women the right to vote years ago.

But the happy mood at Oak Park stopped at Wright's front door. The more Marion learned, the more she began to appreciate the full horror of Wright's actions. There were rumors that Wright had left his family with an unpaid grocery bill of several hundred dollars.

As she now realized, Wright's distraction in his last few months at Oak Park, and his complicated planning for such an extended absence, had an ulterior motive. He was not going to be coming back soon. It was a decade since Wright had carefully posed Kitty and Marion so closely together in a photograph, almost like two sisters. Now, they were together again under much more traumatic circumstances. A lot had happened since that memorable photo. And now, *The House and Studio of an Architect*, which Marion herself had helped to create, was being torn apart.

The media attention to the unfolding saga continued unabated, with reporters tracking down Wright and Mrs. Cheney in Europe. It was a delicious scandal, which provided plenty of newspaper copy. Three years before, the popular press in America had plenty of juicy fodder from the scandal about a prominent New York architect, Stanford White, the designer of Madison Square Garden, the Washington Square Arch in New York, and the Boston Public Library. White was shot dead at Madison Square Garden by millionaire Harry Kendall Thaw, the irate husband of one of White's young lovers, Evelyn Nesbit. Thaw's trial was covered in great detail, revealing all sorts of salacious details about White's womanizing ways, such as the red velvet swing he had installed in his loft apartment in New York. The apartment was decorated with heavy red velvet curtains and fine paintings. The swing was in an upstairs studio where Nesbit and other young women would sit for him in varying stages of undress.[12] Wright did not have a red velvet swing. But, as his son wrote later, maybe it was his jalopy, the Yellow Devil, which did the trick for him with Mrs. Cheney. John Wright wrote, "One night he took his fair companion riding and kept right on going."[13]

If Oak Park was shocked and outraged, so was the tight architectural community in Chicago, particularly the Steinway Hall set and its alumni who knew Wright well. Dwight told people that he had "loved that man [Wright]" until he left his wife.[14] But Walter, who now had a growing practice from his office in the loft at Steinway Hall, might have been a little less surprised. He knew from his own experience how Wright could be. Marion thought she knew Wright well, but she was still shocked to learn he was deserting his family for another woman.

Wright's affair shattered Marion's comfortable professional life and ended a relationship that spanned 15 years. Marion had joined his office as a raw 24-year-old architect just a year out of university, and she was now a 38-year-old experienced professional. The Oak Park studio was now closing for good. Marion had spent some of the most productive years of her professional life working with Wright. She had left the "little university," the close-knit drafting room where she had spent so much time with Wright and the talented group of people who worked in his studio, and there would be no going back.

But the change was also liberating for her. She was no longer in Wright's shadow or subject to his dominating, all-confident personality. She also liked working with von Holst, who respected her architectural and drawing skills and gave her space to do her own thing. Marion had a long-time passion for things German, which would also have helped in her relationship with him. Chicago had a big population of German migrants. At the time, the city had more than 500,000 German-speaking citizens, several times the number of the next largest foreign language speaking groups, the Poles, and the Swedes.[15] Von Holst spoke with a distinct German accent, although he and his father regarded themselves as Americans. But, while they got on well together, Marion and von Holst soon found out that the business they had agreed to manage for Wright had more problems than they could have imagined. Wright had collected as many fees in advance as he could get from his clients before he left for Europe to finance his trip. Von Holst also had to deal with a host of angry clients who had paid good money to have a "Wright House" and did not want to deal with him.

To the outside world, Wright's practice was now being run by von Holst and his engineer partner, James Fyfe. Von Holst liked to keep it that way, and Marion had never worried about who got the credit for the work.

Despite her anger at Wright for leaving Kitty, she still expected to have some sort of professional relationship with him in Europe as she finished off the work for his clients. But to Marion's surprise, Wright never replied to her letters. She was angry at first when she didn't hear from him. After all the years they had worked together, now he was ignoring her letters about the projects she was working on from his office. Everyone back home in Chicago had to pick up the pieces of his life while he was away in Europe with his new lady love. At the least, he could be professional about the work she was helping to finish off for him. But it seemed that Wright was severing their professional relationship as well.

But, over time, with no contact from Wright on her professional queries, Marion took her own initiative. It was a liberating experience, and she saw herself in a new professional role with von Holst and his partner. She said:

> When the absent architect didn't bother to answer anything that was sent over to him, relations were broken and I entered into a partnership with von Holst and Fyfe. For that period I had fun designing.[16]

Twelve

Out on Her Own

Von Holst's agreement with Wright listed 19 projects, divided into three groups: Work under Construction, Work in Hand, and Probable and Prospective. Work under Construction included the supervision of the final work on projects such as the Robie House in Chicago and the Park Inn Hotel and Bank in Mason City, Iowa. Work in Hand included sketches for a house for Mr. Irving in Decatur, Illinois, a town 40 miles east of Springfield. The Probable and Prospective group included another house in Decatur for a Mr. Mueller and another for a Mr. Amberg in Grand Rapids, Michigan.[1]

The Park Inn project was well underway when Wright left. Drummond was making the visits to the city to oversee the work while Marion focused her energies in the office, overseeing the design work for the interior such as the metal grates, the furniture, and fittings.[2] She was also working on the design of a house for a Mason City builder, Joshua Melson, one of the many clients who had visited the Oak Park studio to see Wright in the months before he left for Europe.

One of those assigned to her group was 24-year-old Roy Lippincott who had been working in von Holst's office. He had studied architecture at Cornell University in New York State and was inspired by a speech made by Dwight to go to Chicago. But he had been unable to get work with Perkins as he was working as chief architect for the Chicago school board and had gotten a job in von Holst's office earlier that year. Von Holst had asked his new recruit to work with Marion. As he later recalled, "I was ... assigned to [Marion's] group and, from then on, life became exciting. She took me in hand and, before long, I was blocking out perspective studies and later even working on the renderings with [her]."³

Now she was an independent, professional woman in charge of her own practice within a practice, and she loved the chance to do things her way. She had never married nor even had a serious romantic relationship. She was happy in her work and with her busy extended family life. Sometimes people would wonder why she had never married, or if she had thrown herself into her work because she had not had any successful romantic relationships.

As she recalled later:

> A friend in the office had said the surmises were that I must have been disappointed in love because I took my work so earnestly. I was devoted to my work and indeed throughout my life have been convinced that work is the one great satisfaction for human beings which means that those women who have not grown up to take a life's work seriously as our men do are being deprived of life's greatest continuous satisfaction.⁴

There were now two different groups of draftsmen working in von Holst's office. There was Marion's group, which was working on the specific projects she handled from Wright's Oak Park practice, and another group which worked directly for von Holst and Fyfe on their business. Marion decided she would take a different approach to managing her group from the traditional autocratic rule in drafting rooms. Instead of ordering her staff to do things, or berating them when they made a mistake, she adopted a more supportive, motherly approach to her charges. She delighted in the fact that her part of the office was not only happier but a lot more productive than the group working directly under von Holst and Fyfe. As she would tell people later:

> Unforgettable was the expression on the face of the engineer [Fyfe] when he saw an instance of [my] method in the office, when [I] leaped at a draftsman and said "Oh you naughty little thing, you have done that wrong," where he would have cursed and fumed. But [my] method was effective where his would probably have failed except on the surface. ...

In fact many times [I] told the younger ones not to work too hard, that the important thing was to "keep themselves alive and wide awake."⁵

Marion had two major design projects on her plate. One was a new house in Grand Rapids, Michigan, for David and Hattie Amberg. David Amberg was in the wholesale liquor business and also managed the estate of his wife's family. In 1908, the Ambergs' daughter, Sophie, and her husband, Meyer S. May, had Wright design a house for them in Grand Rapids. The Ambergs liked the house and approached Wright in 1909 to design a house for them nearby on a corner block. But Wright had left for Europe before doing anything on the house, and the project now fell to Marion.

Having the chance to design the house from scratch was a great challenge for her. The land was a corner block with a slight embankment. Marion used the natural topography to create a house that stretched along two sides of the corner, maximizing the view.⁶ The sloping land allowed the house to be built largely on one level with a driveway entrance and some rooms underneath on the lower side. The house was built in orange brick with a roof of red clay tiles with dark brown wood trim.

Marion was able to give full rein to her passion for stained glass windows, running them all along the front of the main story on both sides. They had geometric designs in colors of yellow, green, and brown, resolving into more elaborate designs with the windows at the ends. She had been unable to carry out her original design for the All Souls Church in Evanston, with its sunken parlor, but in the Amberg House she was in control. She put the living room, the central room of the house, at the corner of the two streets, several steps down from the dining room. She also installed high vaulted ceilings, giving the living room a floor to ceiling height of about 12 feet. The room had a dramatic sense of space with light streaming in from the outside through the colored glass windows. But Marion went one step forward with her use of light and art glass. She also put recessed colored glass in the ceilings of the living and dining rooms in warm colors of yellow and brown. Lit from above, they looked like internal stained glass windows or an autumn-toned skylight, spreading a warm light into the room below. The cozy atmosphere inside was accentuated by the orange brick.

There was the central fireplace, of course. Marion knew it had to be a feature of the house. It was in the living room projecting out about 10 inches from the wall. It was made even more dramatic by two brick columns running up on either side of the fireplace, from floor to the ceiling. She arranged for George Niedecken, who had done a lot of internal decorative work for houses designed in the Oak Park studio, including a mural for the dining room of the Dana House, to do a painting of pine trees around the fireplace.

There were other examples of Marion's fine attention to detail. Above the stained glass windows, on the outside of the house, set into the four gables of the house, were colored geometric ceramic tiles. Out the front of the house were several of Marion's trademark planter boxes. In keeping with Wright's approach, Marion also oversaw the design of furniture for the house. The house had a feeling that was both spacious and warm. It was Marion's most dramatic and impressive house by far. Chicago architect Marion Mahony was at last coming into her own.

The other project was a much larger, more complex proposition. It was in Decatur, Illinois, some 200 miles southwest of Chicago, on an estate which had just been bought by Edward and Florence Irving. It was due east of Springfield, where Wright had worked on the lavishly redesigned house for Susan Lawrence Dana and about 65 miles from Tremont, where Marion's grandparents had lived and she had spent some time as a young girl. Edward Irving, who ran the Faries Manufacturing Company, one of the city's largest businesses, gathered together a group of wealthy local business people to develop an upmarket residential estate on the edge of the town. Those interested included Robert Mueller and his brothers. Their father had founded another large business in the city, H. Mueller Manufacturing.

Under the plan, each person who bought a block of land had to organize for the design of their own home, but Millikin Place, as the estate was called, would be designed as a "harmonious whole" by a landscape architect who would coordinate the streetscape, driveways, and entrance.[7]

The Irvings had approached Wright to design their house in Millikin Place, not knowing he was about to leave for Europe. Wright had sketched out a design for the house before he left. Irving had mentioned that one of the Mueller brothers might also be interested in a house on the estate. Wright never met them but he put "Mr. Mueller, Decatur" down as a Probable and Prospective client in the list he gave to von Holst.

Marion took charge of the project and began the working drawings for the Irving House. But before any houses could be built, there was the broader issue of the landscaping for the estate. The Millikin Place investors had approached the famous Chicago landscape architect Ossian Cole Simonds to do the work. One of the leaders of the new American school of landscape gardening, Simonds had won high praise for redesigning Graceland Cemetery in Chicago. He was mentioned in the local paper in December 1909 as the landscape designer of the Millikin Place Estate who had already made some sketches for the site.[8]

But Marion knew a good landscape architect much closer to hand. Her old colleague, Walter Burley Griffin, worked only a few floors above her at Steinway Hall. Marion was in regular contact with William Drummond, who worked in the same office, and was overseeing the Park Inn in Mason City they were both working on. She soon began talking to Walter as well. She knew of his passion for landscaping, having worked alongside him for several years at Oak Park. She had not kept in touch with him since he left Wright's studio, but she soon discovered that he had been doing very well since going out on his own.

She found Walter had designed some 35 buildings in his three years of practice on his own and seen 20 of them constructed. His houses included one for the Peters family in western Chicago, which featured a spectacular diamond-shaped window for an upstairs bedroom that overlooked a garden. He was also working on plans for his first major showing at the Chicago Architectural Club in 1910. Somehow, over the next few months, the idea of getting the much more famous O.C. Simonds to do the landscaping for Millikin Place disappeared, and Walter became the landscape architect on the project. Having her former colleague help her on the project also gave her a trusted person to discuss her work with outside of von Holst's office.

Marion's first task was to complete the work on the Irving House. Wright had done a preliminary pen-and-ink sketch of a two-story structure with long, low hip roofs. It was to have a wide band of color between the two stories, accentuating the horizontal look he was so fond of. Marion found the Irvings wanted the house to be built in brick rather than stucco. She added to the design with two solid vertical piers of brick at the front, inset from the side walls, changing Wright's horizontal look to something more box-like and solid. The house would have stained glass windows, of course. Between the piers were stained glass doors on the ground floor with another wall of stained glass windows above them on the second story. There were similarities with what she had done with the design of her brother's house in Elkhart.

She selected a warm color scheme for the interior, highlighted by dark brown wooden trim around the doors and ceilings. Marion commissioned George Niedecken to do a mural for the living room, and she designed furniture for the house including an unusual combined study desk with an attached couch and bookcase and a desk lamp, as well as the carpets, curtains, radiator screens, and the stained glass windows.[9] Outside, at the back, she decorated the second-story windows with two panels of tiles, in a combination of square and rectangular shapes, set into the wall between the three windows, giving it a touch of color.

As she worked on the Irving House, Marion found that there were two Mueller brothers, 46-year-old Robert and 44-year-old Adolph, who also wanted to have houses designed for land they had bought at Millikin Place. Unlike the Irving House, where Irving and Wright had already agreed on the preliminary design, Marion was in charge of the design of the two Mueller houses from the start and was growing more confident in her style.

The house she designed for Robert Mueller was a more imposing structure than the flatter, more horizontal design that Wright had sketched out for the Irving House. She used this taller canvas to produce an integrated design for the front of the house. The middle part of the house, which was brick, was extended out into the garden, creating a dramatic centerpiece. It was accentuated on either side by two large brick piers, which went from the ground up to the second-story windowsills, giving the house a solid, powerful look. Between them were four narrower brick pillars. Between the pillars, on the ground floor, were floor-to-ceiling stained glass windows. Above these windows were vertical rectangles of colored square tiles and above them, on the second floor, were smaller stained glass windows. It came together in one artistic whole with the six strong vertical pillars showcasing the stained glass windows and the tile designs in between them—a very different look from Wright's horizontal bands. Marion also used a similar technique as she had done in the Amberg House, installing a rectangular colored glass panel with geometric patterns in the ceiling, projecting warm light into the room.

By the time she got to the next house, sometime in the second half of 1910, Marion's confidence in her own style was growing. Her design for Adolph Mueller's house was another big step forward. His block of land was almost double the size of the other two, which gave her more space to work with and maybe the fact that he was two years younger than Robert allowed her to be a bit more adventurous. She designed a wide, two-story stucco house with a distinctly Japanese flavor with some overtones of the Dana House only 40 miles away. It had a projecting entranceway covered by a gabled roof with upturned gutters. Above it, to the right, on the second story, was another larger gabled roof with two strong brick pillars going from top to bottom. She made lavish use of stained glass windows on both floors using variations of the chevron design, which was popular in Wright's office, an evolution of the motifs of a stalk of wheat. The windows in the second story, under the gables, stretched up to the roof, allowing the light to flood inside.

The living room, which was designed to face a side garden, was its most spectacular showpiece. It had strong overtones of the Amberg House in Grand Rapids, with an inverted V-shaped tentlike ceiling, almost 10 feet high in the center. The living room was a few steps down from the rest of the house, giving the room a greater feeling of space. The ceiling was inset with two leaded stained glass windows, one at either end of the room, in warm colors of yellows and orange with tinges of green, with square and rectangular patterns highlighted with the occasional red rectangle. The glass doors of the living room, which faced the garden, were inset with delicate chevron-like designs, highlighted with colors of gold and yellow. Together with the cream interior walls, which were highlighted by dark wooden trim around the doors, it produced a look that was both dramatic and breathtaking. The stairwell had stained glass windows, allowing the light to stream in. It was a step up in design and creativity from the Robert Mueller House nearby.

She had designed an elegant house with flowing interior spaces, which was not only livable but brought together all her decorative skills. She put stained glass windows on three sides of the living room, with their chevron and rectangular designs bringing the spirit of the natural world into the house. The light flooded into the living room from three sides through the delicately designed windows. Looking very different from the Robert Mueller House, did its design reflect some input from Walter? Or was it just a more confident Marion at last given a free rein to develop her distinctive style with a supportive client?[10]

To the outside world, the houses were being designed by von Holst or maybe even the increasingly famous Wright himself. Von Holst himself never went out of his way to introduce his chief designer to his clients.[11] But Marion appeared to be happy to do her own work, behind the scenes, without claiming the public credit.

Marion also designed lampposts to mark the entrance to the estate. They were brick pillars with cube-shaped Japanese-style lanterns on either side, which had overtones of the interior lights designed for the Unity Temple a few years before. Marion prided herself on her knowledge of the natural world but as she got to know Walter more, she found his knowledge of plants almost encyclopedic. He had studied the volumes of the *Cylopedia of American Horticulture* by Liberty Hyde Bailey, published from 1900 to 1902, learning the names of as many plants as he could.[12]

Inspired by a newfound admiration for the work of her former workmate, Marion was able to direct some other landscaping projects in the office to him. The Moe House in Gary, Indiana, which was being completed under the supervision of von Holst's office, was another example of them working together. Marion arranged for Walter to design the gardens around it while she enhanced Wright's original design for the house with art glass doors in the bookcases, art glass wall sconces in the living room, and art glass doors on the sideboards in the dining room.[13] The two began spending an increasing amount of time together. With Wright gone, and their social and architectural circles turning against her former mentor, Marion began to see Walter in a very different light.

Top: Japanese-inspired lamp marking the entrance to Millikin Place, Decatur, Illinois, designed by Marion Mahony.

Bottom: Adolph Mueller House. Millikin Place, Decatur, Illinois. Photographs by Vin Plant 2013.

Tented ceiling of lounge room in Adolph Mueller House featuring stained glass. Stained glass also on doors and windows. Decatur, Illinois. Photographs by Vin Plant 2013.

Thirteen

The Serpent's Wisdom

As her attraction to Walter increased, Marion's life took on a sense of urgency. There had been no spark of attraction when they were working together in the Oak Park studio. Walter was interested in Maginel and was hurt by her rejection of his proposal, while Marion had her own busy life and her attention was very much focused on Wright. As she explained later, when she looked back on things, "during my early life I was led by the passing Will o' the Wisp in what I did—drawing, dancing, drama, architecture."[1] But now she was approaching 40 and discussed her projects with Walter. She began to appreciate his talents and could feel herself changing.

She realized how much they had in common. Walter was as passionate about nature and the environment as she was. He had a strong sense of idealism and commitment to the interests of the ordinary man, which made him very different from the self-centered Wright who loved courting rich clients. Walter's vision for architecture started with the land itself and its natural settings. While Wright continually strained the budgets of his wealthy clients with his elaborate houses and detailed interiors, Marion could see that Walter had a much higher social purpose to his work. He wanted to design communities for families to live together, in houses which fitted into the natural environment with safe areas for children to play. As she began to reacquaint herself with her old colleague, Marion developed, as she described it later, the wisdom of a serpent.[2] The book of Genesis describes the serpent as being "more subtle than any beast of the field which the Lord God had made." It tells the story of how the serpent cunningly lures Eve into the Garden of Eden with the promise of forbidden knowledge.

As her feelings for Walter grew, Marion began to discover wily new skills that she had never used before, feminine skills that had nothing to do with her work. She was now talking regularly to Walter about the Millikin Place project and plotting ways of getting closer to him. The one thing she did know, from years of working with Wright, was that men were dependent creatures.[3] Wright had come to depend on her drawing skills and her talents, talents which she knew would soon be on display with the publication in Europe of Wright's portfolio by Herr Wasmuth, talents she knew were as good as any other architectural drawer in America. If only Walter could get used to spending more time with her, he would begin to need her more. Marion now had a very clear goal. She planned to get closer to the unsuspecting Walter, step by step.

Marion discovered that Walter liked the outdoors as much as she did. He was a member of a Saturday afternoon walking club with others, including Dwight, who went on rambles along the rivers around Chicago. But Walter had never been quite as adventurous as Marion. Once she was planning to visit her brother Gerald in his farmhouse in Indiana on the St. Joe River, and she invited Walter to come along.[4] As they canoed along the river away from the big city, they felt relaxed. It was an idyllic place where the two could really get to know each other.

As they became closer, Walter began to reveal more about his life. He confessed to her that he had always loved spending time on the water, but his overprotective mother, Estelle, had forbidden him to swim in the local ponds and rivers. Occasionally, he told Marion, he would sneak off with other boys to swim in a pond some distance away from the family home. Marion took all this in. Walter had always been the quiet, serious person in the Oak Park office but she was pleased to learn that behind his cherubic face there was a much more adventurous spirit. Marion imagined Walter as a "tow-headed, blue-eyed suburban child,"[5] exploring the western suburbs of Chicago in Maywood and Elmhurst, wishing for more adventures. Marion felt it was her duty to liberate Walter's true spirit from the constraints of his conservative family background. Hopefully, by this means, they might also come closer together.

Marion knew Walter loved their weekend trips to Indiana, canoeing along the river, but their relationship was not advancing as fast as she wanted. Her inner emotional serpent, becoming stronger by the day, began to work out the next step as it studied its innocent prey. Walter and Marion were both hard at work in Chicago, often also working on Saturday mornings. It would be better, she said, if they could do some canoeing around Chicago on the weekends. She suggested they buy a canoe together so they could explore the rivers and streams around the city.

If they had their own canoe, they could enjoy the waters around Chicago whenever they wanted. The Chicago River was just down the street from their office in Steinway Hall. They could put the canoe in the river at the end of Van Buren Street and set off. Walter agreed, and they bought a white Canadian canoe and called it *Allana*. It was, as she told people later, an Irish word meaning "Beloved."[6] Another interpretation was "Dear Child." Marion had her eyes firmly set on her first real love. It is not hard to think that the prospect of having children may also have been on her mind.

In the beginning, they took *Allana* out on Sundays for the day, but they loved canoeing so much they decided to take advantage of the whole weekend, particularly when the weather was good. If they put *Allana* in the river on Saturday after they had finished work, they could stay out overnight and canoe all day Sunday as well.

Walter would bring two canvas sleeping bags with blankets, and Marion would bring the food, most often bread and bacon, as well as the frying pan and a bucket. They paddled along the rivers and explored the streams, escaping from the dirt and noise of Chicago, in their own world together. Marion watched in amazement as the normally quiet Walter came alive. "So many times they paddled for days with no consciousness of mankind," she recalled later.[7] They felt like they were the French explorers who had come down from Canada into Illinois. As Marion wrote later, Walter "immediately saw worlds to discover and conquer ... to rediscover domains in the same pristine state of loveliness as in centuries gone by when [René-Robert Cavelier] La Salle and [Jacques] Marquette journeyed through the Mississippi Valley."[8] By this time she had made up her mind to marry him. He hadn't, she knew, but that was not going to stop her.[9]

They became increasingly adventurous, trying out new and more complicated routes on their weekend trips, pushing farther and farther afield. Each trip had its new challenges. One weekend, they paddled along the Chicago River, until they came to a bend in the river close to the Des Plaines River, a well-known link between Lake Michigan and the Mississippi River. Walter knew there was a portage, an area where they could carry their canoe across the land to the next river, coming up soon. The area was so swampy that in wet weather, in the days gone past, the native Indians could easily paddle through from one river to the other. They had shown the route to the French fur trappers who came down from Canada. But now it was dry and Marion and Walter would have to carry *Allana* across the land as best they could.

It was hard work for Marion. She was tall, but not physically robust and had small wrists. When Marion was a child, her mother did not even like her lifting a hot kettle of boiling water from the stove for fear that her wrists would not be strong enough to hold it. But, with only the two of them out in the wild, Walter and Marion had to manage. They carried the canoe across the land to the river and paddled for home.

The river system around Chicago presented many challenges. There were many places where they would have to carefully maneuver *Allana*. "A stretch of shallows, a ruthless dam, a barb wire fence thrown across by some self-centered farmer to keep his cows from wandering around the end."[10] One weekend, they found themselves in the shallows and had to carry *Allana* across some farmland where they came across some barbed wire. They were carefully lifting it over the wire, taking great pains not to disturb anything, when an angry farmer came rushing down to the riverbank.

He yelled at them from the other side of the bank not to cut the wire. Marion was furious. She and Walter had just been going out of their way not to damage the fence. She gave the farmer some of her "Greek eloquence."

"Don't you know it's against the law to put in such a fence?" she demanded. "We have a good mind to report you and have you prosecuted."[11]

She continued berating him as they carried *Allana* to the river. The farmer stood there speechless, watching them paddling away upstream.

As they became more adventurous, they explored down toward the southern end of Lake Michigan. A unique area, it offered a number of attractions for the adventurous couple. There were flowing streams coming in from the surrounding areas, sand dunes along the lake and a network of railway lines. One Sunday afternoon, they were paddling along a river when Walter had an idea. He knocked on the door of a house and asked the farmer who owned it if they could leave *Allana* with them. They would come back for it the next weekend. The farmer agreed, and it opened up more worlds for Marion and Walter to explore. Rather than having to paddle the canoe all the way back to Chicago every Sunday night, they could leave her with a friendly householder or farmer and catch the train back home and come back the next weekend. Most farmers were happy to let them leave the canoe in a barn or somewhere on their property. Walter would always offer to pay them some money for storing it, but they would refuse.

But one afternoon, when they were a long way from home, their carefree plans came unstuck. Having had such good experience with the local farmers, they had paddled far, thinking that they would have no problem finding a place to leave the canoe. The weather was getting bad and a storm was coming up. At last, they found what looked like a good place, the naval station on Lake Michigan. They asked someone on the base if they could leave the canoe at the base, but they were refused. They persisted. They were sent up the chain of command but to no avail. No one would let them leave *Allana* on the base.

The weather was getting worse and the sky was getting darker. A storm approached and the waves came up. They would have to paddle all the way back to Chicago. Eventually they set out onto the lake, into a dark night, in the face of an oncoming storm. As they paddled back home in the dangerous waters through the rough weather and the rain, Marion was furious. She was tired and angry. She felt the men at the naval base would not have cared if they were lost in the storm. They eventually got back home safely, but Marion would never forget the lack of help they received. Marion's political philosophy was always pretty liberal, but she later insisted that this was one of the reasons she and Walter became pacifists. "Militarism breeds beasts, not humans," she argued.[12]

As the weekends went on, Walter and Marion became closer. They had many adventures, getting to know each other along the way. Sometimes, particularly if it rained, they would sleep together in the canoe overnight, covering themselves with a blanket.

> Two people on a cold night sleeping in a bathtub with a plug in and the water turned on ... the weight of the rain gradually depressed the blankets to form a reservoir and the crack in the middle formed a permanent outlet ... into the canoe.[13]

Marion wanted to become closer, but Walter was happy with things the way they were. After his rejection by Maginel Wright, he told Marion he had sworn off interest in any other women and his work became his life's passion. If Walter would not take the initiative, Marion's inner serpent, which was by now becoming very insistent, told her to take the next step. She just had to wait for the right time to strike.

Marion was also considering the next step in her professional life. She knew the work on the projects that had come out of Wright's office would come to an end and, at some point, she would have to think about developing her own practice. It appears that she had discussed setting up a studio with the sculptor Richard Bock. They had worked together in Oak Park and again on the Park Inn in Mason City where Bock did a sculpture of Mercury. William Drummond designed a double studio for Marion and Bock and was so proud of it, he put it in a Chicago Architectural Club exhibition in 1911.

But then Marion thought of going into partnership with Walter. She had been thinking for some time what a good match they made. The more she knew of him and his work, the more she admired him. She was impressed by his extensive knowledge of plants and trees. She knew his clients appreciated his work, but, unlike Wright, he was a quiet, modest man. By helping him, she could show his true genius to the rest of the world. Walter always had such wonderful ideas, and Marion was a great illustrator.

Walter's chief draftsman at the time was a young architect called Harry F. Robinson. A graduate of the University of Illinois, Robinson had worked at Wright's studio at Oak Park but left to join Walter's practice in 1908. But as Marion became more interested in Walter's work, she also knew that she could use her own, far superior drawing skills to show his work off in a much more stylish way.

Marion loved Greek philosophy. Sometimes she saw herself in a Greek play. She came to see Walter as Socrates, the wise Greek philosopher. "Socrates was, in every domain, an adventurer."[14] She began to think of herself as Socrates' wife, Xanthippe. As she explained later, "Xanthippe was well-known for her renderings and the work of Socrates was lying hidden away, known only to immediate clients."

Marion planned to change all that. It was just a matter of waiting until the right time to ask the question. One weekend, Walter and Marion got a cart to carry *Allana* up north to the headwaters of the Fox River and drop the canoe into Grass Lake, near the Wisconsin border. Marion always sat in the front of the canoe with Walter, the stronger paddler, at the back. The Egyptian lotus flowers were in bloom. She was happily admiring the flowers when she looked ahead. Suddenly, she could see the river was about to drop away sharply. Marion was afraid.

"We can't go here!" she said from the front of the boat. "We can't go here!"

"We've got to!" Walter shouted behind her.

And so they went over the drop together. There was no other choice. They survived the drop safely and paddled on.[15]

The next morning, they woke early in the cold morning and paddled down toward the Illinois River. It was a magical scene with the river covered in mist. The couple watched, transfixed, at the vista before them. "They watched veil after veil of the mists rise from the bluffed and forested banks, each veil revealing a new and even more beautiful universe..."[16] They continued paddling and soon the sun came up, burning off the mist. They pulled into the riverbank for a rest. Walter decided to take a swim in the stream. He found it very refreshing, and Marion could see he was in a happy mood. She took a deep breath.

"Why don't I join your office?" she said.

Walter was silent. She waited for his reply.

"I never dreamed you would do that," he said at last.

"All right, I'll arrange it," she said.[17]

And so they became partners, professionally at least. They agreed on what they described as a democratic form of partnership, which allowed them to work together but also to have their individual clients as well. Marion moved up to Walter's office on the 11th floor of Steinway Hall.

She was determined to prove the value of her artistic skills to Walter. Walter had been working on a house for F.P. Marshall in Kenilworth, an upmarket suburb 15 miles north of Chicago, near Evanston. Marion drew the house in a vertical presentation like a Japanese scroll, using the technique she had developed in Wright's office. She put the house at the top, set among the trees, the floor and garden plan in the middle, and a cross-sectional drawing of the house at the bottom. She added her trademark hanging vines and flower beds. Both drawings were signed Walter Burley Griffin, architect, but above and to the right, nestled in the garden, she drew her initials, MLM, in black ink, like a little spider in the corner.[18]

Working side by side with him, Marion became increasingly impressed with Walter's professional skills. She recalled her feelings at the time:

> And now, on coming into his office, [I] had revelation after revelation, thrill after thrill. Problems which [I] had struggled over in office after office and never solved were being solved one after another.[19]

Marion had her own work to do, but she became increasingly absorbed in helping Walter with his work. As she recalled later, she "became deeply centered in the task of lending a hand in all the emergencies that arose. Truly I lost myself in him and found it completely satisfying."[20]

Fourteen

Madness When It Struck

Marion's move to Walter's office brought them closer together. Marion was feeling happier and more in charge of her own destiny than she had ever been before. She was embarking on a new life and, for the first time, falling in love. As she wrote later:

> I was swept off my feet by delight in his achievements in my profession, then through a common bond of interests in nature and intellectual pursuits, and then with the man himself. It was by no means love at first sight, but it was madness when it struck.[1]

Walter was now a successful architect, developing his own style. He was still living at home with his parents, despite being in his mid-30s. Marion was not going to let his protestations about swearing off women after being rejected by Maginel stop her.

As they spent more time together, Marion learned more about what had happened to Walter in the years since he had left the Oak Park studio. She learned that his big commission to design a city in Shanghai had fallen through when his contact, the man he had met at the St Louis World's Fair in 1904, had died at sea on the journey back to China. She also learned more about the details of his acrimonious breakup with Wright.

Walter had recently taken the Japanese prints Wright had given him to be valued and found they were worth much less than Wright had claimed. Walter was fuming about it. Marion wrote an angry letter to Wright in Europe. Wright was furious about her allegations. In June

1910, he drafted an angry letter to Griffin referring to "an unpleasant rumor ... concerning the prints I turned over to you." That letter was never sent and remained in his papers.[2] Wright may have sent another version to Walter. But this was another sign of the increasing bitterness between Wright and his former staffers.

In October 1910, Wright came back to Chicago. Short of cash, he approached von Holst for money, which he argued he was due for the work on his practice. He filed a lawsuit against von Holst, claiming he owed him money, although it was von Holst who had suffered financially from their dealings. Wright had no office and no practice and was angry that his former employees were getting on well without him. Many clients would not do business with him because his reputation was tainted by scandal. He became increasingly angry, accusing his former staffers of taking clients away from him and attacking their work as second-rate imitations of his work. Marion's ill feeling toward him turned from anger to hatred.

Walter visited at her home, and she learned a lot more about the man she was falling in love with. He was born five years after her, in 1876, the eldest of four children, in Maywood, a suburb west of Oak Park. His mother's maiden name, Burley, was given to him as a middle name. His parents were a conservative couple. George Walter Griffin worked for an insurance company, and they were both members of the local Church of Christ. Walter had a passion for plants as a young child, where he would follow his mother around the garden. When the family moved into a new home, the 17-year-old begged to be allowed to design the garden, allowing him to experiment with different plants.

He also had a fascination with designing cities as a child. Ever since Chicago had to rebuild itself after the Great Fire, there had been much talk about the design of cities. Walter would draw them in his schoolbook, so much so that he was held back a year by his teachers who felt he was not paying enough attention in class. He wanted to be a landscape architect and had sought out the famous O.C. Simonds for advice. But Simonds had advised him against it, saying there was no money in landscape architecture, which he argued was not a profession, and urged him to study architecture instead.

Walter took his advice and studied at the University of Illinois under Professor Nathan Ricker. Ricker had been the professor of engineering before taking on the role of professor of architecture. Under his supervision, Walter was given a much more structurally rigorous education than Marion's classically focused education at MIT.[3] At the university, he had done a project where he designed a capitol building like those in the capital cities of America and in Washington, DC. But to Marion's disappointment, he had not kept a copy of his design.

One evening, they discussed their time together in the Oak Park studio. Walter told Marion how he and Wright had a competition to design a house. Wright had won the competition with his design, which was later used to build a house in Chicago for a man called Joseph Walser. Marion laughed when she heard the story.

"It was I who won the plan," she told Walter. "It was my plan that Wright used for the competition. The Walser House was built to that plan."

Toward the end of 1910, the first volume of the portfolio of drawings of Wright's work was published in Germany under the title *Ausgeführte Bauten und Entwürfe von Frank Lloyd Wright*. In the book, Wright wrote a long preamble, ending by thanking three wealthy clients who had continued to support him. There was no mention of the fact that more than half the drawings had been done by his talented assistant, Marion Mahony. The drawings were retracings of ones in his office, a process which had begun in the Oak Park studio but which was largely done in Europe by Wright and an assistant. Marion's monogram was erased from the copy of the K.C. de Rhodes House, but her spidery MLM remained on the copy of her bird's-eye view of the Como Orchards Summer Colony, snuggled under some trees at the bottom.

Wright may have been arrogant and egotistical but, when it came to architecture, he was always perceptive. He finished the preamble with an astute observation of Marion's drawings:

> The drawings, by means of which those buildings are presented here, have been made expressly for this work from colored drawings which were made from time to time as the projects were presented for solution. They merely aim to render the composition in outline and form, and

93

suggest the sentiment of the environment. They are in no sense attempts to treat the subjects pictorially, and in some cases fail to convey the idea of the actual building. A certain quality of familiar homelikeness is thus sacrificed in these presentations to a graceful decorative rendering of an idea of an arrangement. ... Their debt to Japanese ideals, these renderings themselves sufficiently acknowledge.[5]

But these were the drawings that Wright himself had chosen for the portfolio. At a time when personal photography was not widespread, Marion's drawings were works of art designed to provide an attractive image of the building for the client. Wright knew how her work impressed his clients and how her trees and spilling vines provided a beautiful showcase for the strong horizontal lines of his designs. Her work was now being used to promote his work to the world. Wright's selection of so many of her drawings for the Wasmuth portfolio was a recognition of how much work Marion had done in his studio as well as their unique Japanese-inspired style.

Wright went back to Europe in January 1911 to finish the rest of the portfolio and no doubt to get away from the continued antagonism against him in Chicago. By this time, the feelings between him and his former staffers had reached a poisonous level. Later that year, he wrote Marion a stinging letter, accusing her of stealing his ideas, taking clients away and betraying him to the world at large.[6] She was furious and wrote him another angry letter, finishing with the words, "Forgive my heat—You should be slower to condemn."[7]

Fifteen

Proposals

Walter's family was less than enthusiastic about their son's interest in Marion, this tall opinionated woman who wore such bright, unusual clothing. Even Dwight described her as "Bohemian" while Walter's sister, Gertrude, told people she believed her brother was still in love with Maginel.[1] Handsome, serious, and successful, Walter would have been a most eligible bachelor. Had he been less focused on his work, he may already have been married.

Marion turned 40 in February 1911. As the year went on, she knew she would have to take action. It may have been the upcoming second wedding of her dear friend Anna, set for later in the summer, which spurred her to action.

"Come along now, we must get married," is how one of their friends described the conversation later.[2] Marion argued that he could not live with his parents and his sister forever. Walter gradually warmed to the idea and finally, in the summer of 1911, they came to an agreement. They planned a canoe trip to Indiana, possibly to visit her brother in Elkhart. They decided to get married along the way. But it would be no grand affair, just a simple event at the courthouse with none of their relatives present. Whatever Marion might have wanted, she was a practical woman and she very much wanted her man. Whatever wedding Marion may have envisaged for herself as a young girl, marrying Walter Burley Griffin was more important than anything else. Having a wedding in Chicago may have risked opposition from Walter's family. So an elopement it was.

On Thursday, June 29, 1911, when summer was in full swing, Marion and Walter walked into the courthouse in Michigan City, Indiana, a town near the bottom of Lake Michigan. The bride was tall and lanky, with long black hair, her skin tanned from the sun. The groom was a little shorter, with thick wavy hair, and a softer face which made him look a little younger than his age. No family members were present. Filling out the forms, Walter and Marion both described their professions as "architect."[3] Asked later about their wedding, Marion described it simply. "We eloped. It was wonderful."[4]

Although it was Marion who initiated the proceedings, Walter was committed to the marriage in his own way. It was not the grand passion of youth, like his feelings for Maginel. This was a union between two people who knew each other very well, both personally and professionally. When the couple returned home, they announced their marriage, to the surprise of many. They moved in with Walter's parents in Elmhurst, not too far from Wright's Oak Park home, where they planned to live until they could build their own house.

Marion embraced her new married life with gusto. She decided her married name would be Marion Mahony Griffin. Her new monogram, which she would place on her drawings in the future, would be MMG. It would still have the same spidery image as her old MLM, with the intertwined M's, but now the G would be down the bottom.

She continued her presentations for Walter's houses in the long, vertical scroll-like drawings that were now becoming her trademark. She redid a drawing of a house Walter had designed for Captain Cooley, a riverboat captain in Monroe, Louisiana, which had initially been done by Harry Robinson. She drew the house at the top, set amid the trees, with a floor plan below it and then, down the bottom of the page, a cross section of the main living room. She did one in pen and ink and then redid it on beige silk, which had been covered in a brown wash. She used white gouache paint to highlight the house and its features, a subtle technique she was now evolving to a sophisticated level. Walter signed the lower right-hand side while Marion put the letters MMG in a square down the bottom of the left-hand side. She also worked on the presentation of the house for Walter's brother Ralph in Edwardsville.

By this time, Wright and Mamah had returned to America. They lived in Spring Green, Wisconsin, on the estate owned by his mother's family, away from the social ostracism they would face in Chicago. Harry Robinson left the Griffins' practice, no doubt finding his role had been partly usurped by Marion, and worked for Wright in an office in the city.

As she worked with Walter, Marion became in awe of her husband's design skills and the way he could solve complex architectural problems. As she recalled later, "When I went into his office it was with astonishment that I watched solutions drop from his pencil one after another, each a perfect little classic and each totally different from the others, like the children of different parents."[5]

It was not long after their wedding that they heard the news that hit their busy lives like a bombshell. It was news that Walter had been watching out for a long time. The government of Australia was holding a competition for the design of the country's new capital. Like the American capital, Washington, DC, it would be a completely new city, away from the big established cities.

Walter and Marion excitedly discussed the news. The architects of Chicago were often debating the design of cities. Daniel Burnham's success in building the White City, the Columbian Exposition of 1893, had led to requests for him to design other cities. In 1902, he had been asked to help revive Pierre L'Enfant's design for Washington. And in 1909, he released his own grand plan for redesigning Chicago. As one of the leading architects in the city, Walter had been involved in the discussions on how much of the Burnham plan, inspired by the work of Baron von Haussmann in Paris, could actually be put in place.

Marion knew that the news of the competition for the design of the Australian capital was an opportunity of a lifetime for her husband. Walter had been sorely disappointed when his plans for a new city near Shanghai had been lost with the death of his Chinese contact, Mr. Wong, five years before. Now, at last, he would get to show the world his true skills and his great passion for designing cities.

The announcement of the design competition for the Australian capital city, they found out, had been made on April 30, 1911, but it had taken until July for them to hear the news. Walter had read about the federation of the Australian states more than a decade ago and predicted that there would be a competition to design its new capital. He had been keeping an eye out for it ever since.

But now it was actually announced, he wasn't so sure. He was preoccupied with all the work in the office. Marion became increasingly frustrated as time passed and nothing was done. Now the competition Walter had dreamed about for so many years had finally been announced, he was having second thoughts about it. It was not the challenge of entering competitions. Walter had entered several competitions already through the Chicago Architectural Club, and his status was such that he was now being called upon by the club to judge them. But he knew if the competition entry was to be done properly, he would have to throw his heart and soul into the project. The Griffins' practice was now growing strongly. Did they have the time to devote to such a major project? As Marion had already found out, Walter was not one to make up his mind quickly.

One of the first projects they worked on as husband and wife was in Grinnell, Iowa. Walter was invited to design a house for Benjamin J. Ricker, whose family had a glove-making business. Walter and Ricker, who was no relation to Walter's beloved Professor Nathan Ricker at the University of Illinois, had become quite friendly, and Ricker was eager to help Walter get more work in the city.

While Walter designed the house, Marion wanted to add her own special touches to it. She had become interested in the use of colored, glazed tiles, which were becoming popular with the Arts and Crafts movement of the time. There was a company that manufactured them, northwest of Chicago, called the American Terra Cotta Tile and Ceramic Company. The distinctive tiles, with their naturalistic matte green, brown, earth-red, and cream colors, were becoming known as Teco tiles. Marion used the tiles to make a vertical rectangular design over the fireplace in the study of the Ricker House. She also designed a landscape mural over the central fireplace of the house. It was a horizontal river scene with green grass in the background and trees on either side. For the outside of the house, she also designed two decorative vertical panels, using the Teco tiles, which were set between some of the windows on the top story of the house. They were similar to what she had done on the Robert Mueller House in Millikin Place. Visible from the street, these colorful tile panels gave Walter's solid house a touch of arts-and-crafts style.[6]

While in Grinnell, Griffin had some frank discussions with Ricker. Should he enter the competition to design the Australian capital or not? Ricker urged him to enter, but Walter was not so sure.[7] Walter's procrastination worried Marion. First weeks, and then months, slipped by since they had first learned of the competition, but Walter did nothing about it. She was ready to help with the designs and manage the team from the office to do whatever was needed to get the project done, but it was Walter who was the town planner, the landscape gardener, and the architect who had been thinking about this for so many years. And Australia was such a long way away. Even when the plans were done, it would take weeks to get them there in time for the deadline at the end of January.

Marion seemed to be more passionate about entering the competition than her husband. Was there an element of competition in her own thinking? Her designs had already made Wright famous with the publication of his portfolio in Germany. Was she wanting to show her talented new husband off to the world while Wright struggled for business, living in sin in Wisconsin? By October, she decided that something needed to be done.

She devised a plan. She knew Walter was happiest on their canoe trips. They were planning a camping trip to the southernmost area of Lake Michigan where they would meet up with Dwight and other friends. Dwight had become a driving force behind the group that explored the natural areas around Chicago, looking for places which needed to be protected from development, and then lobbying the city or the state to preserve them for public spaces.

Dwight and the others had gone before them. Marion and Walter set out in the morning. They had a long way to paddle in a day and planned to meet Dwight's group by nightfall. At one point, Marion and Walter had to go upstream against the flow of a river, which required some strong paddling. Marion wanted to stop to study the snails.

"Oh, look at the myriads of gastropods on the logs on the bottom!" she said to Walter, bending her head low toward the water to look into the river.

"Don't look!" he said from the back of the boat. "Paddle!"

"But I've got to look," she said.[8]

Walter continued to paddle furiously. They came to a shallow part of the river where they had to get out of the canoe. They rolled up the legs of their trousers and pulled *Allana* behind them. They turned a corner and suddenly came upon a terrible sight. Before them was a municipal gas plant, which had "let its waste material flow into the stream, a black sticky mass ... a waste of byproducts."[9] As they waded through the water, the black sludge stuck to their legs. When the river was deep enough, they got back into the canoe, but they had to keep their trousers rolled up so the sludge would not dirty their clothes. The horrible sight of industrial pollution stayed with them for a long time. It was a reminder of what could happen if some of the most beautiful areas of the state were not protected.

The sun was scorching, but they kept paddling, their exposed legs getting sunburned. They finally met up with Dwight and the others and slept, exhausted. The next day, the sun was still fiercely hot. As Marion recalled later, the sand was "as hot as the top of a stove."[10]

The group spent the whole day in the water. When it was time to eat, they would scurry out of the water, get their food, and run back in, eating it with only their heads and their hands above the water. Marion's sunburned legs hurt her, but she had more important things on her mind. Walter was now in the company of friends who were as passionate about city planning as he was.

As the day wore on, the tension rose inside her. They had all been happy and relaxed in the water, but now they were back on the banks of the lake, ready to make their dinner. Walter was getting ready to cut the wood for the fire. Marion knew if she didn't speak up now, it would be too late. She turned to her husband and exploded.

> For the love of Mike, when are you going to get started on those plans for the Australian capital? How much time do you think there is left anyway? Do you *realize* that it takes a solid month to get them over there

[to Australia] after they have started on their way? That leaves exactly nine weeks now to turn them in. Perhaps *you* can design a city in two days, but the drawings take time and that falls on *me*. ... It isn't possible do them in nine weeks.[11]

Walter said nothing. By now Marion was in full swing, determined to have her say once and for all.

Perhaps I am the swiftest draftsman in town, but I can't do the impossible. What's the use of thinking about a thing like this for ten years, if, when the time comes, you don't get it done in time? Mark my words, and I'm not joking either, either you get busy on that this very day, this very minute ... or I'll not touch a pencil on the darned things! Serve you right if I refuse to take it on, even now.[12]

There was silence. Walter picked up the saw and starting cutting the wood. But Marion's verbal arrows had hit their mark. Socrates was wise enough to know that Xanthippe was right. By making her point so passionately in front of their friends and professional peers, Walter knew he could never say afterward that he did not have the time or the will to do it. As soon as they got home, they got to work, and a "new adventure was started."

World's Columbian Exposition, Chicago 1893. Eric Nicholls collection. National Library of Australia.

Sixteen

Fetching Up the Genii

About 30 years before that eventful canoe trip, American writer Mark Twain summed up the spirit of Chicago when he wrote *Life on the Mississippi*. Chicago's citizens, he wrote, are:

> ... always rubbing a lamp and fetching up the genii ... contriving and achieving new impossibilities ... [Chicago] outgrows her prophesies faster than she can make them, she is never the Chicago you saw when you passed through the last time.[1]

Once they got back to their office at Steinway Hall, Walter and Marion furiously rubbed the magical lamp, fetching up the genii they both knew were within them. Working up the plans for the competition would be a monumental task. The project would require many drawings, from rough sketches to detailed drawings and perspectives. Then they would all have to be packaged up securely and sent on the long journey by train and sea to Australia. While the ideas for the plan of the city would largely be Walter's, their visual production, their transition from Walter's rough concepts and sketches to the detailed, carefully inked and painted works, would be the responsibility of Marion and her team.

What happened next was the result of a unique partnership between architect and architect, town planner and delineator, man and woman, husband and wife, two lovers, working side by side to achieve a life's vision, working together with all the instinctive movements of two highly trained dancers. The new bride and groom were coming together for the biggest challenge of their lives.

The new nation of Australia, as their friends at Jane Addams' Hull House well knew, was more advanced than America when it came to social policies. Women already had the right to vote in Australia, but only a few states in America had achieved that milestone. If women had the vote, Addams and others like her believed, there would be more attention paid to the proper design of cities and protective laws for workers and children. There had also been other moves by the courts in the fledgling nation to protect the interests of its workers, including the concept of a fair minimum wage. It seemed that this new country, which had once been a collection of British colonies like the American states, was starting out on its own with a fresh vision for a better, more equal society. And Marion and Walter had the skills and the vision to help design its capital, a world-class city that embodied all their ideals.

As a dear friend was to write later of the Griffins:

> Never, they felt, had there been a better opportunity to create anew, free from the debris of old mistakes and the shackles of dead tradition, than in this wonderland, with its forward looking and independently minded democracy.[2]

Exactly what went on between Marion and Walter over that time has never been documented. Walter was the town planning expert, but it would be Marion who would oversee the drawings needed to display her husband's grand designs, just as she had done for Wright. While it was Walter who had the lifelong dream of designing great cities, Marion had some of the best architectural drawing skills in America at the time. She was determined to use all her skills and energy to see her husband realize his long-held dream. But she was also an experienced architect in her own right, experienced in perspectives of places she had never been to, and brought her own vision to the project. Walter had never left America, but Marion had already seen some of the finest cities in the world.

Marion would have deferred to Walter's superior knowledge of town planning and landscaping but, as she had done at times with Wright, she would also have been his strong-minded sounding board as he worked through his ideas.

Roy Lippincott later described how the two worked together:

> Marion was always experimenting with new methods of rendering and presentation, rather I should say they, because there was the closest accord between them and every suggestion that Walt made was seized eagerly by her, and developed and modified between the two of them.[3]

For the next nine weeks, the newlyweds put their busy architectural practice on hold, while they focused on the competition. Roy Lippincott came up from von Holst's office to help out in the evenings and, before long, he was working on the project almost on a full-time basis.

At first, the Griffins worked out of their office in Steinway Hall, but it was soon clear they needed to work on it day and night. Walter took over a large room in the Griffin family home in Elmhurst and put up sketches and plans around the walls. Walter's two younger sisters, Genevieve and Gertrude, helped out with the drawings. It was all hands to the pump.

Walter got a long wooden box from the British Consulate in Chicago which was specially prepared with lots of details for contestants. The consulate had a yellow plaster model of the site, a wide plain with surrounding mountains, and a blue river meandering lazily through the middle. The box included a contour plan of the site, a map of the state of New South Wales, and rainfall and temperature statistics. There was also a copy of two paintings of the site done by Australian artist Robert Coulter.[4]

Like Washington, DC, the selection of the site for the Australian capital, away from the main established cities, had been a compromise decision to keep the different interests involved happy. The newly independent American states had considered several sites for the capital but chose an area near George Washington's beloved Mount Vernon, carved out of the states of Maryland and Virginia. The Australian states had decided that the capital should be in a completely new site, somewhere between the two main cities of Sydney and Melbourne. Chosen after years of argument and deliberation, the site was almost barren limestone plains, used mainly for grazing sheep, far away from any sizable towns. The Griffins studied the wide cycloramic works, trying to imagine what the site was like, what Australia was like, a place on the other side of the world. As Marion said later, "If you project a line from America through to the center of the earth, it will hit the realm of the ancient Lemuria whence Australia sprang."[5]

The instructions suggested planning for a city of 25,000 inhabitants, which could eventually expand to cater for around 100,000. It was a fraction of the two million people who lived in Chicago. The second largest city in America after New York, Chicago had a population of just under half the population of the whole country of Australia. And yet its land mass was roughly equivalent to that of the continental United States.

Louis Sullivan's lecture of 1900 had inspired Walter, urging young American architects to have the courage to create a new form of architecture. And now, thanks to the prompting of his new bride, Walter was accepting his hero's challenge.

The vision of Daniel Burnham's White City, the World's Fair of 1893, was still imprinted in their minds. Marion and Walter had both been to see it. Walter had cycled to the site many times as a teenager as it was being built, watching how Frederick Olmsted, the designer of Central Park in New York, had created a beautiful site with lagoons and a wooded island from a swampy land. He knew that carefully crafted, stylish water features were an essential part of any city of status, and the river in the middle of the plain, the Molongolo River, provided the opportunity for just that.

Burnham was inspired by Georges-Eugène Haussmann, the man who undertook the great work of redesigning and opening up the old city of Paris, 60 years before, in the mid-1850s. After the success of the 1893 Fair, Burnham was in demand as a city planner. In 1909, he and others drew up a bold plan for the redesign of Chicago. Burnham argued that city planners should look to the example of Paris, with its wide boulevards, elegant city buildings, and an extensive system of parks. He incorporated many of Haussmann's ideas into his plan and also wanted to see more extensive use of cultural facilities around Chicago's massive lake.

Marion and Walter started with a fresh sheet of paper, a wide, flat, almost barren site, but the ideas of the two city planners were still fresh in their minds. Their challenge was a lot closer to that faced by Major

Pierre L'Enfant, the French architect and civil engineer, chosen by George Washington to design the new capital city of America 120 years before. The District of Columbia was a diamond shape of 10 miles by 10 miles, which had quickly outgrown L'Enfant's original plan. Walter was determined to produce a plan for a larger area, of around 25 miles by 25 miles, to prevent the land speculation he felt had gone on in Washington.

The Griffins believed that cities should be carefully designed to fit into the landscape, following the contours of the topography, with as little damage to the natural surroundings as possible.

As Marion explained later:

> City planning, as founded by Mr. Griffin, was not a mechanical drafting board affair later to be imposed upon the earth, destroying whatever got in the way. ... In planning Canberra, every detail of the natural conditions was thoroughly studied in order to preserve them and to make the most of each and everything so that the City can indeed be a living thing, a healthy, growing thing.[6]

The site, with its wide river floodplain surrounded by hills, was a natural amphitheater. As they began to imagine a new capital, it was not hard to see that Marion may have been reminded of the idea of the seven hills which surrounded the ancient city of Rome.

The focal point of the city, they decided, would be Mount Kurrajong, which had a commanding view northward, across the river and up to the grand higher Mount Ainslie. In Washington, DC, the Capitol building on Capitol Hill, housed the US Congress, which was roughly equivalent to the Australian Federal Parliament. But the newly created Federation of Australia had a slightly different political system. Its parliament had a house of representatives and senate, like Congress, but its political leader was the Prime Minister, who was a member of the lower house, and it also had a representative of the British king, called the Governor-General.

The Griffins decided that Mount Kurrajong should become the site of the Capitol but it would not be like Capitol Hill in Washington. Their concept was like the Capitol in Rome. In ancient Rome, the Capitoline Hill was one of the citadels of the city. By 1896, when Marion walked around Rome with her brother, it had become an impressive space, designed by Michelangelo, with a central piazza surrounded by museums, which stored some of the city's treasures. It was a place of the people, while the forum, where the business of government took place, was set in the city below. As Walter had not left America, it was not hard to believe that Marion's own experience in seeing Rome would have played a part in this crucial decision for the focal point of the city.

Their Australian Capitol would have a grand building and public spaces on Mount Kurrajong. There would be two official residences on either side, one for the Prime Minister and one for the Governor-General. In the center, as in Rome's Capitol, there would be public areas with a striking public building storing national treasures and the official archives. The houses of parliament would be situated below the Capitol, on Camp Hill, with other government buildings farther down, set around a central water basin, like the Court of Honor in Daniel Burnham's White City. The basin would connect to the central lake through a water gate. They decided there would be five wide avenues radiating from Capitol Hill. Two would cross the river basin to the two other main centers servicing the people—a municipal center and a market center.

The plan, they decided, would have two main axes—the land axis from Mount Kurrajong north to Mount Ainslie, with the government buildings on the south side and most of the people living and enjoying life on the north, and a perpendicular water axis along the line of the river. Inspired by Olmsted's transformation of the land for the World's Fair, Walter decided that the river would be dammed to form a series of five ornamental lakes which would become the central water feature of the city. The Griffins imagined Australians strolling along the water, just as the citizens of Chicago enjoyed Lake Michigan and its surrounding rivers.

As Walter focused on the city design, Marion worked on the drawings. Her years of experience working for Wright had taught her how a beautifully rendered drawing could bring an architectural concept to life. Marion's lush use of trees and foliage in her renderings of his architectural ideas had worked to complement the strong horizontal lines in Wright's work. Translating Walter's grand plans for a new city would be a greater challenge for the new bride who had great ambitions for her talented husband.

They worked on a portfolio of drawings. There was the one of the city plan set into the official contour map, a requirement for all competitors. Then they did a bird's-eye view of the site, called City and Environs, which looked down on the city from a far greater height. Five foot tall and two and a half feet wide, it was done in ink on cloth, colored with a sepia-toned wash and lightly varnished. Looking a little like a series of interlocking snowflakes, it highlighted the powerful geometry of the plan.

Then they did three cross-sectional depictions of the city showing their detailed plans for the city layout and its important buildings. Walter believed that Australia should develop its own style of architecture. Exactly what it would look like he did not know, but the drawings themselves made exotic suggestions. In an explanatory pamphlet that he prepared to go with the drawings, he suggested the architecture might take in the "last word of all the longest-lived civilizations" such as "Egypt, Babylonia, Syria, Indo-China, East Indies, Mexico, or Peru."[7] The designs may also have been inspired by the temple of Angkor Wat, which had been rediscovered just over 50 years before by French explorer Henri Mouhot. There was also an increasing interest in North America in the ancient civilizations of Central and South America. Only a few months before, in July 1911, American explorer Hiram Bingham had discovered the remains of an ancient Incan settlement at Machu Picchu in Peru. The most important building in the Griffin plan, the Capitol, was shown as a stepped pyramid or ziggurat, rising 80 feet above Mount Kurrajong, with its entranceways covered by Japanese-style roofs like those in the Adolph Mueller House. Other buildings were a mixture of classical architecture with a flavor of Aztec styles.

Marion coated the linen cloth with cream wash and drew the buildings in fine black ink. The cross sections showed each building in detail, carefully set into the landscape, in line with Walter's plan. There was a university, a printery, a city hall, a mint, the zoological gardens, museums, a hotel, cathedral, railway station, markets, and a military college.

The buildings were drawn to a miniature scale, which taken together looked like a magical fairy kingdom. The drawings of the military college and the cathedral next to it could have been scenes from a medieval village on a distant hill. There were two wide panoramas made up of four panels each, which were to be joined together. Just to make it clear to those assembling them, they were highlighted by a horizontal, burnished gold band, which stretched across the width of the horizon across the panels. It looked as if it could be a wide, flat mountain range in the distance. Or, with some imagination, the dark gold band could have been a wide shallow river, with the tiny buildings set into the creek bed below it, like the miniature world in the rivers around Chicago, which so fascinated Marion when she and Walter used to paddle along. It was another world that simply demanded a closer inspection.

The third cross-sectional drawing, just one panel, was the view from the central water basin looking southward to the all-important buildings of the government sector, from the water up to the Capitol and the hills beyond. It showed the magnificent, exotic Capitol pyramid-like building, set against a backdrop of brown mountains, a commanding, regal presence over the site, with the other government buildings below.

Marion also used white gouache paint to highlight aspects of a building, bringing in another dimension of light onto the work. She used it on the buildings in the cross-sectional drawings, in some instances with tiny, almost imperceptible crescent-shaped brushstrokes, which gave them a shimmering, luminescent quality. The cross-sectional drawings were colored with yellows, golds, and copper, with hints of green in the trees and bushes, giving them an autumnal tone against the cream backdrop. Marion also used fine black dots to show the reflections of the buildings in the water, so finely done that they appeared to be shimmering.

Marion worried about getting everything done to meet the competition deadline at the end of January, but Walter argued that if the government of Australia really wanted a fine capital city, it would not mind if they were a little late. But even though they worked around the clock, time was tight. On one cross-sectional drawing, showing city hall, the white lines highlighting the buildings in the water only extended across one side. Maybe there was no time to finish it, or maybe it was a detail that escaped Marion's eagle eye. Even so, the three cross-sectional drawings were exquisitely drawn depictions of Walter's ideal city, an exotic, elegant, magical kingdom just waiting to be built.

As they worked on the plans, Marion and Walter knew that they would most likely never again see all the wonderful drawings and artwork once they were sent to Australia. So, they decided to make copies of the drawings for themselves. Just as Wright had done with Wasmuth's portfolio, the Griffins knew that having copies of a major work like this would be important in showing their work to the world to help sell Walter's credentials as a city planner. While the main drawings to be sent to Australia were to be done on linen, Marion set herself an even more demanding task for the drawings they planned to keep for themselves. They would be done on silk, using the techniques that Marion had honed from years of work.

Roy Lippincott later described the process:

> When I first worked with Marion she was making drawings on the silky Japanese vellum with a crow quill pen and brown ink. The hairy surface would catch the pen unless it barely skimmed the surface, in which case *blot* and finish for that sheet—start all over again. The Federal capital drawings were made on linen tracing cloth, lithographed on window shade Holland, and rendered with watercolor and photographic dyes. The next step was to lithograph them on satin, dip the satin in thin glue size and stretch it smooth on a board. When dry, the rendering was done with the dyes, and when stripped from the board and lightly dusted with a soft cloth, enough of the size was removed to show the practically unchanged satin surface.[8]

Then there was to be Marion's masterpiece, the piece of art which would simply stun the judges many thousands of miles away, so they simply could not ignore Walter's plan. As she imagined this ideal city, Marion knew there was only one view which showed it to its full advantage—the view from the summit of Mount Ainslie. It was this view that showed the grand panorama of Walter's city to its best advantage, down to its foothills where there was a casino and then a parkway, like the mall in Washington, across the river to the government buildings, up to the parliament buildings on Camp Hill, and then the exotic Capitol. It was all part of one carefully designed integrated whole, nestled into the natural landscape.

They knew the drawings would have to fit in large boxes. The view they wanted was very wide. They decided it would be made up of three panels, a wide piece in the middle, and two smaller panels on either side that would be hinged together so that they could be folded inward to fit in a long box. Then, when they arrived in Australia, they could be opened up into a vista 10 feet wide, displayed to show the full panorama.

Marion approached this with a very different style to the cross-sectional drawings. It drew on her inspirations from Japanese art, highlighting Walter's geometric design for the city and its buildings with trees and foliage. While the cross-sectional drawings were colored with autumnal tones of white, creams, yellows, and golds, she decided that the *View from the Summit of Mount Ainslie* would be a washed watercolor in purple tones. Why did she choose this color? Was she thinking about the view of the city in the evening, in the moonlight, just as she had seen Rome and Venice so many years before? But the clock was ticking, and the work was almost overwhelming. They were not going to be able to finish the *View from the Summit of Mount Ainslie* in time to meet the ship for Australia to meet the competition deadline. There was no point doing the most beautiful drawings in the world if they did not get there on time. The *View from the Summit of Mount Ainslie* was not strictly necessary for the competition, but it would be, Marion hoped, the masterpiece.

They decided to send off all the drawings and perspectives as well as a sketch drawing of the *View from the Summit of Mount Ainslie* in the one box but hold back on the actual painting to give Marion a little more time to work on her masterpiece. They attached a note to the drawing that said the drawing had been "delayed by accident [and would be] sent by next shipment." The drawings were boxed up and a taxi called to take them to the train station, which would take them to the West Coast and then by boat to Australia.

Marion later recollected the scene:

After nine weeks of driving work, toward midnight of a bitterly cold night, the box of drawings, too long to go in a taxi, was rushed, with doors open and men without their coats—no time to go up 16 stories to get them—across the city to catch the last train that could meet the last boat for Australia. The imperturbable Mr. Griffin himself was the only one not quite frantic because to him if Australia was serious about the matter of their Federal Capital, they wouldn't let the moment of the arrival of the plans be a determining factor in their choice.[9]

With the main drawings sent off to Australia, they worked frantically to finish off Marion's masterpiece, the real *View from the Summit of Mount Ainslie*. Marion's imagination of the site began to expand. Behind the Capitol in the distance was a snow-covered Mount Bimberi, looking a little like Mount Fuji in Japan. They could have done with more time to finish off the drawings of the trees and the bushes near the top of the mountain, but it would have to do. They carefully packed up the drawing and sent it off. At last they could relax.

Walter Burley Griffin working on drawing of Ralph Griffin house Circa 1910. Eric Nicholls collection. National Library of Australia.

Drawing of proposed Capitol Building. Part of Griffin competition drawings for Australian capital. Section B-A. Southerly side of Water Axis. Government Group. The Federal Parliament is below the Capitol. National Archives of Australia. A710, 43.

Seventeen

News from Australia

It was a few months later, at the end of May, when they received the telegram from Australia that would change their lives.

The news spread quickly. There was much excitement among the Griffins' friends and colleagues. The bustling city of Chicago prided itself on its architectural achievements. It was the home of skyscrapers and some of the most modern buildings in the world. To have one of its architects win the design for the capital of a new country was a fitting tribute to the city's growing international reputation as one of the architectural centers of the New World.

Walter's success was chronicled in the newspapers in Chicago and beyond. *The New York Times* wanted to talk to him. "American Designs Australian Capital," *The Times* wrote on May 25, 1912. In the interview Walter expanded on his vision for the new capital, making it clear he would love to go to Australia to make it happen.

> It affords me pleasure to know that my work has been chosen as the best plan for the building of a national capital—the first time that anything has been attempted on any large scale. I do not know whether I shall be called to Australia to superintend the construction of the new city. I hope so. I rather expect I shall. It would be only fair to me. There is nobody in the world who can work out my ideas like myself. I do not know what type of architecture I should adopt. I have planned a city not like any other city in the world. I have planned it not in a way that I expected any governmental authorities in the world would accept. I have planned an ideal city—a city that meets my ideal of the future.

115

Walter was praised for his winning plan, but there was also an immediate recognition of the power of the drawings themselves.

Writing in the *Town Planning Review*, a British critic expressed his surprise that an unknown American architect had won such a distinguished prize. "The drawings are beautiful but eccentric," he wrote. "Were the assessors carried away by the mere charm of the display?"[1]

Not long after the telegram, they received a phone call from an Australian woman called Miles Franklin. She and her friend Alice, another Australian, had been living in Chicago for some years and were excited to learn that an architect from Chicago had won the prize. Could they pay a visit?

Soon afterward, two excited Australian women made their way to the Griffins' office in the Monroe Building, a 16-story skyscraper, which had just been opened, overlooking Lake Michigan. Franklin was in her early 30s while her friend, Alice Henry, was in her mid-50s. The two Australians looked around the office in awe. As Franklin and Henry wrote in a joint article for a Sydney newspaper later, the room was "flooded with light from spacious skylights" and had a "regal view of the lake." They also noticed that this was very much a husband-and-wife architectural team and the relationship between Mr. Griffin and his wife was no ordinary marriage. "It is plainly apparent that their ideals are happily interwoven," they wrote.[2]

The Griffins showed them the wonderful drawings on silk that Marion had painstakingly prepared. The site of the capital was, as Miles would have explained, not far from where she herself had grown up as a child in the Brindabella Valley in New South Wales.

Mr. Griffin, the women reported to their Australian readers, was enthusiastic about the opportunities ahead. "It's the newest of the great Commonwealths, already the most advanced economically with the fewest steps to retrace," he told them.

Walter pointed out the details of the plan. "Here's the governor's palace," he said.

"Palace?" said another architect in the room, struggling to understand the Australian political system. "Is not a palace somewhat out of keeping with democracy in the 20th century?"

"Not a bit," Marion interposed, quickly backing up her husband. "Is not democracy the supreme monarch in our day and a palace is none too good to house democracy?" she said.[3]

The Griffins soon realized they had much in common with the two Australian women who were both closely associated with Jane Addams' Hull House. Hull House had become a center for a wide circle of people in the city who were interested in social activism. Australia's advances, including giving women the vote, gave them a platform to help push for the same thing in America.[4]

Franklin, they found out, was an Australian writer famous for her novel, *My Brilliant Career*, published in 1901. She had left Australia four years later, traveling to San Francisco, where she met people who urged her to visit Chicago and see Jane Addams. She arrived in the city in 1906 and met Alice Henry, a social activist from Melbourne who had arrived a month before.

Franklin and Henry both found work in the Chicago office of the National Women's Trade Union League. The Griffins discovered they had some mutual friends with Henry and Franklin, and they had all attended the same meeting of the Single Tax conference in Chicago the year before. They all agreed to keep in touch, all four of them now having a special bond with Australia. Franklin and Henry expressed their happiness in their article:

> We two Australians felt pride all round ... Australia is leading the world in how far she may prevent many of the evils that follow in the train of great cities, if she first of all builds her great city aright. We are happy that an American has won the prize, for we have not lived here five years without realizing how much these two young countries have in common.[5]

The excitement in Chicago continued. Walter was invited to address the Illinois chapter of the American Architects' Association where a resolution was passed congratulating him on his success. The June 1 edition of *Construction News* carried a long article about him. It reflected the slight sense of surprise among the city's architectural community that Walter had been able to win such an important competition.

> It is not often that a young man jumps into fame overnight, or to express it mildly, so quickly as Walter Burley Griffin, who has just been awarded first prize in the competition for the capital city of the Australian colonies.[6]

The author realized there might be more to Mr. Griffin's success than first met the eye. "Jumping into fame overnight, however, does not do Mr. Griffin justice. There was the latent talent, backed up by push, energy, enterprise and industry, and these, awaiting the opportunity, made good when the time came," the article observed. These ingredients, of course, had also been supplied by his devoted wife.

The article noted that Walter was eager to go to Australia to discuss his plan. "According to Mr. Griffin's understanding, work upon the new federal capital is to begin immediately. It is to be hoped that he will be retained to execute his plans."

One of the next big architectural events would be the design of the new capital of India following its move from Calcutta to Delhi. The article noted that, "The success of Walter Burley Griffin ... should encourage others to take more than a passing interest in the construction of the new capital of India at Delhi."

On September 22, the writer Harriet Monroe hailed Griffin's plan in the *Chicago Tribune*, describing it as:

> ... remarkable for its completeness and beauty, taking advantage of every rise of ground, every depression, every fine view, so simply as to seem almost obvious in its selection of the best possible thing to do.[7]

As the accolades flowed, the Griffins eagerly awaited news on what might come next from Australia. But there was nothing. Walter wrote a letter to the Minister for Home Affairs, Mr. King O'Malley, who had sent him the telegram, indicating his willingness to come to Australia to discuss his plans and provide advice in implementing them.

Marion was also excited, but there was other work to be done. The Griffins were working on a house in Winnetka for a schoolteacher named Harry Mess. She designed a landscape mural to go over the fireplace in the living room, very similar to the one she designed the year before for the Ricker House, using her favorite green-and-brown Teco tiles.

The Griffins also worked on the development of a subdivision in the Trier neighborhood of Winnetka. It was not too far from Marion's childhood neighborhood of Hubbard Woods, near Rogers Park, where Marion's mother, Clara, and her sister, Georgine, were living with eight-year-old Clarmyra.

Dwight had designed the New Trier High School in his role as chief architect of the Chicago school board. Walter was planning to design a neighborhood nearby, which took into account his passionate views about communities with plenty of public parks and gardens. Marion drew a picture of a "model dwelling" for the neighborhood. It was a solid box-like design set in a natural setting of trees, which saved space by bringing the dining room and the living room together.

The Griffins planned to move into the area themselves. With their prize money from the Australian capital competition, they could build their own house on the estate. Marion had already drawn up the plans for their two-story house, another beautiful drawing with her monogram MMG in one corner.

While they were designing their new home, they moved into the house at Rogers Park with Marion's family. Their business was going well and, at last, they could start to dream of having a home of their own.

Perspective view of Melson House, Mason City, Iowa, by Marion Mahony Griffin. Circa 1914. Note initials MMG in middle right-hand side. Mary and Leigh Block Museum of Art, Northwestern University. 1985.1.120.

Eighteen

Mason City

Another major project was afoot. While working in Wright's office at Oak Park, Marion had been involved in designing a house for Joshua Melson, a businessman from Mason City, Iowa. A builder, developer and self-styled architect, Melson had visited the Oak Park studio in 1909 and may well have met Marion then.[1]

Distracted by his plans to leave the country, Wright gave Melson the design for a house he had already built before near Oak Park. Melson was not happy with the design and had not gone ahead with it. The scandal surrounding Wright's departure no doubt also affected the thinking of Melson who was devoted to his own wife. Some time after Wright left, Melson came back to Chicago and spoke to Marion.

The site for the land, Melson explained, was an unusual one, on the outskirts of Mason City, on the high side of the creek. He felt Wright's plan had not taken into account the potential of the site. He had a grander vision. He had bought 18 acres on the banks of the creek, Willow Creek, with one of the leading lawyers in the city, and needed a design for the whole estate, not just a house.

Marion's interest was sparked by his plans. The best person for him to talk to, she suggested, would be "Mr. Griffin."[2] She was fond of Melson, whom she privately nicknamed Don Melancolio for his outlook on life, and believed Walter could help him. Walter went to Mason City to take a look. As soon as he arrived, he could see that Melson was right—it was a special site. The land was on either side of Willow Creek, on the edge of the city. Walter believed there could be as many as 20 houses, carefully placed between the trees, on the land on both sides of the creek. He signed up Melson and the other owners of the land to a contract, which would give him control over its design, and began to work on the project.[3]

Marion accompanied him on another visit to the city. In 1912, she drew up a perspective of how the site could look. She chose her favorite bird's-eye view to depict the pocket of land along the creek. Her perspective of Rock Crest-Rock Glen was a dramatic wide panoramic view, like the one she had drawn for *View from the Summit of Mount Ainslie* the year before, with strong elements of Japanese painting.

She drew a magnificent wooded estate, with the creek meandering through it. There were houses nestled under the trees, on either side of the water, with trees that looked like Japanese bonsais. There was a large area between the houses on the lower side going down to the creek for a communal parkland. Marion did the drawing on green silk with black ink, with a colored ink wash, and used gouache white paint to highlight the houses.

It was a work of art, which gave the investors an idea of how good the area could look if the houses were properly designed and the area properly landscaped. Close observers of the drawing could see the Griffin partnership at work. On the left-hand side, at the bottom, was Walter Burley Griffin's signature. On the right-hand side, down the bottom, was a small square with Marion's spidery monogram, MMG, in a box.[4]

Walter began work on the first house, a T-shaped design made of rough-hewn limestone. It had dark eaves with upturned ends, giving the roofline a distinctive Japanese appearance, and large picture windows facing the park. Walter was particularly excited about what he wanted to do for Melson's house. The Griffins had become very fond of Melson. His land was near the old quarry, perched on the crest of the land overlooking the creek bed.

Walter designed his house with an entrance on the top of the cliff and built out from the street and down toward the creek. Made out of local stone, it looked something like a rock castle set into the cliff. Walter insisted that it have a flat roof, but the challenge was how to make it more attractive. The Griffins decided this would be done by having tall-stepped keystones, or voussoirs, over the upper windows, projecting above the roof line.⁵ Years later, a colleague, Barry Byrne, would tell an interviewer that many of the ideas for the Melson House came from Marion.⁶

Marion drew an exotic Japanese scroll drawing of the house in black ink on white satin. Showing the house side on, it highlighted its integration into the cliff, surrounded by lavish trees and bushes, and a cascading garden. Below it was a finely drawn reflection of the building in Willow Creek with Japanese-style branches. Marion placed her monogram, MMG, beneath a tree, two-thirds of the way down on the right, while Walter signed the drawing in the bottom right corner. Just as Wright had done for his houses, the architects also designed some of the furniture for the house. Marion designed a table for the library and a tablecloth featuring the triangular voussoirs over the windows.⁷

It was one of the most dramatic houses Walter had ever designed. When it was finally built, Walter proudly climbed up the outside of the house "from the lily bed below to the top of the building hanging on by hands and toes."⁸ Melson was delighted. As Marion noted, "Melancholy flew out and an enduring enthusiasm filled its place in our Don."

But a little later, he appeared in the Griffins' office in Chicago, putting on a sad face. Marion recalled the meeting.

> He was going to have to charge up his electric light bills to Mr. Griffin —and then the smile crinkles began. Everyone, and that was the whole town, who crossed the bridge—which connects "down town" with the residence district—whether pedestrian or motorist—stopped to look up the river at the fascinating sight of Rock Crest's initial building—a castle indeed for it was a unity with the whole precipice—completely reflected in the smooth waters above the old dam; and he couldn't resist the temptation of keeping his whole house lighted up to make the most of a spectacle of it.⁹

Walter designed several other houses, including one for James Blythe on the other side of the creek. While the Melson House was a vertical rock castle, the Blythe House was a two-story flat-roofed, horizontal concrete box shape on a stone base. It had a large wide picture window in the living room, which faced onto the park. It had decorative motifs on the outside with overtones of Aztec designs. Its front fence was also decorated with Japanese-style lanterns and concrete planter boxes, another of Marion's design touches. The Griffins were coming into their own with a new confident style, showing what they could do with the right site and the right clients.

Melson House, Mason City, Iowa, with reflection in Willow Creek. Circa 1914. Eric Nicholls collection. National Library of Australia.

Nineteen

The World Turned Upside Down

As time went on, the Griffins' euphoria faded. Walter's winning design had brought him national and international fame and the prize money could be used for their new home, but there was no word from Australia. All their friends and colleagues asked Walter when he would go there. It was embarrassing, to say the least, that the government of Australia just seemed to be getting on with its business without him.

In November 1912, the chief architect of the Commonwealth of Australia, John Smith Murdoch, visited Walter in his office in Chicago. He was passing through the United States on his way back from a visit to London. An austere Scotsman, Murdoch was a member of a board set up by the Minister for Home Affairs, King O'Malley, to review Walter's plan. Walter learned, to his horror, that the departmental board had come up with its own very different plan for the city, which was being considered by the government, instead of his plan which was being criticized for being far too expensive.[1]

A few months later, in January 1913, Walter was even more agitated to learn that the board's plan for Canberra had been adopted by the Australian Federal Cabinet. He wrote again to King O'Malley, offering to come to Australia to discuss his plan, but he heard nothing. Things in Australia were going ahead without him. In March, there had been a grand ceremony to lay the foundation stone for the city, which was now officially called Canberra.

Then, in June, there was interesting news. There had been an election in Australia and a change of government. Prime Minister Fisher and his Labor government were gone, replaced by a more conservative government led by Joseph Cook. King O'Malley was no longer the Minister for Home Affairs, the minister overseeing the development of the new capital, and had been replaced by Mr. William H. Kelly. Walter wrote to Murdoch, telling him he was coming to Australia to discuss the plan.[2] Marion was torn. She understood her husband's reasons for wanting to go to Australia, but she did not relish the prospect of months of separation as he went on the long sea voyage across the Pacific. Walter left Chicago in July and in San Francisco was excited to get the news that the new Minister for Home Affairs, Mr. Kelly, welcomed his trip and would help pay his expenses. Marion was pleased for her husband, but she wished he did not have to be away from her for so long.

While Walter was away, Marion continued to run the office. Another project had come into von Holst's office, which Marion was handling. After Wright left for Europe, Henry Ford had followed up about commissioning a grand house on the Rouge River in Michigan. He approached von Holst's office, and Marion worked on the design. In 1912, Marion drew up a two-story house for the Fords who planned to call it Fair Lane. She designed a long building, which stretched over the land, carefully fitting into the slope of the land. It made extensive use of natural stone, similar to the Melson House, with ribbons of stained glass windows along the building. One could imagine light streaming in from all sides through windows highlighted with colored glass. In Marion's drawing, vines grew over the stones and plants draped from its stone balconies.[3]

Ford approved the plan and all seemed to be going well. In early 1913, an agreement was reached with local contractors to pour the foundations. Marion and von Holst traveled to Michigan to see how it was going.[4]

But by this time, Marion's mind was not too focused on her work. She was finding the separation from her husband increasingly hard to bear. She wrote letter after letter to him, like a lovesick teenager. Where was he now? Was he passing some island in the Pacific? Pango Pango was it called? Could he drop her a line when the ship docked in Honolulu? "Do tell me everything," she wrote. But then she worried this might be asking too much, saying that a short note would do. "No, just drop me a line. It's a pity to spoil a good outing by writing letters, but a line I must have."⁵

She would wake up at five in the morning and lie in bed until eight, just thinking of him, wondering where he was and what he was doing. "Have you decided by now to leave me in the States for the next few years while you get Australia straightened out?" she wrote plaintively.

Clients would come into the office and ask for Walter. The Griffins had been working on plans for a library in Anna, a town south of Chicago. A representative from the city came into the office to discuss the building of the library. On learning that Walter would be away for some time, he invited Marion to come to Anna to meet the board of trustees, telling her that they valued her opinion very highly. But Marion said she would wait and go with her husband when he returned from his trip to Australia.⁶

Marion's letters to Walter continued. "My thought is with you constantly, my love, your love, Marion,"⁷ she wrote. Walter wrote back to her, sending newspaper clippings of his visit. Marion was able to read about Walter's welcome at Sydney Harbour and the coverage of his visit to the site of the capital in Canberra. The press had surrounded him, wanting to know what he thought of the site that he had spent so many months considering.⁸

Walter confessed that the scenery reminded him of work by American landscape painter George Inness. A wealthy Chicago businessman had recently bought several of Inness's landscapes and put them on display at the Art Institute of Chicago, not far from their office. Walter had clearly seen them (most likely with Marion), noting that "every one of them came back to me as I looked at Canberra."

Walter also told his wife that Australian natural flora was a lot more beautiful than he had expected. While Australians tended to downplay their native flora as being rather drab compared to the bright flowers of the northern hemisphere, they were in fact, he said, a lot more interesting than he had expected. But Walter kept delaying his return.

One night, as the weather was getting colder, Marion was particularly depressed. She wrote Walter a letter, telling him to come home straight away, but for some reason it was not delivered and was sent back to her. By the time she got it, she was feeling a little better, but only just. "I have decided," she wrote, "I might just as well be the wife of a sailor as a city planner."⁹

Walter took with him some letters of introduction from Miles Franklin to friends in Australia. One was to Henry Hyde Champion, a socialist, a supporter of the campaign for women to have the vote and of English social reformer Henry George and his Single Tax concept. Walter was a strong supporter of the Single Tax movement, an economic philosophy which argued that the only form of tax should be on land and natural resources. A person would not be taxed on their work but the wealthy would pay tax on the value of their land and use of mineral resources which was then used by the government to help the poor. Talking to someone with similar social and political views, Walter was more open in his comments. When they met in Melbourne, Walter told Champion about the role his wife had played in the designs for the Australian capital.

Writing of their meeting in his monthly magazine, the *Book Lover*, Champion noted that:

> His wife is an architect, too, and did not come with him because they could not leave their joint business, both at the same time. He says, with a suspicious twinkle in his eye, that he has always contended that the ideas of his plan for the building of the new city of Canberra are more than half due to his wife, and that she ought to have much more than half the credit for winning the competition.[10]

Champion's recollection of Walter's comments was clear. Marion had not just overseen the drawings of the plans, she had contributed ideas for the design of the city itself. Walter also took some of Marion's drawings to Australia. He organized an exhibition of them in Melbourne, the temporary national capital and seat of government.

The unusual works prompted one reviewer to note:

> All the works were executed on silk, and in all cases, colored. The perspectives were accurately developed whilst the working portion of the drawings (for each sheet represented the entire drawings of a building) were finished in various media. In some cases, sectional work

was brought out in gold. The environment was highly developed, and the foliage was undoubtedly based on a Japanese motif.[11]

In October Marion received some exciting news. Walter had been favorably received by the new Prime Minister of Australia, Mr. Cook, who had appointed him as Director of Design and Construction of the federal capital of Australia. At last, he would be able to carry out his dream of building his own capital city. He had signed a three-year contract and would be given six months' leave to come home and get his affairs in order and return to Australia.

The Griffins would be moving to Australia. But Walter would be postponing his trip back to Chicago for another two months to start his new job. Marion was devastated.

> Walter me darlint, I can't write to you about business. I don't care anything about business. I want you. It seems as if I'd suffocate, there are bands of iron around my heart so it can't beat. The joy in my soul over your beautiful success can't entirely keep me from being sick to see you. I wish I could have gone over with you. ... Two months more is a dreadful long time. Each week seems like a month. I keep counting wrong, thinking two weeks have gone when only one has and then it seems as if time was standing still and you would never be back again. I'm trying to feel that this postponement is the last one. Please come home. Marion.[12]

Finally, Walter sailed for America. On the way back, he went to see their friend, architect William Purcell, who had moved from Chicago to Minneapolis. The next big project would be a competition to design the Parliament House for Canberra, and Walter wanted to help his friend win the project. It was not until the middle of December that Marion's husband finally came home—a good five months after he left. As she was to describe it later, her world had just turned upside down.

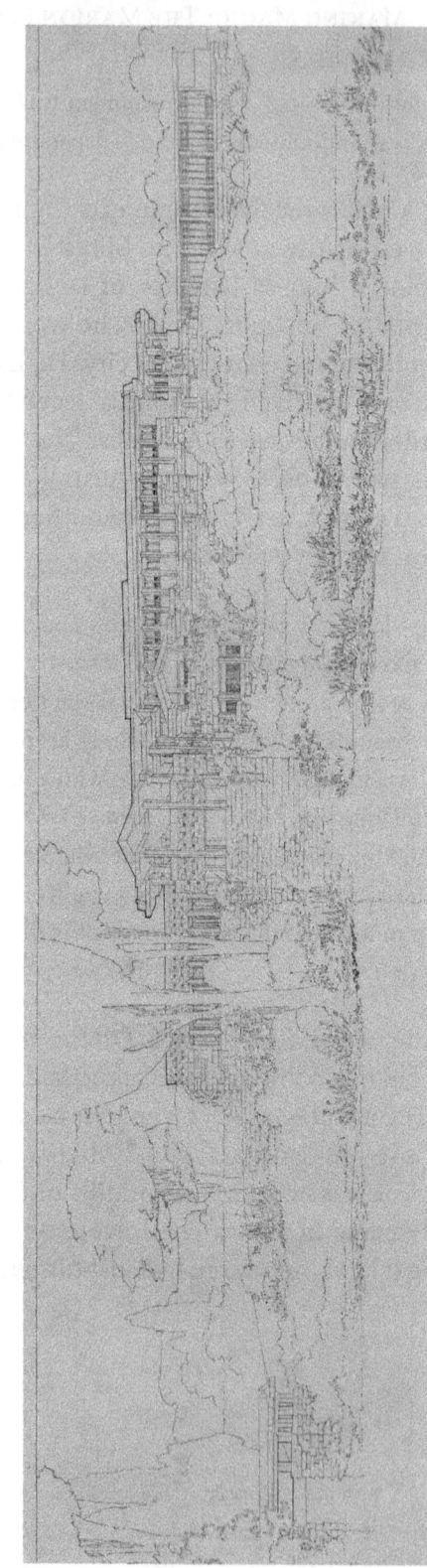

Drawing for proposed house for Henry Ford, Dearborn, Michigan, by Marion Mahony Griffin. 1912. Mary and Leigh Block Museum of Art, Northwestern University, Evanston, Illinois.

Twenty

Leaving Home

It was a grand evening at the Club Room of the Chicago Art Institute on Michigan Avenue. Marion and Walter were at a farewell dinner given by the Illinois Chapter of the American Institute of Architects.[1]

It was the first gathering of the chapter for many years to be held with "ladies" present. It was a very specific recognition by this high-powered group of Chicago's leading architects of Marion's own talents. Her work was well-known to many of its members, some of whom had worked with her. They, more than any other group, would have had a good idea exactly how important Marion was to Walter's unexpected success in the competition.

Walter's proud parents were among the guests, as was his sister Genevieve, and Roy Lippincott, who was now working with the Griffins in their practice after they had offered him a junior partnership. After working so closely for many months on the plan for the Australian capital, Genevieve and Roy had fallen in love. They were soon to be married and would be making the trip to Australia with Walter and Marion.

Covering the walls of the Club Room were some of the Griffins' sketches of their plans for Canberra, including Marion's beautiful silk drawings. It was duly noted in the speeches that Mrs. Griffin was the first woman licensed to practice architecture in the state of Illinois. *Construction News* reported on the night:

> The guests of the evening were unanimous in lauding the works of both Mr. Griffin and Mrs. Griffin. They also remarked, with considerable

delight on the method of exhibition, there being a number of sketches and drawings in satin.

Those present included the cream of Chicago architecture. After dinner, there were speeches of praise for the Griffins and Marion was called upon to say a few words. *Construction News* reported that Marion had:

> ... told of her plans in the most delightful way and declared that, in working together with her husband on the plans for the new Australian capital, she has more than realized her ambitions in an architectural way.

Those in the room might have wondered at her comments, which deliberately downplayed her role, given her talents and energy. Or maybe, in the male-dominated profession they worked in, they may have felt her sentiments were entirely appropriate. The Griffins were leaving for six weeks in Europe. Walter was going to learn more about the latest techniques in building cities and to speak with some leading architects, some of whom Walter wanted to be judges on the competition to design the building that would house the parliament in Canberra.

Marion and Walter got the train for New York and set sail for Europe. It was their first big trip together as husband and wife. Their dear friend, Joshua Melson, would also be joining them in Paris.[2]

As Walter had learned when he went to Australia, the competition for the design of Canberra had been controversial. When King O'Malley, the minister in charge of the project, had announced he would have the final say in the competition in the event the judges could not make up their mind, there were complaints by local architects. The British Institute of Architects, whose views held sway in Australia, had suggested its members boycott the process. It meant that many architects in Australia and Britain did not enter, provoking resentment in architectural circles about the competition. The Griffins' plan had been selected from a field of more than 130 entries, including 41 from Britain, 20 from the United States, and others from South Africa, France, Canada, New Zealand, and Scandinavia. But Walter and the Australian government wanted to ensure that the competition to design Parliament House would have the widest international support. Having a panel of respected judges from around the world would help ensure this.

Walter had no doubt who he wanted to be the American judge—his architectural hero, Louis Sullivan. He also chose John James Burnet from Britain, Victor Laloux, the architect of the Gare du Quai d'Orsay in Paris, and Otto Wagner from Austria.

In Paris, they met Laloux. They also met Louis Bonnier, a senior city official who had requested some of Griffin's work to display at an exhibition at the Musée des Arts Décoratifs in Paris in June that year. Walter had come well-prepared with a roll of drawings and gave Bonnier over 25 of Marion's works for the exhibition, including 20 silk drawings of his houses. There was another exhibition on cities to be held in the French city of Lyon in May.

The organizers asked Walter to send them copies of their design for Canberra for the exhibition. Marion hastily retraced some of the drawings, but it seemed they also sent their precious silk drawings of Canberra to Lyon.

In Germany, they went to Berlin where Walter met with the famous Herr Wasmuth, publisher of Wright's portfolio. In London, Walter met Burnet and addressed a dinner of the Royal British Institute of Architects, which promised to support the competition for the design of Parliament House. Marion and Walter returned to Chicago, excited about their new life ahead.

Walter's contract with the Australian government was for three years from late 1913. The Griffins wanted to keep their practice going, planning to return to the United States a few years later. Walter wanted William Purcell to take over their business, but he was not available. So they asked Barry Byrne, who had worked with them in Wright's studio in Oak Park, to oversee their practice from their office in the Monroe Building. Walter had specifically negotiated in his contract with the Australian government that he could also work on his private practice. It was envisaged he would be spending half his time on his job as Federal Capital Director and half on his own work. Having designed the Australian capital, Walter was eager to play a part in the evolving architectural style of Australia. Just as Louis Sullivan had urged young American architects to develop their own style, Walter felt that Australians should also develop their own local architecture. Marion could help to run their private office in Australia and work on their American practice, and Genevieve and Roy would be coming with them to help. The excited party of four set out for Vancouver to catch the ship for Australia.

By now, Marion would also have learned that the arrangement with Henry Ford to build his country house in Michigan had ended badly. At some point, toward the end of 1913, relations soured. Ford had approved Marion's idea of a massive building in natural stone, but the cost of the material was causing problems. Somehow word got out in the town that Ford was building a two-million-dollar marble mansion. Marion's proposal was for a house of stone, not marble, but the reports upset Henry and Clara. When the bill arrived for the stones, Ford complained that it was too much. It came at a time when Ford was becoming increasingly sensitive about people's view of his rising wealth. His wife, Clara, had also become interested in the Gothic designs she had seen on their trip to Britain the year before. Marion's design may have been a little too radical for their liking.[3]

Ford dismissed von Holst and Fyfe as the architects on the job on February 18, 1914. He paid the firm $142,300 in fees and took legal action against the contractors who were beginning to pour the foundations of the house. The action did not involve Marion, and the Fords' behavior may well have been partly driven by Mrs. Ford's newfound passion for English castles, spurred on by embarrassment about local criticism of the unusual house as being a marble palace. Marion's design, which had overtones of the Melson House in Mason City, would have fitted more naturally into the environment than the gray English Gothic mansion which was eventually imposed on the site. But it was not to be.

Marion did not have much time to lament what could have been as she and Walter and Roy and Genevieve set sail for an exciting new life ahead.

Twenty-one

The Arrival

On May 12, 1914, the *SS Willochra* was reaching the end of its long journey from Canada to Australia. The four Americans were readying themselves for their arrival in Sydney Harbour. Like the Indian brave in her father's poem, Marion had traveled to a new southern land.

The country they were about to set foot in had the distinction of being the world's smallest continent and its largest island. It was just a little smaller than continental United States in area, but it had a population of less than 5 million compared to the 100 million living in the United States. It was a democracy like America but, as Marion and Walter were discovering, its political system was very different. Marion was eager to visit this new country her husband spoke so enthusiastically about and to see him, finally, have the chance to carry out his dream. Walter was now 37, and Marion was 43. As far as she was concerned, her husband was at last on the edge of achieving the greatness he so richly deserved.

Their ship would enter through the Heads, the two rocky sandstone cliffs on either side of the harbor. Twenty years before, writer Mark Twain had sailed into that same harbor, extolling its beauty to his American readers. He described Sydney Harbour as being "shaped somewhat like an oak leaf—a roomy sheet of lovely blue water, with narrow offshoots of water running up into the country on both sides, between long fingers of land, high wooden ridges with sides sloped like graves." Sydney, he said, was "an English city with American trimmings," noting that its climate was the counterpart of Columbia, South Carolina, or Little Rock, Arkansas.[1]

They were going to stay with George and Florence Taylor, a well-connected couple that Walter had met on his first trip to Australia, until they found a place to rent. George Taylor had been a strong advocate of the idea of bringing Walter to Australia. Taylor was active in building and town planning circles, publishing a magazine called *Building*, which he and Florence used to promote their views on building and town planning. He was interested in ideas from America and was most impressed with a visit from the US Navy's Great White Fleet to Sydney Harbour in 1908. The visit had been made after Prime Minister Alfred Deakin had made a request to US President Theodore Roosevelt. In a country still part of the British Empire, it was a sign of a new interest among some leading Australians in the importance of developing military and political links with the United States. Walter was now aware of the intense politics around his role and the plans for the new capital city. Having Taylor's support would be invaluable.

When they arrived, Walter had to go ashore to borrow some money from Taylor to tip the staff on the boat. On the dock, Walter was surrounded by reporters. There was still much controversy over his plans for Canberra, including the cost. "If people will back me and take as much interest in the capital city as I do—we'll get along all right," he said. The reporters continued to quiz him, but Walter knew better than to be drawn in. "I'm rather out of touch," he said diplomatically, before excusing himself.[2]

Florence Taylor was tall and statuesque. She was 35, 8 years younger than Marion. On the face of it, the Taylors had a lot in common with the Griffins. They were both confident, energetic, professional couples with no children, actively involved in local debates over architecture and town planning. Like Marion, Florence had also begun her career as an architect at a time when it was almost unheard of for a woman to do so. But she had met with opposition when she applied to become a member of the Institute of Architects in New South Wales. Around the same time she married Taylor and left the profession. They set up a magazine publishing business, specializing in the building industry with a flagship publication *Building*.[3]

The Griffins and the Lippincotts were taken to the Taylors' house in the suburb of Neutral Bay on the north side of the harbor. The Taylors were planning a visit to America, including spending some time in Chicago, which George grandly declared would be "the Mecca of their ten thousand mile pilgrimage."

They were most enthusiastic about meeting the famous Frank Lloyd Wright. The fact that Walter was seen as a member of Wright's broader circle of architects was important in Taylor's eyes. "We hail Frank Lloyd Wright and his missionaries in the cause of architecture," he had written. He saw Walter as one of those missionaries.[4]

While Walter's work as Federal Capital Director was based in Melbourne, 600 miles south, the Griffins planned to make their home in Sydney. Walter had been taken with the city, its spectacular harbor, and foreshores on his first visit the year before, and it had a milder, more Mediterranean climate than Melbourne. He had also agreed to set up a private partnership with Florence's former employer, Sydney architect Burcham Clamp.

Clamp had met Walter on a trip to the United States after his plan for Canberra was chosen. Walter saw the arrangement with Clamp as a good way of setting up in a local practice in Australia. Marion and the Lippincotts would remain in Sydney helping out with their private practice while Walter would work in his role as Federal Capital Director in Melbourne, traveling back to Sydney on the weekends. Or at least that was the plan.

Marion was befriended by Florence, who was full of praise for her. Florence wrote an article on Marion for the May edition of *Building* magazine which positively gushed.

> The Federal prize was a triumph for a great architect and his life-mate, who happens to be, as I, one of the women of today performing, according to her accomplishments, her highest duty as the help-mate of a husband. ... Who, more than a wife, understands the workings of a man's brain, and having artistic skill, is better able to portray his thoughts? Griffin is a man of genius, and it is his gifted wife who gives that genius its best interpretation. And in this art of architectural delineation, Marion Griffin has proved to be one of the most distinguished in the world. One cannot easily forget the remarkable series of satin-painted studies by Marion Griffin of her husband's designs.[5]

The article included a picture of Marion's Church of All Souls in Evanston which was praised as "an extremely simple and beautiful design." Florence asked Marion to write some articles on "democratic architecture" for two upcoming editions of the magazine. Marion was grateful for Florence's support. But, for the first time in her life, she realized she was being feted because of her husband's role. Both Marion and Walter had been farewelled in Chicago as equals by their architectural peers, many of whom knew Marion's extensive professional experience, but now she was in Australia as Mrs. Griffin, wife of the Federal Capital Director.

Twenty-two

Storm Clouds

The Griffins and the Lippincotts rented a house near the water with wonderful views over the harbor, in a suburb called Greenwich. It was on the north side of the harbor and could be easily reached from the city by ferry. The garden terraced down to the water to an enclosed pool where they could swim safely protected from the sharks in the harbor. Marion loved the view from their house which looked out on distant mountains. "On clear days we get a glimpse of the Blue Mountains across the water. Our yard has flowers in bloom all the year round. We get the full benefit of gorgeous sunsets across the harbor."[1]

Like her husband, Marion took an interest in the very different native flora of Australia. She joined the Naturalists' Society and was increasingly fascinated with the different native trees in Australia, particularly the gray-green gum trees with their gnarled white trunks. The society organized walks on the weekends through the bushlands around the city, like Walter's walking club back in Chicago. Walter had already decided the national capital should be planted with Australian trees and was interested to learn as much as he could about them. Expert botanists accompanied the Griffins on their long walks so Walter could study the Australian plant life in detail, as he had done in America.

But while they were beginning to fall in love with their new home, the Griffins' life wasn't turning out quite the way they had expected. They had thought Walter would be spending about half his time on his job as Federal Capital Director in Melbourne, allowing him to spend the rest working on his private practice in Sydney. But Walter soon found he was spending most of his time in Melbourne and only just managing to come home by train on weekends and not every weekend at that. Marion was the one effectively in charge of their private practice.

In Melbourne, Walter found his efforts hampered at almost every turn by the public servants he was supposed to be working with. Many of the bureaucrats he had to deal with were much older and had been in their positions for many years. They resented the young newcomer from America. Some had been involved in the department board that had been set up after Walter's plan was chosen to produce a new plan for Canberra. They wanted to implement that plan, not Walter's. The highly unstable nature of the new federal government, which saw frequent changes of political leadership, gave the bureaucrats more power than the elected politicians. Joseph Cook was the country's sixth Prime Minister since Federation in 1901. His election in 1913 was the ninth time the nation's leadership had changed hands since the states had come together.

The two most obstructive public servants were Colonel David Miller, the secretary of the Department of Home Affairs, and his friend Colonel Percy Thomas Owen, the Federal Director of Public Works. Miller was 57 when Walter arrived and Owen was 50. Both had served in the Boer War in South Africa around the turn of the century. Miller had been secretary of the department since it was established in Melbourne in 1901 and was now based in Canberra overseeing the development of the site. The two had been working closely together since Miller hired Owen from the Defence Department 10 years before.

Miller had chaired the departmental board appointed by King O'Malley, which had reviewed the Griffin plan and came up with its own plan for Canberra. Owen was another member of the seven-man panel. But when the government changed and the new Minister for Home Affairs, Kelly, had appointed Walter as Federal Capital Director, the board was dismissed. Walter was given complete authority over the establishment of the new capital. But there was considerable resentment amongst those whose views had been cast aside. The two veteran bureaucrats were strongly opposed to Walter before they even met him. Walter's decision to leave Australia for six months, after his appointment in 1913, had also allowed the forces working against him, including Miller and Owen, time to regroup.

The Griffins were soon to get a firsthand lesson of unstable politics of their new country. Just as Walter was settling into the job, Prime Minister Cook, the man who had hired him as Federal Capital Director only a year before, called an election. Neither Cook nor Kelly, who had appointed Walter, had any time to hear his concerns about the difficulties he faced in the job.

Meanwhile, the clouds of war were gathering. On August 4, Britain declared war on Germany and the young country of Australia also found itself at war. It was less than three months after the Griffins had arrived in Australia, so full of optimism. The political climate in Australia changed overnight.

Cook transferred control of the Australian Navy to the British Admiralty and offered to send 20,000 troops to support the war effort in Europe. Every able-bodied Australian man was urged to sign up for the military. Walter and Marion were aghast that this new democracy was suddenly at war, at the beck and call of Britain. America, under Democrat President Woodrow Wilson, was staying out of the conflict.

While Britain argued that its involvement in the war had been provoked by Germany's actions in Europe, the Griffins and many others believed that Germany itself had been provoked into taking the action it did and that other forces were to blame. Chicago itself, with its big German population, was split over which side to support. Walter's university studies had had a strong German influence and both Marion and Walter respected Germany's leading role in European architectural circles. But the Griffins soon found their opposition to the war, and their sympathy for things German, put them at odds with the Australian establishment, which was still very English.

In September, Prime Minister Cook was defeated in the election, replaced by former Prime Minister Andrew Fisher. Fisher appointed a new Minister for Home Affairs, William Archibald. A tough man with strong views, Archibald had no time for the young, educated, softly spoken American, and sided with his head of department Colonel Miller and his friend Percy Owen.

Archibald moved to marginalize Walter. He abruptly canceled the competition for the new federal parliament building without consulting him. Alone in Melbourne, Walter vented his frustrations in frequent letters to Marion who got to know the names of the various public servants and political players long before she ever met them.

With Walter in Melbourne, Marion oversaw their Sydney-based work and the ongoing work for their American clients. She worked on the plans for a house in the Sydney suburb of Double Bay. It had strong Japanese overtones with flared roofs, similar to the Adolph Mueller House Marion had designed in Millikin Place. She also got to know a senior public servant in the New South Wales state government, Leslie Wade, the state commissioner for water conservation and irrigation. Wade had approached Walter during his visit to Australia the year before to design a town in an area in the southwest of the state, which would be part of an inland irrigation project called the Murrumbidgee Irrigation Area.

Wade wanted to develop several inland towns in the region, starting with one which would be called Leeton. Walter had visited the site and worked on the plans for the town on the journey back to America, sending them back to Wade. He designed the town with a circular road system and two water towers with plans for a railway connection.

The town's striking features had been a success. When the Griffins arrived back in Australia in the next year, Wade wanted Walter to continue working on the town and design another one nearby, to be called Griffith. With Walter in Melbourne so much, Marion spent some time with Wade and became fond of him.

Marion was frustrated at the versions of world politics appearing in the Australian press which Australians so readily seemed to believe. They were finding Australia was a far cry from the independent-minded young nation they had imagined during the cold nights at the top of Steinway Hall when they worked on the drawings for Canberra.

But, somehow, these frustrations were more than compensated for by their growing love for their adopted country. After the bitter winters of Chicago, Marion loved the mild Australian climate where shrubs and flowers seemed to grow so easily, blooming almost all year round. And, when Walter did get back to their home in Sydney, it was like a holiday for him.

The Griffins looked for a place in Sydney to build a home for themselves. They bought a block of land on the south side of the harbor, in a waterside suburb called Vaucluse, and thought of what sort of house they might build.

The outbreak of war also changed their relationship with the Taylors. A strong supporter of the military, Taylor was angry at President Wilson's refusal to join the war on the side of Britain and his love for things American began to dissipate. After years of idolizing Frank Lloyd Wright as one of the great new architects of the time, Taylor was less than impressed when he met him in person. Wright and Taylor eagerly exchanged information about the Griffins. Bitter at being socially ostracized from many of his former clients and colleagues, Wright seized the opportunity to disparage the Griffins, whom he blamed for taking clients away from him and accused of producing second-rate designs.[2]

The Griffins got a letter from their friend William Purcell in Minneapolis who had also met the Taylors on their visit. He warned them that while the Taylors were pretending to be their friends, he felt they were deliberately trying to use their visit to dig up dirt on the Griffins to take over the federal capital project for themselves.[3]

Meanwhile, Marion was overseeing their work back in Chicago, keeping in contact with Barry Byrne who was supervising the construction of more houses in Mason City. Soon she was assisted by the arrival of architect George Elgh, who had worked for the Griffins in their office, to help in their private practice. Elgh had left the Griffins' office in 1912 and went to work for Wright, living at Wright's new home in Wisconsin, which he called Taliesin, Welsh for "shining brow".[4]

Still shunned in many circles in Chicago, Wright was developing a new studio in his home at Spring Green. Walter had invited Elgh to come to Australia to help him. He accepted, marrying his sweetheart Nellie in July, and then traveling to Sydney. Elgh's departure from Taliesin was more timely than he could have imagined. In August, while Elgh and his wife were on the ship for Australia, those at Taliesin were struck down by a horrible fate. While Wright was away in Chicago, an angry servant had set fire to the house, killing Mamah Cheney, her two children, and four other people. The servant had locked the doors to prevent people from escaping the fire and attacked those inside with an ax as they tried to escape through the one door which was not locked. It was an awful tragedy.

In Melbourne, Walter was finding himself increasingly isolated by the new government. Minister Archibald and his bureaucrats were doing their best to frustrate him with all sorts of petty tricks. As the war intensified, anti-Americanism was beginning to creep into the debate over Walter's role, making his task all the more difficult.

But Walter was also winning some supporters. One of the judges on the plan for Canberra, James Alexander Smith, who lived in Melbourne, had taken Walter under his wing. A consulting engineer, Smith had been president of the Victorian Institute of Engineers from 1908 to 1911. He appreciated the strength of Walter's plan, and they had struck up a relationship during Walter's visit in 1913. He could see how badly Walter was being treated and gave him advice on how to handle local politics. Walter wrote about him often in his letters to Marion and she grew very fond of Smith from her distance in Sydney. In one letter to her husband in Melbourne, Marion said, "I hope you told Mr. J.A.S. I love him. It's good to find one person in a country you can love."[5]

Twenty-three

The Dogs of War

There was little time for the Griffins to celebrate their first New Year in their adopted country. Sometime in January 1915, they received the sad news that Leslie Wade had died. Walter had designed Leeton and Griffith, two regional towns in the Murrumbidgee Irrigation Area in southern NSW for Wade. The Griffins regarded him as the kind of energetic, visionary bureaucrat they could see driving the new country of Australia. Only 51, Wade died unexpectedly at his home from heart complications. Marion was very fond of him and wrote that his death "broke our hearts."[1]

Marion disliked the rising tide of militarism she saw in Australia. America had seen the horrible carnage of the Civil War. Australians, who had never faced war on their own territory, were being fed tales of romance, heroism and patriotism and the need to fight in a war thousands of miles away in Europe. President Wilson's steadfast refusal to enter the war in support of Britain was making Americans increasingly unpopular in Australia.

"There is a very strong anti-American feeling here," Marion wrote to a friend back home in March 1915. "The Australians find the Americans as inscrutable as the Chinese." She blamed former President Roosevelt's decision to send a US naval fleet to Australia in 1908 for stirring up latent militarism in the country. In a letter home, she criticized Roosevelt for "his pompous sending around the world of the US fleet with its flip assurance—which, of course, he had no business to make—that if Australia ever needed assistance, the US fleet would be on hand to help." Even worse, she argued, the US fleet visit "was a large element in starting [Australians] on the battleship building fever and military movements which are getting an appalling grip on the spirit of the people."[2]

The Griffins found their letters home subject to wartime censorship over the mildest of comments. Once Marion wrote to her brother about a lecture she had attended by a social activist who urged government financial support for health clinics for young children. Marion had seen firsthand the work of Jane Addams in Chicago and her own mother's social circle helping the poor. She opposed the view in Australia that the government should be the one to help tackle all social problems. The attitude, she wrote to her brother, was "but one of the many ways of pauperizing Australia." After she sent the letter, she was called in by the police and warned that she could be jailed for her critical views of the government.[3]

On one occasion Marion took particular pleasure in sheer orneriness at official attitudes. After the war began, the government required "aliens" to be registered with the police. It was primarily aimed at people from countries now on the side of the enemy, such as Germans, Italians, and Turks. One day, she decided she would go into the local police station to register. She cheerfully retold the story in a letter back home.

> A big husky officer sat at his desk with a huge volume in front of him. I told him what I had come for and, to his question as to my nationality, said I was an American.
>
> "Oh," he said, pushing the book aside. "Then you are not an alien."
>
> "But I am," I said. "If I don't register, I'm likely to get into trouble."
>
> "But I mean," said he, "what country do you belong to?"
>
> "I belong to the United States of America," I said.
>
> "Well then, you are not an alien," he said settling back in his chair.
>
> "But yes, I am an alien," I said.
>
> "What country do you belong to: like Italy or France or Germany?" he said.
>
> "Yes," I said. "The country I belong to is not Italy nor France nor Germany, but the United States of America."
>
> "Then you're not an alien," he said.

"Yes," I said. "It's this way. The Canadians are Americans too but they still belong to the British Empire so they are not aliens. But the United States of America does not belong to the British Empire so they are aliens."

And wide eyed and full of astonishment he said, "Ohhhhhhh!" and permitted me to sign the book.[4]

The war changed everything. New building work dried up, cutting back on the potential work for Walter's partnership in Sydney with Clamp. Walter also had little time to work with Clamp because of his role as Federal Capital Director and the partnership was dissolved.

As times became increasingly uncertain, the Griffins shelved their plans to build a house in Sydney. Marion's letters home reflected a combination of social isolation and a painful realization that the cultural differences between Australia and America were larger than she initially thought. In her letters home she described Australia as "utterly European in its ideas." It was "a nation of pessimists full of fears; ideals are rarely to be found in the country. All their policies are based on fear." There was, she believed, a deliberate "freezing out of strangers. ... There is no chance here for any foreigner (and any new-comer is considered to be a foreigner) to prosper in any field, trade or profession (except dentistry)."[5]

There was a lot more class consciousness in Australia than she had expected. "There is bitter class feeling, the political parties being purely a class division with no difference of principles."[6] Always a hard worker herself, Marion was appalled at what she saw as the poor work ethic of some Australians. "There is not, here, a vestige of the feeling that it is a joy to work. No one has enthusiasm in what he is doing. The interest is merely in getting the money out of it. Of course we see that feeling in America, but here there is nothing else." One well-meaning person had advised Marion that Walter should just accept his salary as Federal Capital Director and agree to compromise on his plans. Marion was frustrated at the comments. "He didn't come over here to draw his salary but to do the work he was appointed to do and do it right. ... That's what we don't seem to be able to make any Australian understand." Her husband, she reported home, was "having the fight of his life in the matter which brought us over here."⁷

Marion was appalled at the power of the bureaucrats in the Australian political system.

> Australian Federal politicians do not understand the motives of the Civil Service which is determined to control everything itself without the embarrassment of outside inspection of its methods or results ... in the ten months we have been here, Walter has not been able to accomplish a single thing. They have no notion of letting any plan but their own be carried into execution, and as they are in power for life, they can gain their ends, they hope, by delay piled upon delay.⁸

She was angry at the internal workings of the Labor Party, the party now in power, under Prime Minister Andrew Fisher, whose Minister for Home Affairs, Mr. Archibald, was going out of his way to make life difficult for her husband. Walter had some letters written to him by Archibald and others he wanted to make public to show how unjustly he was being treated. There should be, Marion wrote home, a "muckraking campaign" to expose the internal machinations of the party.

> We are hopeful that the [Labor] Party will realize, before too late, that the publication of Mr. Griffin's correspondence with the ministers would make them the butt of the ridicule of the world, that their failure to fulfill the government's contract with Mr. Griffin ... will seriously impair the nation's credit.⁹

In early 1915, she visited Miles Franklin's mother in Sydney, pouring out her heart about her problems. As she wrote to Franklin, "I am afraid I got the uplift from her and she nothing from me but depression as, you see, the tale I have to tell is not a pleasant one."¹⁰

Marion spent her time overseeing their American practice. She worked on a plan for the campus of the University of New Mexico and another for the town of Mossmain in Montana. She supervised the drawings, working with Genevieve and Roy, and sent them off to Barry Byrne in Chicago.

She was pleased to hear that Genevieve and Roy were expecting a baby, but she was still in need of more outlets for her considerable energies. Marion began to make a few friends in Sydney with like-minded women. One of those was Ada Holman, the wife of the state Labor premier, William Arthur Holman. Ada Holman was a journalist and a strong feminist. The two had much in common. Ada was having trouble coping with a husband whose time was taken up with his job as state leader, as well as the constraints on her ability to speak and write because of his job. Florence Taylor was also continuing to cultivate Marion's friendship, mainly because of Walter's role.

The Taylors had been involved in founding the Town Planning Association of New South Wales in 1913, which was chaired by their friend, the well-connected town-planning expert, John Sulman. Florence wanted to set up a women's division of the TPA. In March 1915, she held the first meeting of the women's section at the Hotel Australia in Sydney. Ada Holman was invited to be its president and Florence invited Marion to become one of its vice presidents.[11]

But soon, it emerged that Marion Griffin and Florence Taylor had very different views of the role of the new women's section. Marion, who had years of experience with the feisty and socially conscious women of Chicago, including Jane Addams, wanted the women's organization to have a strong independent voice away from the male-dominated TPA. But Florence saw it more as a low-key women's committee. As Marion and her friends tried to steer the women's section to take on a more independent, proactive role, Florence was horrified to find her nice little project was fast getting out of her control.

Soon, two factions developed in the women's section—one backing Florence and the other backing Marion. As the war progressed, the Griffins were finding the Taylors to be much more right wing and officious than they had ever imagined. One day, when Walter was away, Marion was summoned to see George Taylor. He instructed her to tell her husband that he should do what Taylor and his friends told him to do when it came to matters concerning the federal capital. Furious, she stormed out of the meeting.

Marion gleefully described the tensions in the women's group in her letters to Walter. There was one particularly heated meeting where she proposed changes to its constitution:

> I passed around my scheme of organization. Mrs. Taylor tried to stop me after I read a sentence or two but, of course, I paid no attention to her, read through and explained as I went. Mrs. Taylor got up and delivered a tirade. It was a pity that the valuable time of the meeting should be taken up with such silly stuff. It was entirely out of order.[12]

One woman said that Marion should be president of the women's association on the grounds that "she's got enough brains to wipe up the floor with the rest of that whole bunch."

Florence, Marion told Walter, was "a really pathetic figure" whose "caretaker [husband George] ought not to let her out of his sight." Florence rang Marion, asking her to resign, making it clear that she had only been made vice president because of her husband. Marion hung up on her.

The under-challenged Marion saw herself as being involved in her own heroic battles in Sydney, along the lines that her husband was fighting in Melbourne. At one point John Sulman visited her home with his daughter, and attempted to advise Marion not to take on Florence Taylor and her friends, but Marion misunderstood his approach. Things came to a head at a rowdy meeting where Ada Holman walked out, to the great embarrassment of Florence and her friends. In the end, after much bitterness, the women's section was disbanded. The Taylors turned from friends to bitter enemies of the Griffins and a potential circle of support from prominent men and women in Sydney, interested in building, architecture and town planning, was closed to Marion.

"Has Mrs. Burley Griffin exceeded her station and presumed to take too much interest in Sydney women's affairs?" the *Woman's Weekly* magazine asked, no doubt briefed by Florence and her supporters. Marion had misjudged the politics of her new country. Those involved at the top levels of architecture and town planning in Sydney were very different to the more idealistic people she mixed with back home in Chicago. Two decades before, a kindly Daniel Burnham had advised

Marion's predecessor at MIT, Sophia Hayden, not to take on Bertha Palmer, one of the most powerful women in Chicago. But Marion had no appreciation of the danger of taking on the well-connected Florence Taylor and her friends in Sydney.

Writing home, Marion said, "The first year in Australia was full indeed with doors opening and doors slamming in our faces. Lifelong friends were made and lifelong enemies."[13]

After the Town Planning Association affair, Marion's life was even more focused on her work. In October, she addressed the National Council of Women in Sydney. She spoke about the need for any women in a profession to throw themselves into their work, but her comments also painted a picture of someone who did not have many social contacts outside of her work.

> As a man did so a woman must—work day times, night times. It must be from the basis of her dreams. She must give it her Saturdays and Sundays and go without holidays. ... At present men had to give up all social life, and women must expect to do the same.[14]

In her letters home, Marion rationalized her split with the Taylors, saying that she had no great desire to be part of Sydney's society anyway. "Fortunately my job as a draftsman made it unnecessary for me to participate in society life," she wrote.[15] But she was still determined that Walter should persist in carrying out his ambitions in Australia. And she loved living in Sydney. It had a temperate climate with many beautiful waterways and spectacular views. It was very different to Chicago, which could be so bitterly cold in the winter and fiercely hot in the summer. She was a determined, energetic woman and could still see opportunities in their new country. After one long letter to her family back home where she poured out all her worries about their life in Australia, she finished with the words, "Now you mustn't think I am so pessimistic as this letter sounds. In fact I am a confirmed optimist."[16] The Griffins were made of much sterner stuff than many people could imagine.

While Marion was fighting with Florence in Sydney, Walter had struck up a friendship in Melbourne with King O'Malley. As he got to know him, he discovered more about this most unusual Australian politician. O'Malley had actually been born in America. He came to Australia in 1888, and, after several different jobs, decided to become involved in politics. But, under Australian law at the time, only people born in the British Empire were allowed to stand for political election. O'Malley invented a wild story about how his pregnant mother just happened to be on a visit to Canada when he was born, so he could stand for politics in Australia. Few people believed him, but he continued to stick to his story. O'Malley had spent time in Washington, DC, and had taken a passionate interest in the establishment of the Australian capital. While his party, the Labor Party, was back in power, O'Malley was frustrated that he was no longer the Minister for Home Affairs, overseeing the development of Canberra. He sympathized with Walter in his battles with Minister Archibald and the federal bureaucrats.[17]

O'Malley and his wife, Amy, had the Griffins over to dinner at their home in Melbourne soon after their arrival in Australia.[18] With Walter in Melbourne on his own so often, he spent a lot of time with O'Malley. As a fellow American, O'Malley felt a special bond with the Griffins. They had similar views on social justice and opposition to Australia's involvement in the war in Europe. Almost 20 years older than Walter, with no children of his own, O'Malley took a fatherly interest in the idealistic young American.

Meanwhile, Prime Minister Fisher was growing weary of his job. The strains of conducting a war, particularly the heavy casualties in the Gallipoli Peninsula in Turkey, where thousands of young Australians were sent by their British commanders to attempt an almost impossible invasion, were mounting on him. In October 1915, he stepped down as Prime Minister to take up the role of Australian High Commissioner to London. His energetic, but sometimes erratic, attorney general, William Morris Hughes, took over as Prime Minister. The shift created a vacancy in the Ministry that saw King O'Malley now back in his old job as Minister for Home Affairs. The Griffins were delighted at the news. The political pendulum in Australia had swung again—this time in Walter's favor.

Twenty-four

Newman College

Marion always looked forward to her husband arriving back from Melbourne, but it could also mean more work for her. One day, Walter got off the train with a sketch on the back of an envelope. It was his idea for a Catholic residential college at the University of Melbourne. He had been approached about the project as a result of his links with some leading members of the Catholic community in the city who had similar views on social justice. He had met them when he attended meetings of the Single Tax movement in Melbourne. With Walter now devoting almost all his time to his work on the federal capital, it would be up to Marion and the others to take his sketches for the college to the next level.

The project was being driven by Irish-born priest Daniel Mannix, who arrived in Australia in 1913, designated to become Melbourne's next Catholic archbishop. He saw education as a way to boost the standing of Catholics in Australia and wanted to build a residential college on land set aside for the church at the university. But the combination of the war, and a drought which had gripped the country, made it hard to raise funds for the project.[1]

He finally found a wealthy Catholic lawyer, Thomas Donovan, based in Sydney, who was prepared to provide the financial support he needed. The 72-year-old Donovan insisted on having a seat on the committee established by Mannix to oversee the project. In July 1915, Walter was approached by Mannix's committee to work on the project. Walter sketched out his ideas for the college on a train journey from Melbourne to Sydney on the back of an envelope, which he gave to Marion after he arrived. As she would tell friends later, "The whole thing was there on that envelope plus what he had in his head."[2] While the basic concept for the college came from Walter, it was left to Marion to oversee the details of its design and the drawings to be presented to the Mannix committee.

Like Marion and Wright, Walter wanted to do something different with his church-backed project than the traditional Gothic style. Walter decided to look to the architecture of southern Europe for inspiration. Maybe he saw its warmer climate as having more resonance in Australia. His basic design involved two L-shaped residential wings, facing each other, around two quadrangles, with a chapel in between. There were long cloisters along the student residences, facing the courtyards on the inside, which would be carefully landscaped with Australian trees.

He designed a rotunda for each of the corners of the two residential wings. One was to be a circular meeting and dining hall with a high ceiling, and the other would be a library. Above each of the rotundas was to be a dome with a central spire-like vertical arrow. The spire was surrounded by four groups of three pinnacles, like the twelve disciples of Christ. The domes had overtones of southern European churches, including the roof of Antoni Gaudi's church in Barcelona. Someone looking at the college from the main road, which ran directly north from the city, would see two long cloistered residential buildings with a church in the middle and two dramatic rotundas with their spires at either end. The windows of the college, facing along the street, were highlighted by keystones, similar to the Melson House in Mason City, looking like the windows of a castle.

As the year progressed, the Griffins decided that the main focus of their work would be in Melbourne. Marion decided to move to Melbourne to be with her husband and help him with the designs for what was being called Newman College and other projects. George Elgh and his wife also moved to Melbourne to help while the Lippincotts stayed in Sydney.

Just as she had done for Wright with his radical proposals for the Unity Temple, and Walter's plans for Canberra, Marion knew that her drawings had to be impressive enough to convince the committee to support her husband's striking design. She produced a drawing of the college, viewed from inside one of the landscaped courtyards. It was a long, wide view with the cloistered dormitory corridors stretching out across the page. It highlighted the striking dome of the rotunda, with the pinnacles on the roof, both a landmark for the site and a protective presence for the students who lived there. On the right-hand side were drawings of gum trees with native plants across the foreground. Each plant was finely detailed. Someone who had seen Marion's drawings in America might have been tempted to look for her signature monogram hidden among the plants, but it was nowhere to be seen. In Australia, Marion was Mrs. Griffin, her husband's loyal helper.

Walter presented the committee with his design as shown by Marion's drawings. While Mannix and other members of the committee were very interested in his ideas, Donovan went out of his way to criticize them, sending off letter after letter of outrage to the committee. He described the design as a "nightmare in stone" and attacked the rotunda concept as a "tower of Babel." He declared that, "You cannot realize the horror with which I regard Mr. G's design, nor the terror in which I live, of its adoption."[3] The Griffins soon discovered he was being stirred up by their former friends, and now bitter enemies, the Taylors. Marion's poisonous battles with Florence were now coming back to harm her husband's work.

Mannix kept above the fray where he could, using Augustus Kenny, the secretary of the committee, to handle the voluminous correspondence from Donovan. "I am assured by his own superiors that he [Walter] was never thought of as an architect, but as a landscape gardener," Donovan wrote, clearly passing on the vitriolic comments that Wright made to Taylor.

Kenny politely replied to Donovan's letters, but one of his letters gave a hint of Mannix's view of the matter. "Since we have waited so long for our college, we are determined that its architecture will show that ... the Catholic portion of the community has a long heredity of success which it will demonstrate by sound progressive ideas."

Donovan made a visit to the Griffins' office, where Marion had put up the designs for the college on the walls. In a letter to Mannix in November 1915, he vented his anger at the masterful power of Marion's drawing. Walter, he fumed, was "careful to decorate the office with Mrs.

Griffin's deceptive and gaudy pictures of our future college." Even as he sought to attack Marion, he acknowledged the power of her drawings. "I saw at once the danger of Mrs. Griffin's dazzling pictures and the unusual model, imposing on some of the committee members." He attacked Marion's drawings for including "pictures of ungrown trees and impossible sky." Donovan had drawn up his own plans for the college but argued that they "would suffer in the committee's eyes from the absence of all those meretricious but unprofessional pictures from the deft hand of Mrs. Griffin, who is an expert in this novel mode of disguising defects."

Mannix remained resolute throughout, which earned high praise from Marion. As she observed, "Dr. Mannix was a power to lean on and could grasp things beyond the customary."[4]

Not satisfied with using Donovan to attack the Griffins, the Taylors also used their magazine, *Building*, to hit out at them. The magazine attacked the design of Newman College, likening it to a railway station, a Luna Park, a suburban cinema, and "like a gaol with exercise yards." Marion may have helped her husband win the design for Canberra, but her ill-judged fight with the Taylors had produced some powerful enemies.

The Griffins could celebrate their second Christmas in Australia with the knowledge that Mannix and the committee (apart from Donovan) were happy with their plans for Newman College. With finances constrained, Mannix's committee decided to start with just one of the L-shaped colleges and called for tenders to build it in a range of building materials including reinforced concrete, brick, or stone. Marion handled the tender process and a contractor came up with some low-cost building options. The Griffins were on tenterhooks for weeks, waiting for the news.

A meeting of the college building committee was set down for 5:00 p.m. one Thursday evening in March 1916. Walter went along while Marion waited for him in their private office on the seventh floor of 395 Collins Street, Melbourne. She lay on the couch half dozing, awaiting her husband's return from the meeting. At 8:00 p.m. Walter came in with a big smile on his face. The contract was signed and building would be going ahead. Marion and the others in their office were elated. "We all danced a jig," she recalled later.

They debated how they should celebrate. Marion and Walter loved the movies. But there was a great discussion. Should they go to a show or be sensible and get something to eat? By this time, they were discovering the culinary delights of Melbourne's Chinatown, which was close by on Little Bourke Street. They decided to be sensible and eat first. "[We] went to a China shop and had our favorite Ki Si Min," Marion recalled. They were finished by nine which was just in time to make the late movie. "Hit a fairly good one so we felt we had spreed it satisfactorily," Marion noted.[5] The celebrations over, there was much work to be done in the Melbourne office.

Construction on the college was soon underway. The Griffins asked Roy Lippincott in Sydney to come down to help out. Marion took particular pleasure noting how Walter's design had won the day, despite the maliciousness of the Taylors and their supporters. If anything, as Marion wrote with some satisfaction in a letter to Ada Holman, the Taylors' actions had achieved the exact opposite of their intentions.[6] The Griffins' relentless energy and creativity could not be put down.

Interior view of Café Australia, Melbourne, showing banqueting hall with balcony and mural by Bertha Merfield. 1916. Photograph by Kerr Brothers. Eric Nicholls collection. National Library of Australia.

Twenty-Five

The Most Beautiful Café in the World

While Walter had his battles with federal politicians and bureaucrats, his high profile was generating an increasing interest in his work in Melbourne, particularly among those who, like him, were newcomers to Australia, not part of the country's established English-orientated elite.

In early 1915, Anthony Lucas, a leading member of the Greek community in Melbourne, approached Walter about remodeling a café he ran on Collins Street. It was in a key location but, with the advent of the war, its name Café Vienna did not have good connotations. The Greek-born Lucas was also aware there was resentment that the King of Greece was supporting the German Kaiser in the war. In the increasingly tense political atmosphere, Lucas wanted to show that he was very much a proud Australian.

Marion was living in Sydney when Walter was first approached by Lucas to remodel his café, but after she moved to Melbourne, took an increasing interest in the project. The challenge appealed to her on many levels. She had long been interested in things Greek, including Greek philosophy and mythology. It was she who dubbed Walter, Socrates, after the Greek philosopher, and herself as his sharp-tongued wife, Xanthippe. At Wright's Oak Park studio, Marion had loved working on the interior design of the houses and the idea of remodeling a café into something quite exotic appealed to her artistic skills. While Lucas was trying to "Australianize" himself, Marion wanted to celebrate his Greek background in the café. She felt his Greek heritage would give him more of an appreciation of something artistic than many others in Australia. As she put it, "He was not Anglo Saxon so was able to appreciate beauty as it developed."[1]

The café gave Marion a chance to draw on the skills she had learned in Wright's studio to bring together the talents of different creative people to create an integrated work of art. As she worked on the café, it is not hard to imagine she would have thought of her days working on the Dana House in Springfield with its many rooms, elaborate stained glass windows, carefully designed furniture, murals and beautiful fountain.

The café was on the ground floor of an office block under the light well of the building. It was an area of five rooms separated by large structural pillars. The Griffins opened up the space, dividing it into three main dining areas. There was a tearoom, called the Fern Room, to be decorated with potted ferns, a fountain court with a central water fountain feature, and a grand banqueting hall, which extended into the ground floor of the adjoining building. They gave the banqueting hall a barrel-vaulted ceiling, which let light in. It was on two levels with a mezzanine area around the sides of the walls where diners could sit and look down on those below.

Marion decided to decorate three of the pillars in the fountain court with sculptures of the three muses of Greek mythology, Daphne, Echo, and Persephone. The life-sized plaster figures were to be standing in sheaves of wheat, rye, and barley. The design had some overtones of the sculpture designed by Richard Bock for the Dana House called *Flower in the Crannied Wall*, which also featured a tall, strong woman, a symbol of creativity.

The central figure, Echo, was the most important, as she would be looking directly at the patrons coming down the stairs from the upper floor of the banqueting hall. Marion knew exactly what she wanted. Just as she had done with Richard Bock in Wright's studio, she sketched out the designs for the plaster reliefs to be made by a professional sculptor. They chose a prominent Melbourne sculptor, Margaret Baskerville, for the job. Baskerville had studied at the National Gallery School in Melbourne and the Royal College of Art in London.

Ten years older than Marion, Baskerville was well established in her profession. So it was particularly difficult for Marion when she visited her at her studio and found something about the sculpture was not quite right. Marion wanted the statue of Echo to be a full frontal nude, from the waist upward. Baskerville had her facing slightly sideward in a more modest pose. Marion retold the story later:

> When I went over to her studio to see the progress on this one [Echo] I found, to my consternation, that she had not molded her facing directly forward as I had sketched, but for the sake of grace, had turned her body slightly. The work was so far advanced I could hardly bring myself to raise objections, but since I was responsible to Mr. Griffin in this matter, I overcame my shyness and explained how, from an architectural point of view, this central figure, directly opposite the stairway, must be markedly different from Daphne and Persephone ... and must be running strait [sic] forward toward the descending patrons. She [Baskerville] saw the point and, without a qualm, ripped out the figure and built her up anew.[2]

The Griffins also wanted to celebrate the natural world of their adopted country. Marion approached Melbourne sculptor and jeweler Charles Costermans to decorate a pillar in the Fern Room. He did a plaster relief of a native Australian fig tree while Marion did another of a ti-tree on the other side. They decided there should be a mural on the back wall of the banqueting hall, on the top story, just as Marion had done for the back wall of her church in Evanston. They approached landscape artist Bertha Merfield for this project.

Merfield was a pioneer of mural painting in Melbourne with a strong interest in the Arts and Crafts movement like the Griffins. Her mural for the banqueting hall was a painting of gum trees in a gully, with the mists and clouds behind them, called *Dawn in the Australian Bush*. Marion found she had a lot in common with Merfield, and they soon became friends.

Each room in the café had a distinct character. The Fern Room had gold recessed lighting, while Fountain Court was more brightly lit. It had four ponds with goldfish and fountains lit by colored lights under the water, surrounded by greenery and boxes of flowers. The Griffins decided that the café should have a grand entrance. The doorway was accentuated by a rectangular box of white quartz-like concrete, with progressively smaller, recessed white boxes, giving patrons the impression of walking into a magical cave. It had overtones of Louis Sullivan's golden door at the entrance of his Transportation Building at the Columbian Exposition in Chicago in 1893.

It was not easy getting Lucas to support some of their unusual ideas. Toward the end of the project, Marion and Walter went to Lucas's café and talked with him about their latest plans until midnight. He finally agreed, but Walter knew to commission the contractor the first thing the next morning to go ahead with what had been decided. Sure enough, later the next morning, Lucas rang back and tried to change his mind. But in the end it all came together.[3]

With Newman College, Café Australia and other projects now coming into the office, the Griffins were very busy. Walter would spend his days in his job as Federal Capital Director and come to their private office in the evenings where Marion and others were working on plans for their other projects. In early 1916, Marion described their workaholic lifestyle in a letter to her family:

> Except for the purpose of going to bed I have no desire to go anywhere. The office looks better than anything else to me. When Walter works at the private office I go to sleep on the couch, when he has to work at the Federal Office I stretch out on his desk and sleep there till he is ready to go which is usually half past eleven or twelve. Then we trail home looking like a couple of inebriates. Sometimes he sleeps on my shoulder, sometimes I sleep on his. Sometimes he keeps on with his work on the train and after he is in bed till one or two o'clock. ... The only thing I take any interest in doing is the work and I keep at it long after I have a curl in my back bone, and am sick with fatigue. ... It's a queer kind of life Walter and I are living, full of a kind of satisfaction but altogether too intense but with all its strenuousness. ... The currents we are pulling against have not yet proved too strong for us and we'll paddle on as long as we can. I have a notion we're helping to clear a way through the jungle, but Lord how the beasts do snap and bite.[4]

While she was happy to be back working side by side with her husband, Marion found herself at the mercy of his demanding schedule. As the workload increased, Marion found herself as the person in the middle, between her husband's dual responsibilities and their office staff. She wrote later of the "agonizing days and months when I had to stand as mediator between Mr. Griffin, who, as designer, had to make all the decisions, and the office force. We could get together only at night when I could put before him each issue and get his instructions and designs for carrying on the work."[5] It was hardly a satisfactory state of affairs for Marion, but she soldiered on, describing herself to some as being a "very useful slave to [Walter's] work."[6]

Meanwhile, Walter benefited from the return of his friend King O'Malley to the Ministry of Home Affairs. The Griffins had become frequent visitors to the O'Malley home in Melbourne. In early 1916, while Prime Minister Billy Hughes was in Britain to discuss the war, O'Malley extended Walter's contract for another three years. Walter's original three-year contract was not due to expire until that October, but O'Malley's canny move preserved his friend's job.

But there was increasing concern at the way Walter was being treated. O'Malley's colleague William Webster, the Postmaster-General, another Griffin fan, called for the establishment of a Royal Commission into the delays in the development of the federal capital. Walter was pleased as he felt it would finally give him a public platform to air the many frustrations he had faced in his job.

Meanwhile in Sydney, the Taylors kept up their attacks on the Griffins. In 1916, George Taylor published a record of his 1914 visit to America in a booklet called, *There! A Pilgrimage of Pleasure*, which was also serialized in *Building* during the year. He used every bit of malice from Wright to attack the professionalism of both Griffins.

> [Wright] blames his pupils, a band of young men and women he employed in his office. ... Some of them took Wright's clients! They are doing works that Wright pathetically describes as "half-baked imitative designs, fictitious semblances pretentiously put forward in the name of a cause." And how he raved to me! "My disciples or pupils, be they artists, neophytes or brokers! I dread to see the types I have worked

with ... cheapened or befooled by senseless changes, robbed of quality and distinction, dead forms of grinning originalities for the sake of originality."[7]

Wright may have been thousands of miles away but his venom was still being directed at the Griffins in their new homeland. Marion's hatred of her former employer only intensified.

Prime Minister Hughes came back from his visit to England in August, arguing that Australia needed to offer up even more of its menfolk to the war in Europe and the Middle East. The true horror of the ill-fated Gallipoli offensive of 1915, initially masked by official censorship, was slowly becoming known in Australia. In a letter home, Marion later described the tragic six-month battle at Gallipoli on the Turkish coast, where almost 9,000 Australian soldiers died and double the number were wounded, after they were sent by the British to attempt an invasion of the peninsula on a narrow beach facing steep cliffs.

It was, she said, a:

> ... ghastly affair where Australian boys were deliberately thrown to the cannon to make a show of conflict where there was no desire nor intention to win, where, in fact, there was an understanding between England and Russia that neither would conquer Constantinople.[8]

Prime Minister Hughes called a referendum, to be held on October 28, 1916, to get support for his proposition to introduce conscription, forcing all able-bodied men to be called up for war service. The move prompted a bitter debate across the country. The increasingly influential Daniel Mannix, who was set to become the city's archbishop the following year, became a vocal opponent of the war and the conscription proposal. The Irish view of the war in Europe had shifted markedly after the Easter Uprising of 1916, when Irish Republicans attempted to overthrow British rule and were harshly put down. Hughes's proposal to introduce conscription split the Labor Party with many of its Catholic members supporting Mannix's position.

Marion was not a Catholic but her Irish-born father was, and she greatly admired the increasingly outspoken Mannix. She and Walter found themselves attracted to a group of socially conscious, liberal-minded friends who also opposed the war. Miles Franklin and Alice Henry in Chicago had put them in touch with some important, like-minded friends in Australia, including social and political activist Vida Goldstein, the first woman in the British Empire to stand for election to a national parliament. Through Goldstein, they met Adela Pankhurst, a young woman whose family was active in the suffragette movement in England. Pankhurst had a falling out with her family in England and came to Australia in 1914. She became a very vocal opponent of the war and the conscription proposals, and her book, *Put up the Sword*, was banned by the authorities in Australia.

Marion described her later as a "lifelong friend" and made sure her copy of Pankhurst's book was always accessible on her bookshelves at home. But the Griffins did not share her more radical views. "We spent a lot of time trying to convert her from communism, really but another form of dictatorship, bureaucratic dictatorship," Marion observed.[9]

It was against the backdrop of this increasingly tense political atmosphere that Mr. Lucas's café was set to open. The event was scheduled for Wednesday, October 25, 1916, three days before the vote on the conscription referendum.

The opening was a grand affair. Marion designed the menus for the banquet. They featured a drawing of the three Greek muses on the pillars, Persephone, Echo and Daphne, all proudly nude from the waist up, drawn in black ink against the light brown paper. There was also much attention given to the star guest, retired opera singer Dame Nellie Melba, who had come home to Melbourne after a successful career in Europe.[10]

At the opening, Lucas was praised for investing so much money remodeling the café, providing the city with such an attractive new venue. Lucas announced proudly that the Café Vienna would henceforth be known as the Café Australia. There were cheers all round. The new café was stylish and modern—an exotic place where patrons could enjoy themselves and temporarily forget the cares of the day. Another magic lamp had been rubbed by the Griffins and another fine genie had been called forth.

One critic was effusive in his praise:

> In the midst of the dull tints of the business buildings of the street, the clear positive tones arrest the eye—green pearl granite, black like the purple grackle's plumage. ... Undoubtedly the handsomest café in Australia, it calls forth constant expression of pleasure and my word, it is beautiful. ... I feel as if I had rubbed Aladdin's lamp. ... [This] is modern Australian architecture.[11]

As Marion herself said, "One could perhaps say it is the most beautiful café in the world."[12] The café set a new standard in style for the city's establishments. People flocked to see it and the famous Dame Nellie Melba became a frequent patron. Lucas was delighted.

As Newman College was yet to be finished, the café was Walter's first major completed work in his adopted homeland. As Marion herself pointed out, Café Australia "introduced Griffin to Australia." It was, of course, the combined creative work of Marion and Walter. If anything, the sense of style and the artwork and interior decoration were largely Marion's, drawing on all the skills she learned in Wright's office. But for Marion, it was more important for her husband to get the recognition she felt he deserved in Australia.

She continued to downplay her own role in his work. Interviewed at the end of 1916, Marion denied her involvement in the plans for Canberra.

> My speciality is, I suppose, what is known as presentation work. Because my work on the plans for the federal capital attracted a little notice, there are some people who imagine that I had a hand in the actual design. That is altogether the work of my husband—I had nothing whatsoever to do with it.[13]

Her comments contrasted with those made by her husband three years earlier when he said the plans were "much more than half due to his wife." Marion was naturally quite modest, but with so many slings and arrows being shot at her husband, and maybe some recognition on her part of the political cost of her fight with the Taylors, she only wanted to help boost her husband's reputation, even if it was at the expense of her own.

Twenty-six

The Case of Mr. Reeves

The Griffins loved walking in the bushlands on the outskirts of Sydney and Melbourne and were enthusiastic students of the Australian plants. They believed Australians should end their love affair with European trees and flowers and use as many native plants as possible.

In his designs for many houses in the United States, Walter had included long lists of the plantings for the gardens with their correct botanical names. Now he wanted the Australian capital to become a showcase for the country's different plants. Many of the hills around Canberra were almost bare of trees. Walter wanted to plant each of the hills with flowers of different colors, including yellow wattles and red bottlebrushes. In America, Walter had studied Liberty Hyde Bailey's books on plants, and the couple decided to create their own guide to Australian plants. Writing home in May 1916, Marion noted that "at present I am doing mostly listing of native plants now for both private work and FC [the federal capital]."[1]

Marion produced eight painstakingly detailed booklets collating Australian flowers by color and time of flowering. In the end, Walter's idea to color code the hills of Canberra proved to be impractical. The experts advised him that many plants from around the vast Australian continent would not survive Canberra's climate. But the Griffins were eager to use their accumulating knowledge of Australian plants in their private practice. Marion threw herself into the landscaping work for the grounds of Newman College, which she declared would be "so planned as to create the impression of a botanical garden."[2] As one writer described it later, the landscape plan for the college:

> ... delineated mass plantings of Australian flora, organized by seasonal floral colors and combinations, including orange, scarlet and yellow, salmon and copper and silver and pink and blue—a botanical color symphony in keeping with Griffin's method of planting together according to color.[3]

Meanwhile Marion had become embroiled in another bitter fight. Early in 1916, she had agreed to design a house for a public servant in Melbourne by the name of Richard Reeves. Unlike the Griffins' entrepreneurial friend Mr. Lucas, Mr. Reeves was a man of modest income on a strict budget. He commissioned Marion to design a house at a cost of no more than £1,400. She designed a modest two-story house. It was her first major commission in Australia in her own right.[4]

Reeves approved the sketch design, but when the bids from the contractors came in, the lowest bid was £1,898. Reeves complained. Marion made some changes to the plan to cut the cost, but he rejected them. She sent him a bill for her services, but he refused to pay, offering less than one-third of the amount they had initially agreed on. Marion was furious. Reeves was not going to pay her for her work, and she suspected he was talking to another contractor to build the house using a plan remarkably similar to hers.

If she could not get properly paid for her work, Marion decided that at least she could try to prevent Reeves from using her design. In November, she went into the Copyright Office of the Federal Attorney-General's Department in Melbourne and registered her design for the house for artistic copyright.[5] Relations between Marion and Reeves soured even further. He began building a house on the site which was similar to her design. She was furious but was prepared to let things slide. But Walter urged her to take legal action against Reeves.

While Marion was fighting her battle with Mr. Reeves, Walter got some good news. In February 1917, the Royal Commission examining the conduct of the development of Canberra finally delivered its report. The Commission's hearings had taken up months of his time. The report vindicated Walter, reconfirming his appointment, and criticized some of his opponents, which was a great relief for the couple.

In April, President Wilson finally decided that the United States would enter the war on the side of the Allies. Socially, it might make things a little easier for the Griffins, after enduring almost three years of anti-American sentiment, but Australia was still bitterly divided on the war and the conscription issue.

The pressures of war had also seen another change in the government of Australia. Prime Minister Hughes lost his referendum to introduce conscription in 1916 but was determined to send more young Australian men to war. His position saw him expelled from the Labor Party, but with support from the conservatives, he formed a new political party which retained power. For a second time, King O'Malley, who opposed the idea of conscription and stayed with the Labor Party, lost his position as Minister for Home Affairs. The change prompted Marion to write home, "How absurd it is to suppose there is a vestige of democracy in the colonial system."[6]

Hughes was reelected as Prime Minister in May 1917 on a tide of nationalism that saw King O'Malley lose his seat. Fortunately, Walter had been able to get O'Malley to sign off on his latest detailed drawings of Canberra before he left office as minister.

Meanwhile, the Griffins were becoming increasingly frustrated with what they saw as Barry Byrne's mismanagement of their office in Chicago. They suspected he had been changing some of the details of the plans they had sent him for their American work. Thanks to O'Malley, Walter's Australian contract had been extended until October 1919. The war and the demands of Walter's job had meant that neither of them had been able to make a trip back to the United States to check on their business. Walter was all too aware of the cost of taking six months away from Australia after he signed his original contract. The Griffins were particularly unhappy with what Byrne had done in Mason City. The clients were disappointed with his work and had complained to the Griffins. And the lease on the office in the Monroe Building was due to expire.

Walter approached some of his other friends in the United States about trying to continue on with a partnership, but with him so far away in Australia in the middle of a war, it was too difficult. In 1917, they closed their office in the United States. With Walter contracted to his position in Australia for another two years, there was probably nothing else they could have done. For the Griffins, it was another cutting of ties with America. They were now, more than ever, committed to their life in Australia.

Marion continued to work on Walter's private projects, including plans for a Catholic women's college at the University of Melbourne. Then she was dealt a harsh blow. On June 7, 1917, in County Court Melbourne, Judge James Grattan Eagleson delivered a judgment against Marion and in favor of Mr. Reeves. The judge's comments were reported in the *NSW Contract Reporter*:

> The Plaintiff knew, from the first that a specific amount stipulated, including a hot water service, was not to be exceeded. Her duty as an architect was to give the best services possible to Defendant, in accordance with his requirements. But instead of producing a sketch plan for a building costing £1,400 or anything like that sum, she produced one, the cost of which would be somewhere near £2,000 or over. Subsequently certain modifications were made to the plan, which amended the plan, however the Defendant declined to accept. In the house, as finally erected by another person, His Honor expressed the opinion that there had been no infringement of the Plaintiff's copyright plans. He held that Plaintiff had not carried out what the Defendant had requested in regard to the preparation of plans for a house costing £1,400 and gave judgment for the Defendant with costs.[7]

Marion was shocked and angry. Judgment against her, plus costs, was a severe blow. There was no recognition for all the work she had done. Unlike Wright, who had regularly and shamelessly exceeded his clients' budgets, Marion was faced with a client who was determined not to pay her fees and a court system that supported him.

The loss in the court case was the culmination of many things for Marion. There was the relentless opposition from the Taylors, the public servants, and others who had conspired against Walter, the criticism of their views on the war, the loss of O'Malley, Walter's strongest supporter in the government, as Minister for Home Affairs, and now a government under a Prime Minister who was cool to Walter and did not appreciate his anti-war views. She felt the Australian establishment was against them. What was the point of doing her own architectural work if the courts and others would decide against them? She had no more heart for dealing with clients in Australia like Reeves and felt it was all part of a broader conspiracy against them.

"The courts of this community," she told her friends later, "have decided that no clients of mine need pay for my services." It was, she said, "a part of the game, of course."[8] But Marion was not a woman to give up easily. She decided to refocus her efforts. She gave up any thought of doing architecture under her own name and threw herself into studying and drawing the Australian native flora and trees. Was she seeking solace from the slings and arrows of life in Australia in something which reminded her of the happiness of her childhood at Hubbard Woods?

A few months after the judgment, she wrote to her old university friends in America:

> I am not bothering my head in my accustomed architectural field, (the practice of architecture in my own name), but am amusing myself with the flora than which there is none more interesting nor beautiful.[9]

The Griffins also found themselves part of an expanding family. The Lippincotts had built a house in an outer suburb called Heidelberg where they lived with their two-year-old daughter, Alstan. Marion loved it. The Lippincotts, she wrote home, "have just finished building a toy of a house in the prettiest suburb of Melbourne—Heidelberg—on the bank of the River Yarra and looking down and out over the hills to the mountains." The Griffins helped them plant the garden. "We are now tucking in plants as fast as we can," Marion wrote.[10]

Their work on planting for Newman College was also going ahead nicely. Marion was delighted to see how easily gardens could grow in Australia. "We are planting the shrubbery there, too, ten acres of it, as the grading is now in shape," she told a friend back home. "One doesn't have to wait long here either for results, so in a year or so it will be looking very lovely."[11]

In October, Walter planned to go to a conference in Adelaide. Marion had never been there, and Walter asked her to come. The spring flowers were in full bloom and Marion loved the place, describing it later to her friend as "a city of flowers and a perfect climate—nestled at the foot of lovely hills from whose slopes you look over the city on to the port town in the shore, and the harbor."

Walter decided to skip the last part of the conference and explore the outskirts of the city with his wife. An enthusiastic photographer, he brought his camera and snapped away at the sights. As Marion recalled, "The last day we ran away from the conference and took a long walk over the hills, getting close to the wild flowers and getting photographs of some most exquisitely beautiful, superb trees."[12]

Marion was a strong woman, more than capable of reinventing herself. If the forces were against her in one area, she would not collapse like Sophia Hayden, her predecessor at MIT who designed the Women's Building for the Columbian Exposition of 1893, but refocus her considerable energies in a new creative direction.

Right: *Eucalyptus Urnigera*, Tasmania. Scarlet Bark, Sunset. Forest Portrait No 11. December 1918. Mary and Leigh Block Museum of Art, Northwestern University, Illinois. 1985.1.117.

Making Magic: The Marion Mahony Griffin Story

Twenty-Seven

An Ancient Land

Marion's expertise in Australian trees and plants was becoming known in Melbourne. She was invited to address the Women Horticulturists' Association of Victoria where she "emphasized the beauties of Australian flora." When considering landscaping, she said, people should use "at least nine-tenths of native flora to one-tenth of foreign material."[1]

From their base in Sydney, the Taylors continued to attack the Griffins. In the March 1918 edition of *Building*, the Taylors wrote: "We take upon ourselves the blame for bringing Mr. Griffin to Australia." Later, Walter was at the opening of the Town Planning Conference in Brisbane where the Governor-General, Scottish-born Sir Ronald Munro Ferguson, warned there was "evidence of a banal, clumsy German architecture, typical of German 'Kultur,' [which] had recently been disseminated over a suffering earth and was reaching Australia via America." Ferguson's words were a carefully cultivated insult aimed at Walter, coming from the highest office in the land, from a man who saw it as his job to maintain the steady supply of young Australian men to support Britain in the war in Europe and the Middle East. His comments echoed George Taylor's criticisms about the German tendencies in Walter's architecture.

But Marion was making new friends in Melbourne. In December, Bertha Merfield, who painted the mural for Café Australia, invited Marion on a painting trip to Tasmania, the island below the Australian mainland. Bertha planned a visit to the island state over the Christmas holidays to meet her friend Mabel Hookey, a local painter and writer, and go on a sketching trip to some of the most scenic parts of the state.

Marion had not been feeling well lately. Walter could not make the trip, as he was too busy, as usual. She felt guilty about leaving him over Christmas, but she knew the offer of the sketching trip to Tasmania was one of those now-or-never moments in one's life. Marion had been drawing the Australian bushland for some time and had begun what she called her *Forest Portraits*. Here was a great opportunity to see a part of Australia she had never been to before and do more sketching for her portraits.

Despite all the attacks that had been aimed at her and her husband, Marion had fallen in love with Australia, or its countryside at least, which was providing a new outlet for her creativity. It was so easy to be a painter in Australia, she told her friends back home.

> I feel that the Archangel who painted Australia was the greatest of them all. Everything is so decorative, and to me, an architect, the function of painting is decoration, mural decoration. You don't have to be an artist there, the picture presents itself to you in perfection. You put it down just as it is ...[2]

Marion didn't bother to ask Bertha much about where they would be going. She was happy to make the trip to the island with someone who knew her way around and to see more of her adopted country. She would have liked to have gone with Walter but she knew her husband was too busy. She always worried that he worked too hard, but it was almost impossible to stop him.

Marion and Bertha were going to get a steamer across Bass Strait, the sea between Melbourne and the northern part of Tasmania, to the city of Launceston. It was due to leave on December 20. In the morning, Marion was in a rush as she made sweets for Walter to take to the office as a Christmas gift for the staff.[3]

She managed to make the boat, the *Loongana*, on time and the two set off across the strait. They had been warned that the crossing would not be an easy one, but Marion had no idea how bad it would to be. A storm blew up and the sea was very rough. It was, she was told, one of the roughest crossings ever. For the next 24 hours, Marion was violently ill and wished fervently she had never decided to make the journey. But then the weather cleared, and the boat arrived in Launceston the next morning. Just over a month before, on November 11, peace had been declared in the war in Europe. On the *Loongana,* Australian soldiers were returning home from the war to their families in Tasmania, many from the Third Light Horse Brigade. None would have had the bright spirit they had when they had left for Europe with such innocence a few years before.

Marion and Bertha got the train south to Hobart, the state capital. Marion had brought an easel and a camera to take photographs. She would turn the photos and sketches into paintings, done in her favorite long Japanese scroll shape, when she got home. On arriving in Hobart, the women went sketching on the slopes of nearby Mount Wellington. They came back to the town two days after Christmas to get the boat for Southport, some 60 miles south, where they were to spend the next two weeks. Marion just managed to send a postcard off to Walter at the local post office before the boat left. "Fine trees. Busy as a bee," she wrote to Walter. "Deserting one's husband makes one keep busy, lest one remember." Marion, as usual, was more worried about her husband's welfare than her own. "Wish I could have made you a second batch of fondant," she added. "Was so disappointed not to be able to."[4]

But the trip also gave Marion the space to focus on her own work. By this time, she already had three tree drawings in hand, "just in pencil, enough to work from," and hoped to get maybe a dozen major studies done on the whole trip. Spending time outside, she felt better than she had for some time. It had been that way since her childhood. She always felt better outside than being cooped up indoors. "You have no idea how much better I am feeling physically," she wrote to her family back home.[5]

They arrived in the coastal village of Southport, the southern-most settlement of Tasmania, which had been the state's second largest town in the early 1800s. Almost at the southern tip of Australia, Marion knew she was as close to Antarctica as she would ever get. She believed that plant life had originated in the Antarctic and felt that Australian "vegetation originated in the Lemurian times, when the partially solidified parts of the earth were still bathed in heavy mists so that the vegetables as well as the animals were still sea creatures."[6]

It was there she saw something that captivated her attention. It was a tall gum tree with a bright red bark. She knew its Latin name, *Eucalyptus urnigera*. Its bark was a fiery red, so fiery, she thought, that the real color could never be reproduced by paint. It was set among other trees, but this one stood out, its red bark captured against the glow of the sunset, like a flame shooting up to meet the setting sun. As she sketched the tree, which she would later paint, she knew she would have trouble convincing people that this scarlet color was actually there in the bark and not the reflection of the glow from the sunset.[7]

Nearby were other gum trees, including one which had a pure white bark with fine dark lines on it. She knew its name too, *Haemastoma*, or scribbly gum as the Australians called it. It was, she thought, as if an insect, a slave insect, had been at work, writing secret messages from the fairies on the bark to the children of Australia.

Marion loved the colors she saw in Tasmania. There, she told her friends:

> ... color runs riot in everything. ... The long lasting colors of the masses of fruits outvying the flowers in their long lasting conspicuousness, we find the barks [of the trees] putting on an amazing show.[8]

Another tree which fascinated her was a Banksia, perched on the top of a cliff face, looking like a Japanese bonsai tree, "decorating the edge of a precipice like a grand cap on top of a majestic column." The sea below was "a vivid blue like azurite."[9] Temporarily freed from the demands of worrying about her husband, Marion was embarking on some of her best ever work.

After about two weeks in the Southport area, they got the boat back to Hobart and visited other parts of the island, including Russell Falls in the Mount Field National Park. There, Marion saw a patch of tree ferns, thriving in the cool of a gully, which took her breath away. They were different from the tree ferns she had seen in her walks in the Dandenong Ranges outside of Melbourne. She had used the tree fern theme in Café

Australia but what lay before her, as she walked through the gully, was simply magical.

> Tree ferns! One of the oldest forms of vegetation and to be found only in Australia, their trunks running up to 30 and more feet in height and their fronds often with a spread of more than 20 feet. ... To walk, entranced, down the long aisle flanked with great golden brown columns, eyes lifted to dwell on the open lace work fretted vault through graceful fern fronds to blue sky. To walk, to stand, to listen.[10]

Marion was also interested in the treatment of the native Aboriginal people in Australia. Her family had been strong supporters of Abraham Lincoln who fought to abolish slavery in America. Founded as a colony to house some of the toughest convicts sent from Britain, Tasmania had a brutal history of white settlement. The treatment of the local Aboriginals was particularly gruesome. Many were killed in clashes with the Europeans and their numbers dwindled. In the early 1830s, George Augustus Robinson, the Chief Protector of Aboriginals, had decided the remaining indigenous people would be better off if they could all move to nearby Flinders Island where they could live in peace.

He was a well-meaning man, and the Aboriginals cooperated with the move. But once they got to the island, they became ill and died out. It was a particularly tragic part of Australian history. Marion knew of the story through her reading of American author, Mark Twain. He had visited Australia in the late 1890s and wrote a book called *Following the Equator*, which was published in 1897. Twain had written that some of the Aboriginals in Tasmania had been sterilized as a way of ensuring their race would die out. Marion had checked this out with a doctor in Melbourne who confirmed it. Now in Tasmania, she wanted to know if the story was true. She asked Mabel Hookey what had happened to the Aboriginals who were sent to Flinders Island. Hookey replied, "They just petered out."

Marion recalled the rest of the conversation later:

> We had been discussing the question of the superiority of one race over another and she had been very positive in her feeling for the superiority

of the whites, I arguing for the dark-skinned people. So I asked her if the aboriginals had been sterilized to which she answered, "Yes."

Then I said, "Do you think that is evidence of the superiority of the white folks?"

She said, "Oh yes; the blacks would have done the same if they had been smart enough to think of it first."[11]

Realizing that she and her Tasmanian host had very different views on race, Marion decided to discontinue the conversation.

Soon Marion and Bertha were on the boat back to Melbourne, their sketchbooks full. Marion had also taken lots of pictures. She could not wait to get home and start painting. She had not forgotten the brilliant red of the gum tree against the sunset or the vivid green tree ferns. She knew how she would show them. The *Forest Portraits* from Tasmania would be done on silk—red silk, gold silk, purple silk. They would be nothing like anything she had ever done before. She had developed very sophisticated techniques for her painting and her work on satin. In some cases, she drew in black ink on the silk but in other cases she transferred her drawings to the silk using a printing process using gel-lithography.[12]

Marion was doing some of the best work of her life, work not done since the cold evenings in Chicago when she and Walter had been working on their plans for Canberra.

Twenty-eight

A Home of Their Own?

After the war ended, Marion and Walter again thought about building a home for themselves. Walter might have been battling with his job as Federal Capital Director, but he was getting an increasing number of private clients coming to him for work, including Café Australia owner, Lucas, who asked Walter to remodel a mansion he had bought in Frankston, a suburb south of Melbourne.

Walter had become friendly with a local real estate agent in the area called William Alfred Towler, who wanted to develop residential estates. Walter had been a long-time advocate of affordable housing. He was passionate about designing smaller houses for people on lower incomes. It was a very different approach to that of Wright, who deliberately courted wealthy clients who could afford his grand plans. Walter was also interested in developing a low-cost building system. In 1917, he patented a system of precast concrete wall units, which he called Knitlock. The units were made of blocks, which could be slotted in together, using steel reinforcing rods, to make prefabricated walls. It meant that houses could be built using only semi-trained labor. The next year he patented a Knitlock concrete tile.

Towler knew Walter wanted to build some houses using his Knitlock system. Based on modular concrete blocks, they would never be as glamorous as conventional houses. But at a time when resources were tight, Walter's Knitlock technique offered a building option that was low cost as well as being fireproof. Towler owned land at Frankston that had great views of the bay, which he subdivided into lots and called the Grange Estate.

In his quest for low-cost housing, Walter had also become fascinated with the idea of a one-room house. Not having children, the Griffins did not need as big a house as many others. They lived a simple life with few material possessions. In June 1915, Walter had addressed the Royal Victorian Institute of Architects on the virtues of a one-roomed house, describing a room which could be divided into four parts by screens or curtains. Now, in the post-war era of material and labor shortages and limited money, his message of a simple, low-cost house made even more sense. Towler let Walter build two of the one-room cottages on his estate using his Knitlock technique. The Griffins called them Gumnuts and Marnham. The houses had a central living area, about 11 feet square, with alcoves along the side for sleeping, a small bathroom and a kitchen. Towler hoped the houses would help to promote sales of land on the estate. While Towler owned the two cottages, he let the Griffins use Gumnuts as a weekend retreat.

The Griffins' life in Australia was forever at the mercy of the shifting political forces affecting Walter's role as director of the federal capital office. Walter's second three-year term expired in October 1919. The minister overseeing the development of the capital was now the Minister for Works and Railways, Littleton Groom, who was eager to get on with the development of the national capital. In late 1919, Groom told Walter he could stay on as Federal Capital Director, but only on a three-month rolling basis.

The Griffins decided to go ahead with building a home in Melbourne. They bought land at the northern end of Kooyong Road, near the wealthy suburb of Toorak. It was a triangular piece of land on a steep railway cutting on the corner of an estate. Most people thought the site was unsuitable for building, but the Griffins loved its great views over bushland to the Yarra River, which wound through Melbourne. They designed a house facing the view, its upper level at street level, which they would use for their residence, and a second level down the slope below, which they could use for their architectural practice. With their home and an office in the same place, just as Wright had done in Oak Park, Chicago, they could spend more time together.

But it was not as simple as that, of course. Nothing ever seemed to be with the Griffins' lives. The Griffins wanted to build it with the

Knitlock concrete blocks, but they had to convince the local council that it was suitable for the area, one of the wealthiest in the city. As his deliberations with the council dragged on, Walter's position as Federal Capital Director was becoming less certain. In late 1920, Walter was told that the government would be appointing a Federal Capital Advisory Committee to consult with the minister. The role of Federal Capital Director would be abolished, and he would become a member of the five-man committee. One of them was the Director General of the Department of Works and Railways, Walter's long-time opponent Percy Owen. Walter would be paid the same salary but would no longer have the independent role of Federal Capital Director. In the future, he was told, Groom's department would take over the work of developing Canberra.

The Griffins were shocked. This was a very different role than the one Walter had been promised when they had come to Australia in 1914 and which had prompted them to give up their American practice in 1917. Henceforth, Walter would just be a member of the committee with his role reduced to that of a consultant. When he found out that the chairman of the committee would be John Sulman, the well-connected town planner and close friend of the Taylors, Walter knew the cards were being stacked against him.

His attempts to speak to Prime Minister Hughes came to nothing. Walter's anti-war views and his friendship with the outspoken O'Malley had not endeared him to Hughes, a passionate supporter of Britain and the war in Europe. On December 23, 1920, Walter wrote to the permanent secretary of Groom's department, saying he was "compelled under protest, and with great regret, to bow to the decision of the Minister to terminate my agreement without the conferences or communications sought by me."[1]

Christmas 1920 must have been a difficult time for the Griffins, particularly Walter, who had worked so passionately and exhaustively on his role as Federal Capital Director for the previous seven years in the face of many odds. Walter had hung on tenaciously to his job with a determination that surprised many people. But now he was finally giving up.

Both Marion and Walter had been focused on the design of the new Australian capital for a decade. Now with this latest news, their current life had come to a painful ending, all their dreams about creating a new capital in a new democracy over. They were forced to put their plans for a new home on hold for a third time in their lives.

The Griffins had been steadily making a new group of friends in Melbourne, and Marion was also working on her *Forest* paintings. Walter was also developing some influential connections in Melbourne who wanted to give him new commissions.

Several decades before the Griffins had arrived in Australia, the town of Heidelberg, northeast of Melbourne on the Yarra River, had attracted some of Australia's leading painters including Tom Roberts, Frederick McCubbin, Arthur Streeton, and Charles Conder. It was an unspoiled rural area just close enough to the city to be visited by Melbourne-based artists who were inspired by the Impressionist movement in Europe.

Walter had first gone to the area soon after arriving in Melbourne, approached by a local businessman who owned two tracts of land he wanted to develop as residential areas. Walter helped to design the Summit Estate for him and later designed the second piece of land, called the Glenard Estate.

When Genevieve and Roy Lippincott moved to Melbourne with their young daughter, Alstan, Walter suggested that they look at building a house on the Glenard Estate. It was close enough to the city by train for Roy to be able to work there but provided a lovely rural setting for their family. Walter and Marion dropped their plans for their house on Kooyong Road and decided to build a house next to the Lippincotts. It would be a replica of the Gumnuts cottage they both loved so much. After the issues with the local council over their proposed Knitlock house in Toorak, the Griffins did not have the energy for another long fight with the council at Heidelberg for their unusual house. The couple decided to apply to the council to build the structure as a "dollhouse." Walter and Marion worked on it on the weekends assisted by a local chicken farmer.

Finally, the house was built. It was, Marion recalled, "the cheapest, most perfect and charming home in the Empire."[2] It was larger than Gumnuts, with the external walls 21 feet square with a series of alcoves off the main area. There was an area by a window for a double bed, which could be covered by a curtain. There was a small bathroom, seven foot by seven foot, in a corner, and other alcoves for a piano and a fireplace. The interior design was done in earth tones. Marion furnished it with a circular table in the middle, rugs on the floor, and wicker chairs. The floor was built in timber directly on the earth, which Marion argued was far warmer than a concrete slab. They decided to call it *Pholiota*, the Latin name for a genus of tiny mushrooms. Marion could not have been happier. As she recalled later, "The one moment of pure romance was that moment spent in *Pholiota*."[3] Then they built a garden around it. It was so wonderful they could barely stand to leave it when they went to work in the city each morning.

As Marion wrote later:

> It nestled far back on its allotment, under the spreading branches of two giant gums, and was so lovely in the midst of its ever blooming garden that Mr. G and I used to walk backward every morning as we went off to the office so as to delight our hungry eyes as long as possible.[4]

But, of course, when it came to the Griffins and their very original ideas, nothing ever seemed to go smoothly. When it came to light that the couple were actually living in the "dollhouse," the local council challenged them. If it did not comply with its building standards, it declared, it would have to be torn down.

But Marion and Walter were defiant. Marion declared stoutly:

> Well, let them pull it down. ... We'll live in a canvas bag (as we had done in our canoe trips) ... and cook our meals over a bonfire. We own this lot. We'll see what they do about that.[5]

Finally, after many representations, an agreement was reached and the council allowed their little mushroom to stand as an "experimental house."

Marion had grown up in a house that was always full of people. Now that she finally had her own home, she was always inviting people to visit. By now, the Griffins had developed an active circle of like-minded friends, many of whom were interested in social justice issues and had opposed the war and the two conscription referendums. They included writer Vance Palmer and his wife, Nettie. Nettie Palmer was the niece of Irish-born politician and lawyer, Henry Bournes Higgins, famous for a 1907 court decision that effectively set down a minimum wage in Australia. Marion was friendly with Higgins' sister, Ina, a passionate landscape gardener. The Griffins were also friendly with another, more radical left-wing activist called Guido Baracchi, who was one of the founding members of the Communist Party of Australia in 1920.

Pholiota was such a curiosity that many people wanted to make the trip to Heidelberg to see it. One day, Marion met Ellen Anderson, the wife of an English surveyor who was visiting Melbourne. Marion immediately invited the couple home to dinner at *Pholiota*.

Mrs. Anderson recalled the evening later in a thank-you note. The scene started in Melbourne around 6:00 p.m., the official closing time for the public hotels when men would stagger into the street drunk. She described Marion shopping for their dinner, "flitting, darting, flashing, from barrow ... to barrow in Collins Street." Marion, she said, was:

> Garbed in restful blue, a saffron scarf waving and curving round her head in the evening sunset breeze. ... In the six o'clock cauldron of Collins Street, her form alone, alluring, obliterating the ruck and muck drew our gaze. She invited us to feast with her, and the magic of her tongue ... made us dizzy and oblivious of our numbers and the trouble we would give. ... Oh that all dinners were so enjoyable. ... Almost thou persuadest me to be a socialist. ... The powers of that Witch Goddess. ... And even the real Socialist present had, by the time our hostess had graciously bowed him out, learned somewhat of culture from the Atmosphere of an Aristocrat-Socialist.[6]

For the first time in her life, Marion Mahony Griffin, artist and architect, devoted wife and aristocrat socialist, finally had a place she could call home.

Marion and Walter in the garden at *Pholiota*, Eaglemont, Victoria.
Child may be the Lippincotts' daughter, Alstan. Circa 1921.
Eric Nicholls collection. National Library of Australia.

Interior view of *Pholiota*, Eaglemont, Victoria. Circa 1925.
Eric Nicholls collection. National Library of Australia.

Twenty-nine

No Fences, No Boundaries

As his hold on the job of Federal Capital Director was becoming more tenuous, Walter turned his thoughts toward an idea that had been with him for some time—he wanted to develop a high-class residential suburb. But it would not be just any suburb. It would be a place that epitomized his view of how people should live together in communities. A place with safe roads, parks, and places where children could play, houses that blended in with the local environment and were enhanced by native plants and trees.

From the moment he arrived in Sydney, Walter felt its harbor foreshores and waterways and its hilly terrain with so many gum trees would make the perfect setting for a new suburb. It was just a matter of finding the right place. Whenever he was in Sydney, he would look for possible opportunities. By 1919, the realization that he may not be able to see his vision for Canberra roll out the way he wanted increased his determination to find some land for a new estate. If he could not see out his dream of building an ideal capital city in Canberra, he would revive his dream of building an ideal suburb in Sydney.

Around this time, Walter was spending a lot of time with King O'Malley. Now approaching 60 and out of federal politics after almost two decades, O'Malley had a lot of time on his hands. He had long been a sounding board for Walter's ideas and frustrations and now Walter discussed with him his vision for establishing an ideal suburb in Sydney.

They hatched a plan to put together a syndicate of investors to buy land for Walter's dream suburb. Walter asked two architect friends in Sydney to begin searching in earnest for a suitable site for his project.

The next year, in 1920, Walter saw some land he liked in an area north of the city. It consisted of land on three almost parallel promontories, in an area called Middle Harbour. About four miles north of the city, the land covered a total of 650 acres. It was owned by investors in London who had long since lost interest in it. As he battled to retain his hold on his position as Federal Capital Director, Walter contacted the local representatives of the owners who asked him to put in a bid. He offered what he thought would be enough for one of the properties and, to his great delight, found he had bought all three pieces of land.

On November 26, 1920, just as Walter was having his final tussles with Minister Littleton Groom, Walter, King O'Malley, and other investors formed the Greater Sydney Development Association (GSDA) to buy the land. The investors in the GSDA, which came to be called "the company," were a diverse lot, drawn from the political, business, and architectural contacts of both Walter and O'Malley. O'Malley made one investor, James Catts, a former politician from Sydney and one of his closest friends, the company secretary.

Forty-five shares in the company were issued at £1,000 a share. Walter was appointed the managing director and held one-tenth of the shares, but his shares had 10 times the voting power of the ordinary shares. The next year, Walter was free of the demands of the federal office and had more time to devote his attention to developing the new suburb.

Walter decided to start developing the land on the southernmost promontory, the one closest to the city. The estate owned by the GSDA was on the south side of a rough track called Edinburgh Road, which ran along the ridge of the peninsula. The top of the ridge was a barren place, as all the trees had been cut down by local residents for firewood. One of the local landmarks was an outcrop of rocks with a great view of the harbor called Edinburgh Castle Rocks after Edinburgh Castle in Scotland. Walter called his land the Castlecrag Estate and the other peninsulas were called Craigcove and Castlecove.

Walter was determined to retain the natural setting and design houses that would fit into the landscape. He planned to design houses with flat roofs, like the Melson House in Mason City, which would be set into the natural landscape, each carefully located so that they could enjoy the full view of the water without blocking the view of those higher up the hill. Walter hated the red-tiled peaked roofs of Australian houses. The ubiquitous red tiles, which were so popular in his adopted homeland, required a peaked roof for support. There was no snow in Sydney, so flat roofs could be easily used. Not only did they fit more naturally into the landscape, there was also the potential to use the rooftops for gardens or for people to gather.[1]

Walter and Marion walked all over the estate. The land fell away from the main road, first very gently, and then more steeply as it went down toward the water. There were stunning views over Middle Harbour, with some spots looking up through the spectacular cliffs, the Heads which guard the entrance to Sydney Harbour, and out to the Pacific Ocean. They no longer had *Allana*, but they could imagine canoeing in the waters, exploring the many bays and inlets of the property. The top part of the estate had been almost stripped bare but this could easily be remedied by planting new native Australian trees.

Walter traced out a road system, which followed the natural contours of the land. They allowed for a dress circle effect, which tiered down toward the water, so all the houses could look out at the view. Between some of the houses would be narrow pathways allowing the local residents to walk down to the water. The roads had to be carved out of the natural sandstone, and the local stone would then be used to build the houses, just as Walter had done with the Melson House in Mason City. He decided to name the streets after parts of castles such as The Parapet, The Postern, The Rampart, The Bastion, The Bulwark, and The Citadel. Walter explained his vision for Castlecrag in a promotional brochure, where he declared that he wanted "Castlecrag to be built so that each individual can feel that the whole landscape is his. No fences, no boundaries."[2]

Walter planned to begin developing a 90-acre tract, which included the "Edinburgh Castle" rocks. To preserve his vision, Griffin also set down a series of building covenants to ensure that anyone building on the estate would have houses that conformed to his plan as he had done in Mason City. The covenants stipulated that the houses could only be built of stone or concrete; they had to be in sympathy with the natural topography and the gardens planted with Australian flora. Roofs were to be flat or low to allow for maximum view of the harbor.

The first two houses built by the GSDA were display houses on Edinburgh Road. They were two small cottages called GSDA No. 1 and GSDA No. 2. Built in sandstone, they set the tone for the houses Griffin envisaged for the suburb. They were single-story and rectangular-shaped with a flat roof. GSDA No. 1 was the showpiece, featuring Walter's distinctive voussoirs, or keystones, above the windows, like the ones he used in the Melson House and in Newman College in Melbourne. The front of the houses both faced the views of the harbor and the bushland, with their kitchens facing the street. It was a radical idea, which the local council disliked. The houses were both built in time for the first big auction of land on the estate on Saturday, November 26, 1921.

GSDA shareholders were offered a free block of land if they built a Griffin-designed house on the estate. Five of them quickly took up the offer. Four houses were built on The Parapet, a circular road which came off Edinburgh Road, in 1922. The owners were Sir William Elliott Johnson, the Speaker of the Federal House of Representatives, Melbourne theatrical entrepreneur Julius Grant, a Chinese businessman and herbalist in Melbourne called Chin Wah Moon, and the Reverend Cheok Hong Cheong, another influential member of the Chinese community in Melbourne. In 1923 a fifth house was built on Edinburgh Road for King O'Malley.

As they were investment properties with absentee owners, the houses were all rented out. This created a very different atmosphere in the estate from more conventional residential developments, which were normally bought by owner-occupiers. Some people who moved there were attracted to the area and were happy to just rent, while others moved to the estate with a view to getting Walter to design a house for them later on.

In August 1922, Marion addressed the Victorian Artists' Society with a speech entitled the "Building of a Garden City." She had brought along some drawings she had done of their plans for Castlecrag, done in ink on satin, which were put up around the walls to show the audience. They were, she said, creating a suburb that would follow the natural formation of the landscape. The streets would follow the contour of the land, "nothing to be straight or right angles." She spoke about how the people in Sydney seemed so determined to "destroy, destroy,

destroy" the city's magnificent natural surroundings by cutting down trees and clearing the natural bushland. Man, she said, was insisting on destroying the handiwork of the Creator and creating ugliness. Their new suburb would be a showcase of what could be done with the Australian landscape. Their imagination captured by Marion's magnificent drawings, the members of the society left dreaming about the ideal suburb now being created to their north.

But back at Castlecrag, sales of land were slow. Walter's unconventional designs were very different from traditional Australian houses. And the strict covenants, which Walter insisted on to maintain the character of the estate, made banks wary of lending money to people wanting to build there. And the area was not so easy to get to for those dependent on public transport.

Some investors in the GSDA began complaining that things had not gone as they had hoped. Chin Wah Moon was not happy with his house, and the company had to buy it back from him. But Walter was undaunted. In January 1924, Marion wrote to her friend Miles Franklin urging her to visit them at Castlecrag, to see "what is in the air for the future if we can fight it through." As always, the Griffins were battling the authorities—in this case the local council—to push for their vision for Australia. "It's enough to make one's hair stand on end how determined the authorities are that nothing beautiful shall be left in Sydney or anywhere else in this beautiful country," Marion wrote. [3]

Interior of Capitol Theatre, Swanston Street, Melbourne. 1924.
Eric Nicholls collection. National Library of Australia.

Thirty

A Crystal Cave

Walter's practice in Melbourne was going well. Since he was freed from the demands of his federal capital job, Marion might have hoped they would lead a quieter life. But the workaholic Walter threw himself into his private practice, eager to prove that he could still make his mark on Australian architecture and carve out a new role for himself as a successful architect in his adopted country.

Walter knew two men from America—Herman and Leon Phillips—who had come to Melbourne to help set up an amusement park called Luna Park in the beachside suburb of St Kilda in 1912. They were part of an organization that had been involved in the first Luna Park on Coney Island, New York. In 1920, Walter designed a second establishment for them in St Kilda, called the Palais de Danse, which became a popular meeting point for young people.

Walter also kept in touch with Café Australia owner A.J. Lucas, whose status was continuing to rise. In 1921, he was appointed the Greek Consul General for Melbourne. The year before, Lucas, Herman Phillips, and some other investors decided to build a new office block in Melbourne on the site of Lucas's 650-seat Town Hall Café in Swanston Street. They wanted to produce an iconic building for the city, something special that would become a local landmark like the Café Australia. They decided it would be 10 stories high, the maximum height allowed in the city at the time. Its showpiece would be a grand auditorium on the ground floor that could seat 3,000 people. The building would be called the Capitol Building and the theater, the Capitol Theatre. The Griffins had not succeeded in building their capitol in Canberra but here was a chance to build one in Melbourne.

Walter and Marion were familiar with the idea of having an attractive auditorium on the ground floor of a building with office space in the floors above. The Griffins had both worked in Steinway Hall, which was originally planned to have a concert hall on its lower floors although it had never quite worked out as planned. And, of course, everyone in Chicago knew of Louis Sullivan's grand Auditorium Building where Walter had sat to hear the lecture from the master himself.

In December 1920, Walter was commissioned to help design the building with another local firm. But it was the Griffins' office which focused on designing the theater. Lucas and Phillips traveled to the United States and Europe to inspect the latest in theaters and to buy fittings for the building, including a Wurlitzer organ.

Walter also had another idea to make the auditorium even more special. Sullivan's Auditorium Building had magnificent proscenium arches around the stage with sparkling lights. The idea grew of having the ceiling of the theater covered with crystal to look like a cave. Walter made inquiries of a firm in Belgium to see what it would cost to buy crystal for the ceiling, but it proved to be far too expensive. But the concept was not forgotten.

By this time, Marion had cut back on her work for the Griffins' private office and was concentrating on drawing her *Forest Portraits*. She wrote detailed notes about the trees in each portrait and was thinking of using them as the basis of a book. But in 1921, Roy Lippincott, one of the mainstays of the office, won a prize for the design of a university building in Auckland, New Zealand. He was spending an increasing amount of time there and eventually moved the whole family to New Zealand to live. Their other American assistant, George Elgh, had already returned home a few years ago.

So Marion again stepped up to become, as she occasionally described herself, a "loyal slave" to her husband. The Griffins designed an auditorium with a magical ceiling. Marion, with her expertise in designing interiors gained in Wright's office and with Café Australia, was very involved in the process. Instead of crystals, they decided to use interlocking crystalline shapes made of fibrous plaster. The ornamental

V-shaped boxes would contain rows of different colored lights connected to a master switch. While the organ was playing, the ceiling would turn into a kaleidoscope of changing colors.

One of the problems with traditional theaters was that the pillars needed to support the building, and the balcony level above obstructed the view of the stage. The auditorium of the Capitol Theatre would be the latest in design, and the Griffins wanted to make sure there would be no internal columns blocking the view.

It was a major engineering challenge to design the unusual ceiling with the wide beams needed to support the structure without internal pillars. The roof of the theater was effectively suspended from the floors of the offices above. Walter decided they could precast the ceiling patterns and then interlock them into place in the ceiling. While Walter and Marion knew what they were trying to achieve, the structural concepts were radical. The plans had to be approved by the Melbourne City Council, which took its time reviewing each part of the proposed building.

Marion took on the massive task of overseeing the drafting for the project, providing the council and the builders with the detailed drawings they needed.[1] While Walter liaised with his clients, the council, and the builders, Marion and her team toiled over the drafting tables. The design and the approval process proved to be a monumental task spanning two years. It involved more than 500 different sketches and design sheets. Of these, Marion Mahony initialed 382 sheets and Walter only 90.[2] It may have been her increased role in the office, particularly her work on the Capitol Theatre project, that prompted Marion to apply for registration as an architect in the state of Victoria in June 1923, more than two decades after she became a licensed architect in the state of Illinois. Asked, on the registration form, to list buildings designed solely by the architect, she wrote, "Residence Mr. J. Scott Jefferies, Surrey Hills. Also in collaboration with my husband in all work carried out by him in his private practice in Australia."[3] The Jefferies House was a simple, square house made of Griffin's Knitlock bricks designed earlier that year.

The Griffins threw themselves into the Capitol Theatre project. They designed a grand entrance with semicircular steps leading up to a sumptuous foyer with a smoking room off to the side. They called on sculptor Margaret Baskerville, who did the three Greek muses for Café Australia, to provide further decoration. Baskerville and her husband designed two large relief panels for the foyer called *The Dance of the Hours*. Marion also designed some stained glass windows for the ceiling of the entranceway. The theater project gave Marion a new outlet for her creative skills. Walter designed a platform that could hold a piano and musicians, which could rise up to the view of the audience to play before the movie started, and then slowly descend out of sight. Progress was slow and there were constant tensions between Walter and Lucas, who was worried about the delays and the increasing cost. It was an exciting project for the Griffins, but it was to take its toll.

Thirty-one

Changes

Early in 1924, Marion decided it was time for a change. There had been strains within the Griffins' marriage for some time, more on Marion's part than Walter's. On the outside, they were the happy couple they had always been—and they were, largely. But after 10 years in Australia, Marion was finding the intense relationship with her husband, where they were both living and working together, becoming difficult. Walter was a workaholic who was only too eager to accept as many commissions as he could. Working on the Capitol Theatre project was a long and time-consuming exercise, much more challenging than anything they had done before. The Griffins had built houses but had never been involved in building an office block before, certainly not one with an ambitious, exotic theater as its showpiece, subject to lengthy deliberations of the local municipal council.

But it was more than that. Walter was the frontman for the business with an increasing number of supportive clients. After years of frustration as the Federal Capital Director, he was enjoying his rising status among some of the more interesting people in Melbourne. He was still deeply hurt at the way he had been treated, and angry at the fact that a temporary parliament house was being built in Canberra in a different location to the one he had proposed. But now he was being approached by new clients in Melbourne, including some influential people in business, and things were going well.

But Walter's success, and his ability to juggle so many different projects at one time, depended on having the ever-reliable, ever-diligent, ever-supportive Marion running their office, handling the detail of the drawings, making sure the office worked around his schedule, and looking after their domestic affairs.

Marion had never wanted any personal status or profile. She was happy for Walter to get the glory and the public attention. Walter was the designer who loved dealing with the clients and being the public face of the business while Marion had been happy to oversee the office staff and let her husband enjoy the limelight. She could not have been more supportive of her husband's grand plans, his vision and his goals, or a more devoted wife.

But, by 1924, even Marion was finding her life as her husband's loyal slave a strain. In the daytime, Walter was focused on his clients and other people coming into their office to see him. But the drafting staff depended on Marion to get decisions out of Walter so they could get on with their work. But often Marion found it difficult to see him during the day, which meant everyone had to wait until he was ready in the evening to get his views. And, she was very much aware, her lack of access to her husband meant that some of the staff would have to stay back late to finish work that could have been done earlier had she been able to give them a decision from Walter.

In the past, when he was Federal Capital Director, Marion would wait until he came back from his work to their private practice in the evenings. Now he was in private practice, she was finding he was busy with clients from about 10:00 a.m. onward and she still had to wait until the evenings to get his attention. The demands of the Capitol Theatre project added to the pressure, but she kept soldiering on.

Finally, Marion decided she had to take action. She asked Walter to get to the office by 9:00 a.m. so she could get some decisions out of him in the morning before he would be diverted by clients. But Walter insisted he was a night owl who did his best creative thinking in the evening, which made it hard for him to get into the office early. Marion could understand his argument. She knew her husband all too well. But where did this place her? She was getting tired of being the devoted handmaiden.

By early 1924, the bulk of the architectural work on the Capitol Theatre was done and the construction was well underway. There came almost a natural tipping point. And with the Lippincotts now in New

Zealand, there were no more family ties to Melbourne. Years later, Marion would only mention the strains with the utmost caution.

> There had been a strange conflict which only a character testing deepening of consciousness brought to an end. After all those years together in work and play, breakfast over and the house in order and leaving for the office together, the busy days with its long hours, return together. Then came that perverse requirement of mine that [Walter] should get down to the office by nine in the morning. By ten there was always a stream of people. It was almost impossible to get hold of him to get the decisions, which must come from the designer, to facilitate the work of the draftsmen and shorten the often long hours of work at night by means of which I could function as mediary the next day between the designer and those carrying out the drawings.[1]

Eventually Marion decided she had to get away. By this time, development at Castlecrag had been underway for three years, but the sale of land there was still not going well. There were complaints from some of the shareholders about lack of progress on the project. So she made a decision. As she wrote later, "It certainly was no pleasure to me and half in temper, half in desperation, I decided to leave Melbourne and go to Castlecrag in Sydney."[2]

In March, she went up to Sydney to live in Castlecrag and see if she could do a better job of selling the project. It was agreed with the company that she would get a commission of 20% for any sales she could make.[3] It was all quite amicable and logical on the surface, but for Marion it was also a break from her life in Melbourne.

When she arrived, she had no real idea where she would live. The company had an engineer based at Castlecrag who lived in a cottage by the water. There was a boathouse nearby, built on a floating pier attached to the rocks at the bottom of a large cliff. If she could live in a one-room house, Marion decided she could easily live in a boathouse. But there was a catch. The boathouse could only be reached by boat, and she didn't have one. The engineer would have to take her back and forth in his boat. She would shout out to the engineer who would come and get her when she wanted and would also bring her food and drink.

Soon after she arrived, Walter came up to visit her with King O'Malley. All three of them stayed in the boathouse. A storm came up in the night. The boathouse rocked up and down violently, buffeted by strong waves. O'Malley kept going out the back door to see if the house was still attached to the cliff. It was fine, but O'Malley vowed the next morning that he would never sleep in the boathouse again.[4]

Walter and O'Malley went back to Melbourne but Marion stayed on. After two weeks in the boathouse, she decided to move into one of the houses on Edinburgh Road owned by the company, the house known as GSDA No. 2. It was next door to GSDA No. 1, which was used as a company office and drafting room. Marion was not one to wallow in her personal problems, and there was plenty of work to be done. Much money had been spent clearing the land, building the roads, and paying the levies to the local council, but there was little new money coming into the venture.

Marion was eager to step up the sales of land on the estate. The area's parkland setting made it a popular place for people to visit on the weekends. She enlisted the help of some local young people to approach the weekend picnickers and sell them the advantages of buying land on the estate and building a house designed by Walter. She made sandwiches, which they handed out to the weekend visitors, using it as a way to start up a conversation. Her strategy began to have some success. Soon the new land sales helped to pay off some of the big debts they had incurred.

Marion was attracted to the challenge of managing the estate. Away from Walter, she also had the space and the freedom to get things done in her own way. She spent much time walking around the bushland sketching the local trees. The views at Castlecrag were stunning, but there was much work to be done to repair the natural landscape. At the end of June, Marion went back to Melbourne, but the vision of what Castlecrag could become remained with her.

On Friday, November 7, 1924, the Capitol Theatre opened with a gala charity screening of a movie called *The Ten Commandments* by Cecil B. DeMille. Just as the Griffins had given Melbourne a most special café in 1916, they had now given the city an iconic building—its first skyscraper and a magical theater that would become the talk of the town. Their work done, Walter and Marion were about to set off on another journey.

One Saturday, after the opening of the Capitol Theatre, the members of the Quarterly Club were having a special gathering in Melbourne. They were farewelling Marion at one of their favorite places, the Botanic Gardens. Marion had spent many happy hours in the gardens. The Griffins would take a rare opportunity of a break in Walter's work schedule to make their first visit back home to Chicago.

Marion's colorful clothes still managed to surprise those who knew her. She arrived at the meeting wearing a "mastic-colored knitted silk frock with a cape effect and a Tutankhamen turban." The women gave her bouquets of brilliantly colored poppies. They all had tea in the pagoda and, it was later reported, Mrs. Griffin "with her dynamic personality, gave a graphic outline of her future plans."[5]

Walter and Marion were going back into the depths of a Chicago winter but they would be back with their families for Christmas. So much had happened since they sailed into Sydney Harbour more than 10 years before—the war, Walter's battles with the politicians and the bureaucrats, their successes of Café Australia and Newman College, and now the magical Capitol Theatre building. Walter's parents had come out to visit them, and his sister and her family had been with them until their move to New Zealand a few years before. Marion's mother, Clara, had managed to visit but none of her other family members had come, despite Marion's appeals.

Clara, now 82, was living with Marion's sister Genie, a schoolteacher, in Rogers Park, with her daughter, Clarmyra, who was now 19. Clara was an energetic woman who had continued to work at her school until well into her 70s, but Marion knew that she could not delay seeing her much longer. Her elder brother, Jerome, had sadly been killed in a car accident in Mexico. The Griffins had no plans to move back to America, at least not in the foreseeable future. They had plenty of work in Melbourne, and now there was the challenge of developing Castlecrag in Sydney. But after 10 years in Australia, it was time to go back for a visit.

Walter had a list of things he wanted to do once he got back home. He wanted to see the Stinson Library in Anna, Illinois. It had been finished while they were away, and he was eager to see how it had turned out.

And he would go to Monroe, Louisiana, to see Captain Cooley who was indicating that he might, at long last, just have the funds to build the house Walter had designed for him long ago before he left for Australia. He also wanted to catch up with Louis Sullivan, his old hero. There was so much he wanted to talk to him about, so many experiences in Australia. He would also be meeting Henry Pynor, a young Australian architect who had worked for the Griffins in their office in Melbourne, who was in Chicago, and he was hoping to catch up with his old friend, architect William Purcell, who was now living in Portland, Oregon.

But when they got back to Chicago, they found much had changed. Walter discovered, to his great distress, that Louis Sullivan had died earlier that year. He had just missed seeing him again. Sullivan had spent his last few years penniless and all but forgotten. It would have been a heavy blow for Walter.

While Marion was busy catching up with her family and old friends, Walter was shocked at how much the architectural scene had changed in Chicago since he had left. The energetic, idealistic atmosphere of the young architects who had passed through Steinway Hall and their peers, and dreams of a new Prairie School of Architecture, seemed to have disappeared. Dwight was all but retired, although his wife, Lucy, had become a famous author, well-known for her series of books on twins from different countries, her income helping to support the family.

Wright had a family estate in Spring Green, Wisconsin. He had an office in downtown Chicago but was spending time working in Los Angeles. He had had a difficult time of things for many years, particularly in America, but he had been getting some attention lately for his work designing the Imperial Hotel in Tokyo. Unable to get much work in the United States and still fascinated with things Japanese, Wright had spent many years traveling back and forth to Tokyo, rebuilding the Imperial Hotel in grand style. It had not received too much attention in the United States until 1923, when a massive earthquake destroyed many buildings in the Japanese capital. While the city was devastated, Wright's hotel was still standing amid the rubble. It was seen as a testimony to his architectural skills and revived interest in his unique style. In a twist of fate, the misfortunes of so many Japanese had served to revive public attention on Wright's architectural skills and in a more positive view than they had been for many years. Kitty had finally granted him a divorce, and the home and studio at Oak Park had been sold. Wright had married his latest mistress, Maude Noel, or Miriam as she was known, and they had already separated.

It may have been on this visit that Walter and Marion learned that Wright had built some houses using concrete blocks in California. The Griffins knew that the Taylors had been keeping in touch with Wright, as they published some of his derogatory comments about Walter in their magazine, and some of the Taylors' associates had visited Wright on trips to America. Chances are Wright had developed the ideas for using concrete blocks himself, but Marion believed he may have stolen her husband's ideas.[6]

Walter expressed his disappointment about the Chicago architectural scene in a letter to Purcell.

> I can't say that the development of architecture here at home is what it should be according to our hopes, if not our expectations. Why is that, in some things so bold, our countrymen are such cowards in aesthetics?[7]

Walter went south of Chicago, to the town of Anna, to look at the Stinson Library, and sent Marion a postcard of the building. Then he headed to Louisiana to see Captain Cooley. He had a fondness for the riverboat captain. It had been almost 20 years since they had first met, and he had designed a house for him. It had not gone ahead, but Walter had continued to write to him. The Griffins had designed the Riverside Club in Monroe, which had opened after they left for Australia.

Down in Monroe, Walter was excited to meet up with Captain Cooley again. He now had the funds and the land. He was ready to go ahead with building his house by the river. Walter assured Cooley that his former staffer, Henry Pynor, would help oversee its construction. Walter wrote another postcard to Marion to tell her about it.

When they left Chicago for Australia at the end of February, Walter's parents came with them. Walter and Marion's visit home had been all too short. Walter had not been able to fit in time to see Purcell in Oregon but wrote to him, telling him that he hoped to be able to get back to the United States more often in the future. If anything, the visit had confirmed to the Griffins that they were better off continuing with their work in Australia. Things had changed in Chicago. Their friends had moved on. There was no role for them there.

Thirty-two

A Community Develops

Sometime after they returned from their trip and Walter's parents had gone back home to Chicago, Marion headed back up to live at Castlecrag. She could legitimately argue that it was important for the investors that she should be there to sell the land and oversee the project. She had already proved her worth in just a few months the year before.

While Walter accepted his wife's move to Sydney and could appreciate the importance of her work to their plans, he was concerned about her welfare. She was a very competent person and not the slightest bit worried about being alone, but he thought it would be a good idea if she had some help in Sydney. And he had the perfect person for the job. The Griffins had hired a young woman, Louise Lightfoot, who had a degree in architecture from the University of Melbourne, to work in their Melbourne office. Walter asked Lightfoot to go to Sydney to be both a helper and companion to his wife.[1]

The 23-year-old Lightfoot was enjoying her life in Melbourne and definitely did not want to go. She had wanted to be a dancer and had only studied architecture because of her father's wishes. She was having a grand time in the dance halls of Melbourne and had no shortage of men friends. She also regarded Mrs. Griffin, as she was known to everyone in the office, as a rather formidable figure. But, she was apprenticed to Walter, and he was her boss, so Lightfoot reluctantly agreed to go. She made the long journey to Sydney by herself and arrived at the house in Edinburgh Road where Marion was living.

She stood outside the door of the house, hesitating. Finally, she knocked on the front door and Marion answered, "Come right in!"

And so her new life in Sydney began. They lived in GSDA No. 2 and worked next door in GSDA No. 1. But Lightfoot soon found that not only was she expected to help with the drafting work, but also she was expected to do the cooking as well. Marion loved having people to her house, but she was not a good cook and neither was Lightfoot. The second day she was there, Lightfoot was cooking the vegetables and accidentally burned her hand with the hot water.

Marion was never idle and she conscripted Louise for her work. On Saturday mornings, they made sandwiches to give to sightseers coming to the area as part of their sales pitch for the estate. Walter then decided to send a second helper up to Sydney for Marion, Amy Kathleen (Cappy) Mahady, who was a typist in their Melbourne office and close friend of Louise Lightfoot.

Later that year, one of the houses around the corner in The Parapet became vacant. It was a rectangular box-shaped house made of local stone, which had been built in 1922 as an investment for Melbourne theatrical entrepreneur Julius Grant. It was designed around a freestanding fireplace with a wide living room at the back of the house. It had a series of French doors opening out to a spectacular view looking east to North Head and the Pacific Ocean. It was built flat on the earth, so the house opened up directly to the garden outside. People loved to visit the house and sit out the back and enjoy the view.

So Marion and the two girls moved in. Marion had spent a lot of her spare time at Castlecrag drawing the native landscape, expanding her collection of *Forest Portraits*. She hung some of her work on the walls and put in some wicker furniture and rugs on the floor.

Later in the year, Walter decided to join them. The Griffins were never flush with money and decided to sell their beloved *Pholiota*, which soon found an appreciative buyer.[2] Selling the land at Castlecrag was proving to be much more difficult. The problems in selling the land created ongoing tensions within the shareholders. Those people who were interested in Walter's unusual designs found difficulties raising the finance from the banks. The banks did not like Walter's houses, which were very different from conventional Australian dwellings, and they did not like the strict covenants he had put on developments on the estate. The financial problems caused strains in the relationship between Marion and King O'Malley. Marion accused O'Malley of "being a liar over a money guarantee" when he was visiting Castlecrag in 1925. But O'Malley felt that Marion had tried to "swindle" him over the sale of a block of land in the area which he said "was so steep they had the lavatory chained to a tree."[3]

In a letter in November 1925, a GSDA director, Charles Cerutty, complained bitterly about the lack of reports from Walter about progress with the estate and his postponement of a meeting with the directors. Marion's antagonism toward some of the board members, whom she now regarded as involved in a conspiracy against her husband, was by this time well-known. Cerutty was worried that Marion may be taking her frustrations out on the other investors by not putting as much energy in selling the land as she might have.

> It appears to me that there is a suggestion of passive resistance in his [Walter's] inaction. I feel that Mrs. G's residence on the property gives her an opportunity for exercising her antagonistic feeling to the Board as now constituted. No other explanation presents my mind the extraordinary slump in sales, considering we are now in the spring of the year.[4]

In reality Marion was as eager as anyone to sell the land and see her husband's designs built. Sales were slow but a little community was slowly developing at Castlecrag. Walter built some shops on the estate near the main road, which had helped bring some services to the somewhat isolated community. In November, the residents of the estate formed the Castlecrag Progress Association. Castlecrag resident Edgar Herbert was elected president and Walter joined the executive committee. The association began to lobby for improvements in services to the area including a local infants' school, better transport to the city, the upgrading of Edinburgh Road, sewage services, and putting the electricity wires underground.

Now Marion had her husband back living with her. They had a simple but lovely stone house, designed by Walter, with a wonderful view. As

Christmas approached, she decided it was time to celebrate. Marion was fond of the local children. By now she knew Australians regarded the celebration of Christmas, in the middle of summer, as more of an outdoor event than it was in the cold, snowy northern hemisphere. Marion organized an "outdoor Christmas Party" at their house for the local children. The parents were told to send a small coin to buy each child's present, which would be placed under a tree.

And so Marion and Walter were together again, carving out another new life, hoping at last to build their ideal community.

Thirty-three

New Friends

The Griffins may have broken their ties with Wright, but their past associations with him were about to catch up with them again in a rather unusual way.

Sometime around mid-1926, a young woman living in Sydney was reading a book published by a Dutch architectural magazine, *Wendigen*, which focused on Frank Lloyd Wright and his work, including the Imperial Hotel in Japan. Its Dutch editor was a big fan of Wright and published several flattering issues of the magazine on the architect, binding them into a book. It had been given to the woman, Ula Maddocks, by a Dutch friend who had recently been home to Holland for a visit. Ula was so enthusiastic about it, she put some of the pictures of Wright's work in the window of a store in Roseville, only a few miles from Castlecrag, where she was working. One day, a lawyer friend of the Griffins, Edward Beeby, walked by the shop and saw the photos. He came in and spoke to Ula, telling her that two of Wright's former disciples were living nearby.[1]

Ula arranged to visit the Griffins at Castlecrag with a group of her friends. They were members of a quasi-religious philosophical group called the Theosophical Society, which had followers around the world, some of whom would meet in summer gatherings in Holland. Ula's Dutch friend, a fellow Theosophist, was a wealthy young man living in Sydney, called J.J. van der Leeuw.

Ula and her friends were fascinated with what they saw at Castlecrag and its liberal, community-minded spirit. They saw the Griffins' beliefs as fitting in with their own views, still spiritual but breaking away from conventional churches and conventional thinking. Ula was a nurse and her husband, Edgar, was a music teacher. Both had been members of the Theosophical Society for some time. Soon after their visit, van der Leeuw went to see the Griffins himself and wrote an enthusiastic letter of recommendation to another Dutch Theosophist friend living in Sydney:

> This morning I went to see the houses built by an architect called Griffin, the architect of Canberra who at present is building and planning what will practically be a new suburb on Middle Harbour, Castlecrag. He is an American and this is the first architect whose work I have seen in Australia and really liked. Personally I have decided that whatever more I build here ... whether Guest house, or Masonic Temple or Church, is going to be built by Griffin. He is the only architect in Australia whose work is really modern and beautiful.[2]

Van der Leeuw's recommendation carried a lot of weight in Theosophist circles in Sydney. He came from a wealthy Dutch family with a strong interest in architecture. Van der Leeuw did not end up commissioning a house from Walter, but the combination of his eager endorsement and the enthusiastic reports from Ula Maddocks and her friends, encouraged other members of the society to visit the Griffins' new community.

Outsiders from the established churches, the Theosophists saw the Griffins as fellow travelers. For their part, the Griffins, particularly Marion, were eager to strike up new friendships in Sydney. Marion was certainly not going to link up with her old friends, and now enemies, in Sydney, Florence and George Taylor. Those doors were firmly closed to her. After having to deal with so much criticism over their social and political views, it must have been a relief for the Griffins, particularly for Marion, to be embraced by a new group of people who were liberal thinkers, but still quite spiritual. Marion had a passionate interest in community and in nature, with a touch of mysticism, including her belief that she could see fairies in the natural landscape if she tried hard enough.

Marion's move to Castlecrag allowed her to create her own community rather than just working as a "loyal slave" for her husband. A canny saleswoman, Marion was also astute enough to see their newfound Theosophist friends were also a potential source of business for their estate, which was always struggling for new investors.

The Theosophist movement in Australia at the time was small but active, partly due to the fact that one of its early leaders, controversial Englishman Charles Webster Leadbeater, had moved to Sydney in 1915. The movement had been founded by Russian-born Helena Petrovsky Blavatsky, who combined an interested in the occult with an interest in the Eastern religions of Hinduism and Buddhism. She founded the Theosophical Society in 1875, Theosophy meaning "divine wisdom." It was a new spiritual philosophy, which sought inspiration from the religions of East and West and came at a time when new scientific ideas, such as Charles Darwin's Theory of Evolution, were raising questions about the teaching of established Western religions.

Charles Leadbeater, a former English priest, joined the society in England and spent time at the headquarters of the society in Adyar, a town just south of Madras in India, before coming to Australia. In India, Leadbeater met a 14-year-old Indian boy, Jiddu Krishnamurti, who he believed had the potential to become the new messiah. The Theosophists took the boy and his brother back to England to be educated, where his supporters included Lady Emily Lutyens, the wife of the architect Edwin Lutyens, who designed New Delhi.

In 1915, Leadbeater moved to Sydney where he founded his own version of Theosophy, which he called the Liberal Catholic Church. It had nothing to do with the conventional Catholic Church, but the name helped to give it some credibility. In the wake of the horrendous carnage of the war in Europe, which had been supported by some of the conventional churches, many people were looking for new spiritual ideas. The idea of seeking inspiration from the exotic East was particularly attractive. Leadbeater and his followers set up headquarters in Clifton Gardens, on the north side of Sydney Harbour. In 1923, the group also built an amphitheater for some of their events on a cliff top overlooking nearby Balmoral Beach. Ula and her friends never quite believed the idea put forward by some that the amphitheater was also a place to wait for the new messiah who would come to them across the water. But other leaders of the movement were adamant that there would be a coming of a new world teacher somewhere, sometime.

Marion was open to new ideas at the time. Her love of nature had a deep spiritual dimension, but Theosophy itself was a step too far for her. Around the time she met Ula, she read a book, *An Outline of Occult Science*, written in 1910 by German philosopher Rudolf Steiner. Steiner had originally been a leading member of the Theosophist Society in Germany. But he espoused a more conventional view, believing Theosophy should teach a more Western spiritual path, more in harmony with established religions. Steiner was also unhappy with the personality cult of some of its leaders. The German was also much more skeptical of the idea that the young Krishnamurti was the new messiah in waiting. Steiner and the majority of German-speaking lodges broke away from the Theosophists to form their own philosophical organization called the Anthroposophical Society in 1912.

Marion had grown up as a spiritual person involved in a very liberal Unitarian religion and was immediately taken in by Steiner's writings. She was at a point of change in her life. She had spent years battling what she believed were forces conspiring against her and her husband, forces which had succeeded in preventing her husband from realizing his dream of creating an ideal city. She could not believe why human beings wanted to destroy the natural environment. Reading Steiner's works, she told her friends, "changed me from a pessimist to an optimist."

As she wrote later:

> Before then, I had been saying what a pity Lord, who had created the wonderful beauty of stone and bush and animal, has made the fatal mistake of creating man who devoted all his energies to destroying these beauties. ... But, now, I grasped the reversal of things and realized, instead of man's standing at the top of a tree of evolution through these kingdoms, they had all, mineral, and vegetable and animal, derived through the eons from him. ... From this standpoint, it was possible to attain a basic purpose for life.[3]

While Marion did not join the Theosophy movement, she had at last found friendship with some sympathetic fellow travelers in Ula and her group of friends. Marion gathered around her an unusual, free-spirited group of people with unconventional ideas. The Griffins were creating a new community at Castlecrag. Walter's passion was in designing an ideal city with houses set into the natural environment. Marion's passion extended into the very spirit and soul of the place, to seeing the forces of God in the natural setting around them. Like her grandparents in Tremont and her parents in Chicago, she opened up her house to newcomers and friends. She was determined to create a new community at Castlecrag and all were welcome.

The association with the Theosophists led to some new business for the Griffins. Walter was hired by van der Leeuw's friend to build a large house opposite the Theosophists' headquarters in Clifton Gardens. This was later rented out to a newly married Theosophist couple, Harold and Norna Morton. Years later, Norna would write about her delight with such an unusual house:

> It was rather like a simple sandstone castle from the ancient past, only it was set in the Australian bushland and draped with wattle and eucalyptus trees. Walter Burley Griffin was a genius when it came to capturing the spirit of the land and making his houses merge naturally with the environment. Inside and throughout, the walls were a restful green, and, appearing in all rooms and hallways, there was a burst of yellow mottling—like wattle in spring. The effect was accomplished with a heavy sponge dipped in a brilliant yellow paint; no need for pictures in these houses.[4]

Harold Morton became the general secretary of the Theosophical Society of Australia in 1928. He also helped to form radio station 2GB where he broadcast his Theosophical views each day. The Mortons became passionate supporters of Walter's ideas about architecture and the natural environment and later moved into Castlecrag themselves. Walter was also approached by another Theosophist, Judy Creswick, to design a new house for her at Castlecrag. In 1926, he built a two-bedroom, flat-roofed Knitlock house in an area well down the hill from Edinburgh Road, called The Barbette.

From the beginning, it was clear that Castlecrag was not going to be any ordinary community. The Griffins presented an unusual sight as they strode around the suburb. They were both passionate about Australian trees and shrubs and eager to replant the estate with native plants. Young Wanda Herbert, who lived in Castlecrag from the age of two, when her family came from Melbourne, would watch the Griffins walking along the road:

> They were walking along, bareheaded, on their way to plant trees in the triangles [areas of land at the corners of the roads to slow traffic]. Stocky Mr. Griffin, pushing a wheelbarrow, was dressed in his gray slacks and white shirt, unbuttoned at the neck, collar detached, sleeves rolled up, and Mrs. Griffin was wearing her red-ochre pajamas of heavy crepe, and brown sandals. In those days Australian women did not wear trousers. It was more or less mandatory for matrons to wear hats. Marion never did. People did not go around planting gum trees either.[5]

Walter continued his work building houses and developing the estate, while Marion threw herself into the local community. He built a house for Robert Guy, a freelance artist, and his wife, Elizabeth, on a street called The Bastion leading down the hill toward the water. It was a small house with only two bedrooms. Made of two interlocking squares, the house was made of local sandstone and had a flat roof. One of the bedrooms was designed to open out into the living room, creating a large combined space. Walter used vertical concrete pipes as columns on three sides of the living room, with French doors in between them, which opened out to the garden giving a great view of a nearby reserve. He painted the columns in a moss green overlaid in gold, making it look like a Greek temple. Marion loved the house, which she called The Temple of Aphrodite. It was, she wrote, "another burst of genius" from her husband. "A tiny house like a tiny temple, [which was] a perfect work of art."[6] The unusual house became a popular gathering place for the local residents.

In 1926, the opportunity came up to buy some land next to the Castlecrag Estate, the Haven Estate, but the Griffins never had much money. Marion's elderly mother, Clara, had bought the house in Elkhart, Indiana, which Marion had built for her brother Gerald, and had written in her will that it should go to Marion. She asked her mother to sell the house at Elkhart and give her the money to help buy the land. Her dear mother did so and the Griffins were able to buy another 30 acres of land next to their property, expanding their ideal suburb. From then on the Haven Estate was often referred to locally as "Marion's Estate."[7]

Developing their ideal suburb had been a lot more difficult than they thought. As it expanded, the Griffins' unusual experiment attracted more attention, but nothing ever came easy for them. Walter planned a group of houses on a circular road called The Rampart. The first was built in 1926 for a young woman, Ellen Mower. It was a small two-bedroom Knitlock house, set down the hill from the road to give it a harbor view. It had a flat roof, which could be accessed from the street by means of a ramp. Wanda Herbert and the other children from the estate watched the house being built from their perch on a nearby rock. It was so unusual that Mower did not move into the house and the company had to buy it back from her. Like most of the other houses, it was rented out.

But Marion loved the house, and its flat roof and great views made it a great place for community parties. "Some houses are so dainty you can hardly believe they are for humans," she told her friends in America, enthusiastically describing Walter's design of the Mower House.

> A bridge across a bit of a chasm takes you under a trellis bower to the roof. What a view! Raking up and down the valley! ... No shrub was allowed to be destroyed as the building was constructed, though it took battles with masons and plumbers to prevent it. Consequently from the moment it was finished it was a bower of loveliness—yellow banksias, orange callistemon, pink ti shrub, golden darwinii as well as stately trees and clumps of Christmas bells and endless other native things.[8]

Right: *Angophera Lanceolota*: A Castlecrag home in a Castlecrag Gully. Drawing by Marion Mahony. Eric Nicholls collection. National Library of Australia.

Thirty-four

Drawing Nature

Louise Lightfoot and Cappy Mahady lived with the Griffins in the Grant house. The two girls slept on box couches on opposite walls of the bedroom while Marion and Walter had two couches in the living room. Each morning, they would fold up the bedding and put it back into the couches underneath. Marion, who had grown up in a large household that was very communal, had no great love of privacy. "Anyone needing privacy was not living right," she would say.[1]

The Griffins did not eat red meat and were not drinkers of alcohol, but Marion loved fish. Lightfoot recalled her experiences living with Marion.

> Marion's style was to pop a dish of potatoes and onions and milk in the oven and a strawberry shortcake. Citrus drinks and salads were in plenty. ... We rarely took meals in town but on such occasions Marion would order "Smawked Cahd."
> "What did she say?" the waiter would ask.
> I would translate her request to Smoked Cod.[2]

They would often get fish from the harbor from their surveyor, Mr. Hudson. But one day, Lightfoot was cutting up a fish in the kitchen. It wiggled and fell on the floor. Lightfoot dropped her knife and almost fainted. Looking at the helpless fish on the floor, Marion declared, "From henceforth no fish, flesh, or fowl to be served in this house!" And she kept her word, although Lightfoot and Cappy did manage to cook some bacon in the house when the Griffins were not around.

Marion was a keen walker and could clamber over rocks at Castlecrag with great agility. Lightfoot recalled, "Mrs. G never tired as she climbed over rocks and through the bush and she expected others to share her enthusiasm."

Walter had an office in the city, which was used to represent the company, but he did a lot of drafting work in their home at Castlecrag where the Griffins set aside one and sometimes two of the rooms for their work. Marion did not often go to the office in the city, preferring to focus on life at Castlecrag. Lightfoot helped out with the drafting work on new houses for the estate, working under Marion's ever-watchful eye. Always a little in awe of Mrs. Griffin, she would later recall:

> She was a remarkable woman, her husband's devoted and capable executrix and the supervisor of his young draftsmen. She was my instructress. I still hear the sound of her ring scratching the paper as she rubbed out the mistakes in my drawing.
> "Keep your mind open to the inspirations of the Creator," Marion would advise. "And then I will come and pick it to pieces."[3]

Marion, who had always been interested in acting and the theater decided they should have a community festival. Everyone was drawn into it in one way or another—costumes, lighting, scenes, acting. Louise did an "Egyptian Water Carrier" dance while her friend, dancer Mischa Burlakov, did a lively Russian dance. The concert was a great success, but in the end the money did not cover the cost of the costumes that Lightfoot, Mahady, and Burlakov had bought. When she realized this, Marion gave them the money. Lightfoot, who often found Marion a little formidable, was touched by Marion's kind gesture.

After the terrible wartime years, the 1920s were more upbeat and adventurous. Women became more daring and changed their looks. Marion decided she would, too, but there was mixed reaction to her decision. As Wanda Herbert recalled later:

> It was the flapper era and women were breaking their bonds and cropping their hair. Not that Marion Mahony Griffin gave the impression of having any bonds to break, unless in her own mind. It was her hair, the long straight black hair, coiled or plaited around her head that so

delighted Walter. One day, Marion returned triumphant from the city with an Eton crop. Walter was devastated.[4]

Was it just that Marion wanted to be in fashion or was she making a personal statement of her own independence? While Walter was not happy, Marion was delighted. Her short hair was part of her plans to dress up for a man's part in their latest play. As she later recalled, "I had my hair cut and dressed man fashion for the occasion. All the ladies fell in love with me."[5] It was reminiscent of her time at MIT when she dressed up as a man for a play and was voted the "handsomest man" in her class.

Marion made many of the costumes for the plays herself and was very proud of her handiwork.

> My own knack of costuming was, I am convinced, the only faculty that ever won the real admiration of my husband who was constantly tickled pink to see the sumptuous and charming effects for unexpected guests or ourselves created from our stray sheets, table or couch covers and oddments. ... When Castlecrag, individually or in groups, entered the metropolitan affairs of Sydney, such as the annual Shakespeare Ball, they frequently walked off with the prizes.[6]

Many different people came to visit the Griffins' house, inspired by their ideals and eager to see for themselves the development of this unusual community. At one of these evenings, Lightfoot was amazed to see Marion dancing around the room for her guests. "I was most interested and asked her to teach me to dance. 'I only make it up as I go on,' she [Marion] replied."[7]

Marion said she was inspired by creative dancer Mary Wigman. The German-born Wigman was a pioneer of expressionist dance, some of which would be done in silence and others done to the sound of percussion instruments. Marion encouraged Lightfoot to learn more about her.

People often speculated about the background of the Griffins, particularly Marion. While they appeared to be very modern, they were also conservative in their own way. They did not smoke and were not drinkers, although Walter would occasionally have some wine when out with friends. When Lightfoot began an affair with Burlakov, who had a wife living overseas, Marion was most disapproving. She was even more unhappy when Lightfoot continued her relationship with him after his wife arrived in Australia.

Some speculated that Marion must have had Native American heritage as her skin was very brown, just as her classmates at MIT had done in their cartoon. When Lightfoot asked her about her background, she said her mother "came from the Bohemian quarter" of Chicago, a comment which led Lightfoot to observe:

> Marion could have been called a square Bohemian. She was unconventional yet strict. There were no arguments in her house, no lies, no unkindness, no pessimism. Any kind of weather was "perfectly lovely." She was sometimes a little bitter of criticism and Waltie's Canberra troubles but used to laugh. ... She was as volatile as Waltie was reserved. She looked after him as well as she knew how, offering him constant drinks of water, reading to him from the many architectural magazines he insisted on keeping up with, stitching his black silk new bows.[8]

As the community evolved, people would have gatherings at the different houses. As Marion recalled later:

> The combination of natural loveliness and beautiful architectural setting, constantly varied as one hostess after another offered her home, and the ingenuity of the citizenry in costuming, made beautiful and brilliant occasions of these community affairs, none of which ever entailed any expensive outlay.[9]

As it was with *Pholiota* in Heidelberg, the door to the Griffins' Castlecrag house was never locked. Marion loved the local children. She kept bowls of fruit in the house and encouraged them to come in and help themselves. Local residents and others attracted by the Castlecrag experience would often drop by. Marion had been unable to return to her childhood life at Hubbard Woods, north of Chicago. But she was recreating a new life and a new community around her, thousands of miles away in Australia.

The Cragites, as they were called, bought canoes and rowing boats and spent time on the waters exploring all the inlets and coves. Louise Lightfoot enjoyed some happy days there.

> There were canoe trips to the beautiful Upper Reaches of Middle Harbour. Misha, the strong dancer, was always recruited for boating. There were office picnics to Palm Beach [in the north of Sydney] and Bulli Pass [on the south of the city]. Sometimes members of my family would come and stay for holidays.[10]

Marion also loved canoeing on the waters of Middle Harbour. There was plenty to explore with all the different inlets. She loved the view of the Covecrag peninsula, the middle of the three promontories where the GSDA had bought land. "Viewed from the harbor [Covecrag] has the constantly changing and lovely effect of Fujiyama, only it is ever blooming."[11] As she had done when she was canoeing with Walter in America, she was as fascinated with what was underneath the water as what was above it. She recalled canoeing on the water looking at the "incredible beauty in the water below us and dripping from our oars, Lucifer lighting the depths."

Castlecrag, with its dramatic and unusual landscape, also allowed Marion to continue with her artwork. Her aim was to record the unusual trees and plants she found in Australia, just as Bailey and others had done for American plants in the reference books that Walter had studied. Years before, she had painstakingly compiled eight books about Australian plants, each covering plants of a different color, for Walter's plans to plant the hills of Canberra. His idea was to prove impractical, but Marion's chronicling of Australian botany continued with her drawings and their detailed descriptions of trees in a work which she hoped might one day turn into a book.

She had a particular passion for the Angophoras, the Australian gum trees, which were a regular feature of her drawings. She did one perspective of a house Walter had designed for Castlecrag but, as usual, the scroll-like drawing was as much about nature as it was about the building. She drew a giant gum tree in the middle of the page, with the proposed house, flat-roofed and made of stone, down in the valley below. It was signed Walter Burley Griffin, Architect, but Marion kept it as part of her collection along with a detailed note about Angophoras. She called it a "Castlecrag home in a Castlecrag gully."

In the caption, she noted that:

> Botanists tell us that this district has a greater variety of blossoms than any other spot in the world. Trees and shrubs are in blossom the whole year round, a constant succession, in endless variety. By planting the proper varieties one can have acacias, the wattles, the goldenrod tree, in blossom all the 12 months of the year, great masses of showy clusters of various shades of gold. This huge tree, too, an Angophora Lancelota, loving the spectacular, chose the edge of a precipice thus dominating the gully. Humans ignorant of spiritual science might well wonder whence it got its nourishment but indeed the plant has no earthly things for its nourishment but only for its support and to maintain its upward position.[12]

She was fascinated by the gnarly trees that clung to rocks and precipices and imagined their origins in ancient times.

> The trunk of the Angophora may be round or it swells out in one direction and then narrows up to a slender oval in section at another according to its passing mood, and the branches pay no attention to the laws of gravity, reaching out, twisting and contorting as if they were in water, indeed in every way often resembling water animals. This pink barked tree often resembles a great octopus with outreaching twisting and contorting tentacles.[13]

In her drawings in America for Wright, she wrote, she had "strained to the point of veracity" many of the trees she drew around the houses. But in her work in Australia, she felt, "nature itself accomplished the decorative character required. ... It needed no stretch of the imagination to make mural decorations of these trees."[14] There was so much beauty around her, her main frustration was not being able to do as many drawings as she wanted.

> There was always a minor strain because I was not able to make a set of at least a hundred of these wonderful decorations so lavishly put forward by the fairies of this ancient continent, the Gnomes dissolving the rocks for tender rootlets, the Undines carrying up the sap, the Sylphs forming the flowers, and the Fire Fairies the seeds.[15]

She loved the native yellow wattle tree, Australia's national flower, noting in her *Forest Portraits* that:

> The Wattles are the Golden Rod trees of Australia, over 400 varieties, whose flowers run the gamut of the yellows from pale cream to deep gold, and there is never a time when they are not in bloom. So, with proper selection, you can have superb masses of bloom every month of the year and forms from the daintiest of shrubs, the perfumed Suaveolens, to the stately Melanoxylon, the foliage of every conceivable shape but always evergreen.[16]

She wished that some philanthropist would plant the American western desert with wattles.

Lightfoot watched her work with admiration. She was amazed when Marion produced a capeweed one day and showed how it was "an example of the perfect symmetry in the work of the Creator." Marion's love of nature infused all her work. The perspectives she drew of Walter's houses would carefully depict the plants and trees around them, the works rendered in silk with her Japanese dyes. But the Griffins' love of nature was not always shared by others. As they replanted many trees, they would awake sometimes to find that vandals had come to Castlecrag in the night and cut rings around the bark to kill them. Marion valued every tree on their estate and taught Lightfoot how to heal the injured trees, cutting splints to put across the scarred bark, binding them with mud and using sacking to wrap around it as a protection.

In 1927, Australia was readying itself for a grand celebration. The new federal parliament building in Canberra was finally completed and was to be opened by the Duke and Duchess of York in May. The Duke's father had been at the grand opening of the Federal Parliament in Melbourne in 1901. Almost three decades after the Federation of Australia, and 16 years after the Griffins had designed the Australian capital, the seat of government would finally be moving to Canberra. The cream of Australian society would be attending the celebrations.

Walter had been a vocal critic of the concept of building a "temporary" parliament house in Canberra and would never be popular with those now building the new capital. He argued that the location of the temporary building, in front of the location he proposed for the permanent one, threatened the symmetry of his plan for the city. If they built a temporary parliament, he argued, it would become part of the capital and never be torn down. When the official guest list was revealed, and it became known that the Griffins had not been invited, there was a furore in the media. Finally they were invited, although they were not part of the official party. The Griffins may have taken some comfort in knowing that the stunning drawings they had prepared for the federal capital competition back in 1911 were also put on display as part of the celebrations.

Actors, actresses, and dancers would regularly visit The Crag. In August 1928, Miles Franklin, who was still living overseas, came to see them on a visit home to Australia. When she got to Castlecrag, she could see immediately what her friends were trying to do. Franklin and Walter went for a walk around the estate. As they walked, Walter unburdened himself to his old friend who recalled later:

> The poor man confessed to me his bitterness, is sorry he did not stay in the USA. (This *very private*, of course). The way he is persecuted and thwarted is shameful—and so terrible that it is typical of Australia.[17]

Marion was not worried to see her husband disappear outside with Franklin who was good friends with both of them. "Mrs. G. is going to come out at night especially so I can talk to *her* and she said she was glad I took Mr. G. out in the air," Franklin wrote later.

In 1928, the GSDA produced a promotional film of the Griffin estates entitled *Beautiful Middle Harbour*. It was a black-and-white video showing the beautiful views of the estate but it also served to highlight the lifestyle. It showed the residents having parties on the rooftops, most likely on the top of the Mower House. A most unusual community indeed.

Thirty-five

1929

The Griffins' social circle expanded to take in some of the more interesting people in the city. Their interest in the theater had brought them into contact with Duncan MacDougall, a Scottish-born producer and actor, and his wife Augusta, known as Pakie, who ran the Playbox Theatre in Sydney, which opened in 1925. Walter and Marion became friendly with the MacDougalls. Passionate about putting on plays, the Griffins were eager to encourage a relationship between the social set around the MacDougalls and the Playbox Theatre and their own community at Castlecrag. The actors and others involved with the theater would often come to parties at Castlecrag.

In 1928, the MacDougalls separated and Pakie and her son Robin moved into Castlecrag, renting a house in Edinburgh Road. Pakie decided to set up her own club, renting two large rooms on the second floor of a building in Elizabeth Street in the city, overlooking Hyde Park. Walter and Marion helped her transform it into a nightclub, called Pakie's Club. They had a grand opening on June 8, 1929, with a group from The Crag putting on a play for the evening, with journalist and poet Mary Gilmore reading from her work.

Pakie's was a bohemian club although it did not serve alcohol. It became a popular haunt for writers, including Xavier Herbert and Kylie Tennant. The Griffins would often go to the club and dress up for its parties and functions. A few months after it opened, they held a Mexican night and Marion and Walter went dressed as Mayan gods. Marion went as Al Puch, the god of death and destruction, wearing a colored robe and a headdress with long golden spikes. Walter went as Itzamma, the chief god and ruler of heaven.

That year another interesting line of business opened up for Walter through a client in Melbourne, Nisson Leonard-Kanevsky. Born in Russia, he arrived almost penniless in Melbourne where he became involved in the clothing business. In the early 1920s, he had approached Walter to design an office building for him which he called Leonard House, one of Australia's first curtain-walled high-rise buildings. Walter moved his office into the building in 1925. When Walter moved to Sydney later that year, the Griffins' Melbourne office was supervised by a talented young architect, Eric Nicholls, who had worked on Leonard House.

In 1929, the local council in Essendon, a suburb of Melbourne, invited tenders for the construction of a municipal incinerator. The entrepreneurial Kanevsky learned about it through a contact in the Russian-Jewish community, Vasilie Trunoff, who knew of a patented design for an incinerator designed by John Boadle, a sanitary engineer for the Melbourne City Council. It was an efficient, low-cost method of burning waste that Boadle had patented in 1926. In 1929, Kanevsky formed a partnership with Trunoff and Boadle called the Reverberatory Incinerator and Engineering Company, RIECo, which bid for the Essendon contract.

But the site was in a residential area, close to parklands, and the council was concerned that the incinerator should fit into the local surroundings. Kanevsky approached Walter to design something that would be pleasing to the eye. While Walter was now living in Sydney, he oversaw the drawings, with Nicholls' help, and the company won the tender. The Essendon incinerator was a striking building, a small triangle fitted into the side of a larger triangle, with a stylishly decorated chimney. It had a diamond-shaped window outlet at the top of the smaller triangle, reminiscent of the window in the Peters' House, which Walter had designed in Chicago after leaving Wright's office.

The entrepreneurial Kanevsky could see the opportunities of selling the concept to other municipal councils around the country, combining his marketing skills, Boadle's incinerator design, and Walter's unique architectural flair to make the industrial buildings attractive. Soon the three began getting approaches from other councils intrigued to see an industrial building that could be effective in disposing waste and look attractive in the local environment. From his base in Melbourne, the 27-year-old Nicholls threw himself into the work, and Walter invited him to become his partner in the incinerator venture.

Meanwhile, in Castlecrag in 1929, Walter at last got the type of client he wanted for his ideal suburb. Thomas Wilson Fishwick was a businessman who moved to Sydney representing a British company, Fowlers, which sold locomotives and rolling stock. Fishwick had lived in Japan before coming to Australia and was more open to more modern architectural thinking than many others in Australia. He bought land at Castlecrag and commissioned Walter to design him a house. At last having a client with money who appreciated his style, Griffin was able to take his architectural designs at Castlecrag to the next level. The land was in a small cul-de-sac called The Cidatel, which had to be carved out of the sandstone to access the view. With a wealthier client, Walter was free to design a house which was much more impressive than any he had ever done at Castlecrag. He designed a two-story building with a large picture window looking out onto bushland and the harbor. The building caused a great stir in the community, particularly when it was learned that Fishwick would be installing fish tanks into the ceiling of the dining room.[1]

Fishwick was delighted with his house, noting later that:

> The house that Mr. Griffin designed and built for us at Castlecrag was full of charm and character and it gave my wife and myself great pleasure to live there. In the hot summer days, it was always cool and at night we often slept out of doors on the rooftop with only the stars above. Much of the stone of which the site was built was quarried from the site by Italian workmen.

If only the Griffins could have had many more clients with Fishwick's combination of money and enthusiasm, their suburb would have flourished. After all his battles, Walter at last had a chance to show the type of house he really could design for his ideal suburb. If the Melson House, made of local stone, was the architectural showpiece of the community of houses Griffin designed in Mason City, Iowa, the Fishwick House highlighted what Walter could really do in Australia.

The stock market crash on Wall Street in October 1929 must have seemed like a long way away from the small community at Castlecrag. As Christmas approached, Marion had many other things on her mind. The estate was full of what the locals called Christmas bushes, colorful shrubs with red flowers, which would bloom around Christmas time. They were so pretty that people would come from all around to pick them to decorate their homes for the festive season. But the Griffins hated to see trees cut down or native flowers destroyed, so they set up a roster of local people to guard the bushes and deter the scavengers.

On Christmas Eve 1929, Marion wrote a note to Miles Franklin:

> Castlecrag has concentrated for the past week on safeguarding the bush. We have all been taking turns about at being out at 4 am and late evening, though Walt had been on duty just about all the time. We think our dozen rangers on duty have made a decided difference to the stripping of the three promontories of Xmas bush and bells, though some rascals have slipped through our fingers. Why don't you write an article for the press suggesting that Australians, instead of destroying the glory of the bush, make a religious ceremony of going out to see the Xmas bush in its prime and establish festivals for its worship? A good religion that would be.[2]

Then, of course, there was the annual Christmas Party. This time it was to be at Pakie's home on Edinburgh Road. It was a party that was to live on in the minds of everyone who attended. The patrons from Pakie's new club came, as well as the extended Castlecrag community. Bernard Hesling, a young Englishman who had not long arrived in Sydney, was one of those who attended. He traveled to an area in Middle Harbour called The Spit, where boats were moored. There, he was picked up by a Castlecrag local in a canoe and rowed to The Crag for the party. He spent the evening squatting on a "damp boulder on Pakie's lawn, spooning up some sort of marzipan with gravy, drinking fresh carrot juice, which is good for you, and watching with half an eye Marion Griffin, all of 50, doing a hula in a horse rug."[3]

Hesling, who later moved into Castlecrag, wasn't the only one who found Marion verging on the eccentric. Many people speculated about her origins. The myth persisted that she had Native American blood in her background. She was a very different woman than most people in the area had ever seen before.

As Lightfoot wrote later:

> People said Marion was of American Indian origin because she was so brown. Actually her skin was very white, but she had dark hair and suntanned quickly. After I had lived in the US and Mexico, I realized there was nothing of the Indian in her.[4]

Hesling reported a similar view:

> Marion—fifteen years older than Walter—claimed Red Indian blood and standing, mounted like the last of the Mohicans at Castle Rock with tomahawk profile and ropy arm flung out contemptuously toward Paleface Northbridge, it was easy to see that her maiden name could have been Pocahontas.
> "Walter and I wanna keep The Crag voigin bush," she drawled in a sort of Boston-Indian.[5]

One doubts that Marion actually ever did tell anyone she was part Native American. She was only five years older than her husband, not fifteen, and came from Chicago, not Boston. But Hesling's comments were typical of the myths and legends built up around Marion and the scene at The Crag. Was it just that she was so different, so exotic that people had to make up stories to explain her background? Was her manner just that little bit formidable, deterring people from asking her too many questions about her past? Or maybe the myths, legends, and rumors were just part of the territory in such an unusual social environment.

Castlecrag's liberal, open house, social environment, its Bohemian atmosphere, and many parties attracted an interesting range of people. At the time, homosexuality was still something that went on behind closed doors and was not widely discussed. But in the late 1920s, the Griffins' community attracted lesbian couple Ida Leeson, who worked at the Mitchell Library, the main library of the city, and her partner, Florence Birch. They bought a block of land on Edinburgh Road in December 1929 with views overlooking Middle Harbour and The Spit out to North Head, where they had plans to build a Griffin house. The next year, they moved into Castlecrag, renting a house on The Parapet, near the Griffins. Leeson and Birch were the kind of artistic and interesting thinkers that Marion liked. They were well connected in literary circles and loved Marion's plays. As Leeson's biographer explained:

> A decision to move to CC was not made lightly. It required a commitment to the Griffins and to a set of ideals. The rocky promontory in Middle Harbour was an outpost, without any of the conveniences most people took for granted. The nearest transport was the tram from Willoughby, a few miles away from Castlecrag to Milson's Point, then crossing the harbor by ferry. ... There was no sewerage or gas at Castlecrag and electricity and even water were not easy to get. There were a few shops near the entrance to Edinburgh Road. ... But for the daring adult, Walter and Marion Griffin's vision of a new way of living in harmony with nature and with other people was compelling.[6]

To the outside world it may have seemed as if Castlecrag was an almost idyllic community, but for the Griffins, life was never that easy. Walter and the company, GSDA, were under constant financial pressure, and the strains with the other shareholders continued. Their architectural and social experiment may have been lauded by the Theosophists and others, but the sale of land and the construction of houses had gone a lot slower than they had hoped. Banks and owners continued to balk at some of the strict convenants that Walter believed were necessary to preserve the unique character of the development. And there were complaints from some other homeowners about leaks from the unusual flat roofs. Some said that Walter should have more closely supervised the construction of the buildings, particularly the Knitlock buildings, to make sure they were built properly. Others said that the some of the local tradesmen did not like his unusual construction techniques and his insistence that things be done his way. There were rumors that some deliberately undermined his instructions, not using the right mix of ingredients for the Knitlock tiles or installing them incorrectly, which led to problems for homeowners.

Walter was also in a constant battle with the local council about his unusual plans. He wanted all the houses to face the view and not the street and kitchens facing the main road. He campaigned to have the unsightly power lines underground and to have floors built in timber on the earth and not, as was initially proscribed by local council regulations, raised above the earth. And the more land the GSDA had, of course, the more levies were needed to pay to the local council, money which the cash strapped company did not have. Walter was determined that about one-fifth of the total land be preserved as parkland to ensure its natural setting, and wanted all the land along the waterfront to be kept free of development. He argued that the company should not have to pay rates on this open land, but the council was unsympathetic to his arguments.

One of the unhappy clients was Judy Creswick, who had a flat-roofed Knitlock house down in The Barbette. She complained about leaks and other problems and took legal action against the GSDA, which was settled in early 1929 when the company agreed to buy her house back from her. Marion stayed in the house for a few weeks to show everyone that it was perfectly fine to live in. The Griffins were gathering a community of like-minded people around them, but financing their dream was never easy.

Cappy Deans, Marion Mahony, and Walter Burley Griffin in the garden of their home in Castlecrag with Walter's father, George. 1930. Eric Nicholls collection. National Library of Australia.

Thirty-six

The Split

Marion soon found herself taken with another new member of the Castlecrag community. New Zealand born Edith Williams and her invalid husband moved into the Moon House, a few houses down from the Griffins' home, around 1929. Williams was a passionate supporter of the teachings of Rudolf Steiner. She had been to Europe and visited the headquarters of the Anthroposophical Society in Switzerland. On her return, she had helped to establish the Australian chapter of the society and became its general secretary. Williams had discussion groups in Castlecrag about Steiner's philosophy. Marion had already read one of his books a few years before, and his message had struck a chord with her. With Williams living nearby, she learned a lot more about his ideas. The years after the Great War, with its heavy casualties, had shattered many beliefs and the 1920s was an era where people looked for new meaning in life. Williams' enthusiasm for Steiner's teachings was infectious and in 1930, Marion joined the society.

Around the same time, there were ructions within the Theosophical movement, which led to some disillusionment within its ranks. Increasingly uncomfortable at being held up as a messiah figure, Krishnamurti broke from the society. It led to some soul-searching within the ranks of its supporters and saw some Theosophists and would-be Theosophists shift toward the teachings of the Steiner group.

Anthroposophy, or "human wisdom," was a more conventional philosophy than Theosophy, or "divine wisdom," and much closer to Western religions. It took what it believed was a more scientific approach to the spiritual world. Steiner argued that a human being, through wisdom and self-development, could unite with the spiritual world. He believed the human spirit would pass out of the body after death and enter a spiritual world before being born again into a new life on earth in a new body. His teachings also had a political aspect to them, arguing for a minimal involvement by government in the economic affairs of a country.

Marion found Steiner's teachings about self-reliance and the need for a limited role for government a refreshing change from some of the attitudes she had encountered in Australia. The government, she would argue, should be like a traffic policeman who would ensure that everyone had access to the roads and policed the speed limit, but it should stay out of the business of making cars. It was a view that focused on the rights and roles of the individual, much more in tune with the lower government tradition of the United States than the prevailing view in Australia.

America had its roots in private enterprise and private initiative, while the white settlement of Australia had been made by the British government. It was an important distinction in the history of the two countries, and the attitude of their people, which is not always obvious at first glance.

The white settlement of Australia had begun its life as a British penal colony. From the beginning, government was a pervasive part of the society. It created a population used to government providing basic infrastructure and administration. The country's white settlers had also imported a version of the British class system, which Marion was surprised to see in the new country. Under the class system as it operated in Australia, she reported, "titles are usually given, or at any rate offered, as bribes to play the game with officialdom."[1]

This, she believed, leads to a working class "who feel greater and greater bitterness that they have to work for what they get, while the most honored and respected elements in the community are heaped with benefits for which they give nothing in return."[2] In her letters home she complained about "that dominating spirit in Australia of eagerness to get something for nothing."

Marion was refining her own view of the world, throwing herself into the study of Anthroposophy. Steiner believed in the concept of the Four

Ethers—Warmth, Light, Sound, and Life, which he said were the spirit-like forces shaping the world. The idea was taken from Hindu teaching and evolved by the Theosophists. Marion wove this way of thinking in with her long-held Celtic view that there were mystical creatures, such as fairies, undines, and gnomes, which helped to build the vegetable kingdom.

Marion had always loved young children, although she never had any of her own. In Steiner's teaching, she also found support for her own long-held view that young children should not be pushed into conventional classroom teaching too early. Steiner believed children should be encouraged to play and explore nature and develop their own creativity before they were corralled into formal lessons in the classroom. Marion had come from a family of teachers who had similar views about letting children explore the natural world and find their own way without having a scolding parent or teacher constantly over their shoulder. Marion encouraged the establishment of a kindergarten at Castlecrag and saw herself as a teacher of the local children. She wrote later that her embrace of Anthroposophy "opened up the real way to make friends with the children whose lives are being parched by the arid teaching of our present communities. Parents began sending their children to me when they asked those 'impossible' questions."[3]

But all was not well in this "ideal" community, particularly between Marion and Walter. Sometime in 1930, there were tensions in the Griffins' marriage, although they kept their problems very close to themselves. Walter did not share Marion's newfound passion for Anthroposophy. He was a more practical man who had a lot on his plate, focused on the day-to-day pressures of trying to keep their practice going and their community financially viable.

But there was another issue. At some point during 1930, it seems, Walter began having a relationship with another woman. Writing in her book, *The Crag*, Wanda Herbert noted that her "Mrs. Griffin had revealed to Grace [Wanda's mother] that Mr. Griffin had an 'entanglement' with a certain woman. Father fell heavily silent on the subject. He truly never gossiped but clearly he knew all about it."[4]

Wanda recalled that her family was "shocked that anyone would ever dream of coming between Mr. and Mrs. Griffin, whose partnership was regarded as inviolable." Who it was with is not known. Could it have been someone he had met through his work in the city? Or could it have been with one of his idealistic followers in the Theosophical Society? Walter was seen as a man to admire by the society. He had addressed one of its meetings and had two articles published in its magazines. It is not hard to think that a young woman would have found the handsome and visionary architect from America very attractive, while his older wife was now very much preoccupied with her newfound interest in Anthroposophy.

In 1930, Walter was only 54 and Marion was about to turn 60. Walter's cherubic looks made him look younger than his age. Walter was also a man with many frustrations. There was his ongoing disappointment at being thwarted in his plans to build Canberra, which was now being developed without him; his battles with Willoughby Council over his plans for Castlecrag; and the lack of finance for his grand plans for the estate. And the financial crash of 1929 was starting to hit home. The world economy was in a downward spiral with building work and finance for new projects drying up. While Walter was under considerable pressure, carrying a heavy burden of supporting a new community in difficult economic times, Marion had joined a rather esoteric philosophical movement with its belief in reincarnation and ethers.

Walter's father, George, came out to visit the Griffins again that year. Walter's mother, Estelle, had died a few years before. George liked coming to Australia and enjoyed the outdoor life, the warmer weather, and the relaxed atmosphere at Castlecrag. But several pictures taken during his visit to Sydney, sitting out in the garden of the Griffins' home, show that Walter was clearly wrestling with a major decision. The pictures show a relaxed George Griffin and Cappy Deans happily sitting at an outdoor table, while Walter and Marion sat behind them, clearly in the middle of some serious domestic issues. Their strained body language is unmistakable.

A relationship with another woman would not have been an easy decision for Walter. His personal, financial, and professional life was largely tied up with the development of Castlecrag, and Marion was an integral part of this. The photos taken in the garden of their house, which were meant to celebrate George Griffin's time there, showed

Marion looking at Walter, her face, as usual, side-on to the camera, and he looking down at his lap, thinking.

Is Marion looking at her husband and asking him what he is going to do? In the picture, a clearly unhappy Walter can only look down.

Walter and Marion had worked hard to build up Castlecrag as a model suburb, an architectural and social experiment that was now underway. Neither of them would have wanted to break up the community they had worked so hard to create.

Young Wanda Herbert recalled an incident, which she believed revealed something of Marion's character. Marion and Walter had had a couple staying with them who eventually moved out to another house in Castlecrag. When they left, the woman had taken one of Marion's rugs and proudly displayed it in her new home. Marion was very upset about it but could not bring herself to challenge the woman "for the sake of the community." Outwardly confident with strong ideas, Marion often let others dominate, Wanda noted.

> Because Marion is not infrequently described as a domineering extrovert, the hardheaded business woman of the partnership, one cannot avoid noticing her inability to confront the culprits in this case implies a contradiction in her nature. Marion was not without courage. Why did she put herself second?[5]

The Griffins both knew the devastating impact that Wright's scandalous affair with Mrs. Cheney had had on his practice in Chicago. His reputation had been shattered, his family distraught, and it had taken him many years to rebuild his business. Marion may have been a radical and outspoken woman to outsiders, but she was also conservative in many ways. She made it clear to Louise Lightfoot that she did not approve of her having an affair with a married man.

Marion's heart was broken. She loved Walter, but clearly he was wrestling with the situation. What prompted her final decision, one cannot say. Maybe it was the prospect of having to face another jolly Christmas together at The Crag, organizing the great festivities and plays she loved so much, knowing Walter's situation. Trying to keep up a happy face in front of all of her friends, when she was broken hearted, may have been too daunting, even for her. She was a proud woman. As Christmas 1930 approached, Marion did not feel like dancing the hula or partying on the lawn.

Finally she came to a decision. She would go away and leave Walter to make up his mind. He would be free to work out what he wanted to do. "In 1930 at the end of that character testing decade of one's forties [by this time she was almost 60] ... I threw up my hand. Now you are a free man," she told him.[6]

"I'm a perfect damn fool," Walter replied, or so she wrote in her diary later, but Marion decided to go anyway.

On November 27, 1930, Marion boarded the *SS Maunganui* at the docks on Sydney Harbour. The New Zealand owned ship was headed for Wellington where Marion took another ship to San Francisco. Marion was private about what was happening. Their split was cryptically mentioned later in her memoirs:

> The many years were packed full of every joy and every anguish, till that demon who sat on my shoulder seems to have run his gamut of possibilities in work and play together.[7]

Her new views on Anthroposophy seemed to be playing a factor, but there were other points of tension as well. They included, she wrote later, a "curious conflict of interests, perhaps best expressed as a warfare of philosophies."[8] Nietzsche was a bone of contention between them, she added mysteriously.

Marion may have been leaving, but she was not abandoning her husband entirely. She arranged for Grace Herbert to look in on Walter while she was away, making sure there was food in the icebox and his shirts were ironed. After Marion left, it appeared that Walter was a lost man. He would travel to his office in the city and return to the house at Castlecrag each night but, as Grace would recall, "his mind was always somewhere else."[9]

Thirty-seven

Fairies and Herons

It must have been an odd sight that greeted the children of the George B. Armstrong elementary school at Rogers Park in the northern suburbs of Chicago, sometime early in 1931. A tall, wiry 60-year-old woman, probably dressed in bright clothes, stood on a table, day by day, painting a colorful mural high on a wall in a corridor. The children walked past her as they went to and from their classes each day. It was hard to miss, the mural being 5 feet high and 20 feet wide. As she explained to the children, it was about fairies helping to feed a family of herons.

Marion was back in Chicago, living with her widowed sister, Genie, and her daughter, Clarmyra, near the school where Genie was a teacher. Marion's expertise as an artist came to the notice of the headmistress of the school, Miss Reynolds, who asked her to do a mural for the graduating class of 1931. Marion called it *Fairies Feeding the Herons*. Estranged from her husband and her life at Castlecrag, she happily threw herself into a new project inspired by her Anthroposophical views and her love of children. More than a decade before, when she had gone on her sketching trip to Tasmania, being freed from the demands of worrying about Walter, Marion found more space for creative thinking and her artwork. Now she was embarking on another artistic challenge. As she recalled later:

> One boy said to Miss Reynolds, the principal, "You sure did hire a good one when you hired Mrs. Griffin."
> "I didn't hire her," she said, "I got down on my knees to her."
> And this was the splendid spirit all the way through.[1]

The mural showed fairies clustering around a nest of baby herons, high in a birch tree, helping the mother heron to feed them. Other fairies were helping the father heron to carry more supplies of fish to the nest, their diaphanous wings spread out against a blue background of sky and water. Could there be some overtones of Marion helping other parents to bring up their young children? Providing them with the educational and spiritual nourishment she believed they needed and that she could supply?

Marion had woven the idea of fairies into her personal philosophy of spirituality, nature, and life forces long before she even embraced Steiner's Anthroposophy. She believed that children up to a certain age could see fairies and adults could, too, if they really tried. While she was painting the mural, Marion had many discussions about fairies with the children. She explained to one skeptical child that fairies were like God's helpers.

When she had finished her mural, Marion gave a talk to the graduating class:

> I explained to them that the kind of thinking that enabled them to see the fairies was the same kind of thinking that made people able to function as geniuses so, if they wanted to be among geniuses in their work, they must be ready to develop the kind of thinking which would someday enable them to see fairies.[2]

Marion had been sure that the fairies were at play in the Australian bushland as well and had developed her own theory about their role in the natural world. In a caption she wrote to go with a drawing of a fig tree, sometime during her time at Castlecrag, she noted that:

> The Fig is a sort of rubber plant and it pours its roots fantastically over the rocks, till the gnomes make some entry point open in the rocks for them to enter. The gnomes don't bother with them till all the other plants have been attended to. Without the help of the gnomes, the roots of the plants could not make their way through the earth nor could the leaves and flowers and fruit develop without the help of the undines, sylphs, and fire fairies. All these things require intelligence, though the blind materialists of today are all like Topsy who thought she just

growed without a father and mother. The fig foliage is a solid mass. It lets no atmospheric moisture pass it by but makes use of it all. That is where the undines are at work. In the waterfalls is where they play.[3]

Sometime after Marion arrived in Chicago, she and Walter began exchanging letters. They went back and forth across the Pacific just as they had done on Walter's first trip to Australia in 1913. But, unlike those days of their early marriage, when Marion could not wait for Walter to come back to her in Chicago, it was Marion who was staying away from Walter. Their exchanges were laced with philosophical discussions, including debates about freedom and relationships and what it meant in terms of their various philosophies. It was a complex, high-level debate between two very intelligent people, with nuances only they could really understand. Their differences may have been painted in philosophical terms, but the powerful emotions between the couple were still there.

In one letter, Marion wrote to Walter about Steiner's *Threshold of the Spiritual World*. "In love, when one really loves a person, there exists in the depths of his being a terrible antipathy to that person. The antipathy is there if the love is real love."[4]

And later:

> Anything that can be proved can be disproved. The only basis for knowledge is perception, checkable perception. Not till that battle had been fought out to the finish was it possible to realize that the close companionship of marriage is the best training for that demon—the Ego—which presently finds it cannot continue to endure submission to any of the external worlds.[5]

In a letter to Edith Williams, she described her frustration with Walter in terms of Steiner's argument about the importance of anger.

> Steiner says without the molding force of anger through which the Ego becomes richer and richer, the Ego reaches a point where it begins to weaken and disintegrate and that is the point where I think Walter stands. ... I think Walter lacks the capacity for anger.[6]

In 1931, Walter joined the Anthroposophical Society in Sydney. It was most likely to pave the way for a possible reconciliation with Marion, but still the couple remained apart. Meanwhile, Walter's business designing incinerators had been growing, providing a much-needed source of income when the residential housing business had all but dried up. Around 1931, Walter and his partners in the incinerator company were tendering to build an incinerator at Sydney's Moore Park. Kanevsky moved from Melbourne to Sydney to better manage the business. By this time, the Fishwick family had moved back overseas again, so Kanevsky and his wife moved into their house, enjoying the best Griffin-designed house on the estate with wonderful views.

Kanevsky loved the house and the community the Griffins had built. Maybe he also found Walter a little lost and sad. Walter's creativity and his unusual, striking designs were critical to the success of their incinerator business. In 1932, Kanevsky paid for Walter and John Boadle to travel to the United States and Canada to research the latest practice in municipal incinerators. The trip would include a visit to Chicago. Was the wily Kanevsky trying to reunite Walter with his wife? It appeared that Walter made up his mind suddenly to make the trip, setting off with only a few days' notice to his colleagues on a Saturday in July.

The year before, Eric Nicholls and his wife, Mollie, had also moved from Melbourne to Sydney. They moved into the Moon House, a few doors down from the Griffins' house, which was vacant after Edith Williams and her husband had moved out. Nicholls would help oversee the business while Walter was away.

Walter's visit to America brought him to Chicago where he saw Marion for the first time in almost two years. But it seems that by the time he arrived, Marion had already decided she would move back to Australia.

Now, after almost two years apart, she wrote to him:

> Your truly human letter speaking to me as a fellow human being crossed mine telling you I was coming home. You wrote to me that you hated my letters and I wrote to you that I hated yours.[7]

Marion acknowledged that, by her actions, Walter would have been entitled not to take her back.

> I jolly well would have deserved a cessation of communication on your part and you would equally have deserved finding me back on your hands unrepentant.[8]

She added as a light-hearted aside, replying to a point in one of his earlier letters:

> Thanks for the distinction on freedom. It is a comfort to know, from words out of your own mouth, that you do not think that Steiner upholds Nietzsche's concept that freedom consists in not doing what your wife wants you to.[9]

In September 1932, the Griffins sailed back to Australia together. In her version of the story, she had signaled her reconciliation with the simple comment, "Well, Walter Burley, that's that."

When she got back home, Marion would find much had changed about Sydney. The much-discussed Harbour Bridge had opened earlier that year, linking the north and the south sides of the city. While it made travel to Castlecrag from the city a lot quicker, Marion hated it. She thought it was ugly and that it would be an obvious target of any military attack on the city. She felt a tunnel under the harbor would have been a much better solution.

Australia was now in the grip of a severe depression with almost a third of the working-age population without a job. Desperate families would line up for the dole. Homeless men would sleep in parks, some would find their way to the outreaches of the promontory where they lived. The radical and outspoken New South Wales Labor Premier Jack Lang, who had been elected just before Marion left Australia, had tried to alleviate the state's budget problems by suspending the repayments to bondholders in Britain. But, in a controversial move, he was dismissed from his position by the state governor. It was a time of great social unrest.

There was a collective sigh of relief at Castlecrag when Marion finally returned. She came back with gifts for many of her friends. Six-year-old

Wanda Herbert wrote a poem celebrating her return. The gnomes, she wrote, had told the fairies that Marion was coming home and they all danced, hand-in-hand. Wanda remembered the feeling of happiness on her arrival.

> During Mrs. G.'s absence everyone had tried to keep things going normally. Now it seemed as if, having held their breath for twenty-two long months, they all suddenly released it in one great shout of joy. ... Mrs. G. brought me three lovely frocks in heavy crepe, hand-ons from her family. Scarlet, turquoise and light-orange, they were gathered from a yoke and had short cape sleeves. I wore them to school, pleased that no one else had anything like them.[10]

Marion's arrival signaled a return of the fun at Castlecrag. The Griffins gave a party at their house, and soon after, there was also a Halloween party and then the Christmas nativity play. Walter threw himself into his work and designed a new incinerator for the local Willoughby Council.

But there were some changes afoot.

Section of *Fairies Feeding the Herons*. Mural by Marion Mahony at G.B. Armstrong School, Chicago. Photograph by Vin Plant. 2013.

Sections of mural *Fairies Feeding the Herons*. G.B. Armstrong School, Chicago. Photographs by Vin Plant. 2013.

Thirty-eight

A New Life

Marion found the Depression was taking its toll on their little community. There were no new houses being built on the estate. The incinerator company work was bringing in some income but financial pressures weighed on everyone.

A salesman for the estate had commissioned a house from Walter in a tucked-away corner down the hill called The Barbette. It was a long rectangular building with an octagonal sitting room at one end and a fireplace and an alcove for a piano, and it became known as the Long Griffin. But the man could not keep up the repayments and he and his family had to move out.

Edgar and Ula Maddocks, who had been living in other homes at Castlecrag for a time, moved into the house. Ula was a great enthusiast for what the Griffins were trying to do, and the octagonal room with its space for a piano was ideal for Edgar, a music teacher who gave piano lessons to the local children. Ula was a warm, outgoing, sociable person but Edgar was shy and avoided people where he could. They were both committed Theosophists, but their marriage had its problems.

Now in her late 30s, Ula was desperate to have a child. She and Edgar had been married for many years and had not been able to have children. Ula had a very good friend, a fellow Theosophist called Ronald Craig. He had been to India for a Theosophist conference at its headquarters in Adyar (possibly on a trip with Ula herself) and met a lovely young Indian girl from Madras. The couple fell in love and wanted to marry. But her father insisted that she finish her university studies before he would sanction the marriage. Craig returned to Sydney and waited for his girlfriend to complete her degree. He planned to go back to India in the middle of 1933 to marry her and settle down there. Sometime in May 1933, just before Craig left for India, Ula and Ron Craig conceived a child. To the outside world, it appeared as if Edgar was the father. With Craig out of the country, far away in India, it was all so much easier. Edgar knew the child was not his, but he was happy to finally be a father.

In February 1934, Ula had a baby girl called Deirdre. Ula was delighted and asked Walter to be Deirdre's godfather. The Griffins knew the real situation about Deirdre's parentage and took an extra interest in Castlecrag's newest baby. Ula was delighted to be a mother at long last, but there were many reasons to keep the truth about her relationship with Ron Craig a secret.[1]

Ula was a serious admirer of Walter. Asking Walter to be Deirdre's godfather was a sign of her devotion to him, and it may have been an extra insurance policy for Ula to have a man of importance nearby, to help look out for her young daughter. Walter was pictured proudly holding baby Deirdre in his arms. Ula became closer to Walter and Marion.

The close-knit world of Castlecrag began to chatter. The word had gone around that Edgar and Ula had been unable to have children. And they knew that Marion had been terribly hurt four years before, when Walter had had some sort of a relationship with another woman, a situation so serious that she had left him for two years. As Ula became increasingly close to both of the Griffins, and Walter took a fond interest in his goddaughter, tongues began to wag. There were those who wondered if Walter was too close with Ula. Some speculated that it was Ula who he may have had the relationship with back in 1930.

But Marion was not worried. She knew the truth. She was fond of Ula and wanted to help her. But, for the sake of both the Maddocks and the Craigs and for baby Deirdre, the Griffins knew they had to keep the secret of her real father. If people on The Crag were not bold enough to ask Marion about rumors that she was part American Indian, they were certainly not going to confront her with the more sensitive issue of Walter's relationship with Ula. Marion had not worried when two young women, Louise and Cappy, had lived with her and Walter for a time, so the idea of another younger woman moving closer into the

Griffins family life was not unusual for them. Marion herself had been close to both Wright and Kitty for many years. Marion had clearly been upset by Walter's relationship in 1930, but she regarded Ula as a close and trusted friend.

The house where the Maddocks were living in The Barbette had been taken back by the company after the original family left. In December 1934, it passed into Ula's name. It was another sign that Ula regarded herself as a woman independent of her husband. Young Deirdre became one of Marion's "babies," as she called the children of Castlecrag. Just as the good fairies in Marion's mural on the wall at the school in Chicago were helping a mother and father heron feed their babies, so Marion kept a motherly eye on Deirdre and the other young children in their little community.

Walter was known for spending time down at The Barbette. Marion's favorite way of calling for Walter, when he was far away on the estate, was to shout out the Australian bush call "Coo-ee"—one long "Coo" followed by a short, sharp "ee"—which could be heard from a long way away. But residents recalled that many times Walter would continue working on whatever project he was doing, pretending he didn't hear her call.

When Marion returned, some noticed that there were still some strains in the Griffins' relationship. Young Wanda Herbert noticed that Marion now had gray streaks in her hair and that her relationship with Walter had changed. As she wrote:

> The process of re-adjusting to the community, knowing that everyone was aware of earlier events, would have been difficult for anyone. It was probably even harder for Marion, given the pride she felt in being this particular man's wife and the special nature of their partnership.[2]

Sometime after her return, Marion had told Wanda's mother Grace that, "Walter's affair had broken her heart."[3] When it was over, and she and Walter were back together again, everything seemed to be all right, but things were not quite the same.

Marion threw herself into life at Castlecrag with a renewed passion, particularly the plays and community activities and her involvement in

Anthroposophy. She began Saturday morning art lessons for the local children at her house, just as her mother Clara had done when Marion was young. She also became close with Lute Drummond, an admirer of Rudolf Steiner's teachings.

Drummond was passionate about opera and had lived in Europe for a while. She heard Steiner lecture and visited the headquarters of the Anthroposophical Society in Switzerland. When she came home, she became one of the founding members of the society in Australia. Marion and Drummond became fast friends and decided to hold Anthroposophical festivals and discussion groups at Castlecrag. Marion also decided to learn German to further her knowledge of Steiner's teachings and took lessons from a woman living in Castlecrag, picking up the language very quickly.

There had been talk for some time of having a theater at Castlecrag. There had been many plays and musical events in the community, but on Marion's return, she wanted to have some grander productions. Walter decided that they would build the theater they had been talking about for so long. They found a spot for it, a triangular area at the fork of two roads, down in a gully in the Haven Estate, the estate which had been bought with the inheritance that Marion had received from her mother. Members of the community helped build it. As Marion recalled later, "The Valley was astir for weeks with Castlecrag 'Bees'."[4] They built rows of seats out of stone into the side of the gully to face the theater on the other side. "Walter pitched in, working as hard as everyone else, enjoying the break from the drawing board." But the work was made the more difficult because of Walter's insistence that it be done by preserving as many of the existing trees and plants as possible. Finished in 1934, the Haven Theatre became the scene for some of Marion's greatest theatrical productions.

With the Haven Theatre at their disposal, Marion and Lute Drummond took the plays at Castlecrag to a new level. They were grand, well-organized events. There would be rehearsals at Lute's flat in the city and on the weekends in the theater itself. Marion worked her creative magic on some elaborate costumes. The festivals became famous and people would come from miles around to see them. They started with *The Sacred Drama of Eleusis* in September 1934, followed by *The Sakuntala* in April 1935, and *Iphigenia in Tauris* in June 1935.[5]

The theater was lit by lanterns as well as the lights from cars shining onto the stage. There was a job for everyone who wanted to be involved, from acting to making costumes to doing the sets and selling the tickets. Ida Leeson and Florence Birch had moved out of Castlecrag after Leeson was appointed to run the Mitchell Library, the first woman ever to do so, as they needed to be closer to the city. But the couple returned to Castlecrag often and helped out with the plays.

Marion was in charge of the productions. A reporter from *The Sydney Morning Herald* described attending a performance of *Antigone* in the theater:

> The choruses took up their groupings among the bush and greenery with complete confidence. At times the effect of all the illuminated figures in the eloquent poses was dream-like and almost incredible, like that of a highly imaginative painting. ... The acoustics of the dell were remarkably good.[6]

Having agreed to join the Anthroposophical Society, Walter would attend local discussion groups about Anthroposophy held in various homes on the estate. But he never seemed to be an enthusiastic participant. One photo shows him at a meeting in a Castlecrag house, leaning against the back of the wall, his arms crossed, looking decidedly bored. Marion is next to him, looking at him, in her usual photographic pose, her face side-on to the camera.

But Walter had more serious problems. One night, around 1934, there was a small fire on the estate. Walter was trying put it out when he stepped out into the darkness and fell over a precipice. He landed on a rock on his side, his full weight on his ribs. He was in excruciating agony and had continuing pains in his stomach. The doctors did test after test but were unable to diagnose any problem. Walter soldiered on.

Walter Burley Griffin with Ula and Deirdre Maddocks in the garden at Castlecrag. 1935. Eric Nicholls collection. National Library of Australia.

Thirty-nine

An Invitation from India

While Marion was involved in her plays, Walter found it difficult getting new business. The tough economic times were biting and their finances became tight. The optimism which had prevailed in 1929, when Walter was building the Fishwick House, was long gone. The Griffins had been able to expand their community by buying the Haven Estate, but it also meant that the company was liable to pay extra council rates. The local council steadfastly refused his pleas not to be charged levies on the undeveloped land along the water.

In 1934, Walter built his first house in the estate in some years, down in The Barbette for Frank and Anice Duncan. The Duncans were members of the Sydney Bushwalking Club and became friends of the Griffins who also loved bushwalking. The Duncans were able to get the house built after receiving money from Frank's father.

The Duncans' small house was built with Walter's Knitlock bricks with corners of stone. It was set in the bushland and, like most of the other Griffin houses, it had French doors opening out onto the garden. Wanda loved the house, describing it as "the tiniest dwelling imaginable, pocket-sized to match their means."[1]

But, fortunately, the incinerator business was still producing work. Walter had returned home invigorated by his trip to America. He began designing a new incinerator for Willoughby Council, not far from Castlecrag, which opened in 1934. Many saw it as one of his finest designs for such a project. It was built into the side of a steep valley. Each incinerator was built on a similar principle but was designed specifically for its site. With the Willoughby incinerator, a horse-drawn cart and later a motor lorry would bring in the garbage at the top level. It would tumble down to a lower level where it was burned, and then the ashes would tumble down to another lower level. The ashes were taken away from the back of the incinerator at the bottom. The building was made of local sandstone, and the roof of its entrance was a wide inverted V with crystalline motifs on either side. The exotic design was continued in the tall chimney and along the sides of the building as it came down the side of the hill. One commentator described the building as "cascading down the cliff face like a frozen waterfall of crystalline shapes."[2]

Walter was also working on a project for a much larger incinerator, in an industrial suburb on Sydney Harbour called Pyrmont. It was to be Walter's largest incinerator, and he wanted to make it a work of art. He designed it with a giant chimney in the middle with Aztec motifs down the side. Marion was excited about the structure. She described it as "beautiful, majestic, as unique as any of the historical records of the past" and predicted that it would "stand as an historical record of 20th century architecture."[3]

She took Lute Drummond to see it when it was done. Marion and Drummond were both in agreement about the presence of fairies and other forces in nature. "We both saw angel forces playing around it as if it was a living thing," Marion recalled later.[4]

Meanwhile, Ula was receiving regular letters from Ron Craig in India. She told him her worries about the difficult economic times facing the community at Castlecrag. Craig knew how much Ula admired Walter's architectural talents. He worked as a journalist on the local English language newspaper in Lucknow, a city in northeast India, but he kept an eye out for potential business propositions.

When he arrived in Lucknow, Craig found a much more vibrant atmosphere than the depressed economy he had left in Australia. It was a city with a rich history, which had once been a regional capital in the past under its rulers, the Nawabs. There was a lot of new building going on. A decade before, the city had been chosen by the British as the capital city of the state, the United Provinces of Agra and Oudh. The elite of Lucknow were Muslim landowners. At a time when there was increasing talk of Indians wanting independence from Britain, the landowners of Lucknow were a lot more favorable to English colonial rule than many Hindus in other parts of the province. The original capital of the state under British rule had been the city of Allahabad, 140 miles away from Lucknow. But radical Hindu forces there were agitating against the British colonial rule and in 1921, the provincial governor, Sir Harcourt Butler, decided to transfer the capital to Lucknow. A new building for the legislative council was opened in the city in 1928 and the shift of the political capital brought a new prosperity to the city.[5]

Craig knew a local builder called Alagappan Mudalir and told him about his connection with Walter, the world-famous American architect who had designed the Australian capital. Alagappan was talking to the trustees of the University of Lucknow who wanted to build a new library. He needed a good design to attract their attention and contacted Walter in Sydney to ask for his help. Marion was proud of the plan Walter had drawn up for the library which, she reported to her friends, "looks and feels quite Indian and yet is the last word in modernism."[6]

In September 1935, Alagappan sent a telegram to Walter.

> Plans accepted. Come by first boat.[7]

Alagappan wanted Walter to come to India to talk to the university about the new library. Walter debated whether he should accept the invitation but Marion urged him to go. He would only be away for three months, and she felt he could do with a break. She was worried that Walter was working too hard. She believed it was time for her husband to take a vacation.

Marion also felt the trip would also be interesting "anthroposophically." Rudolf Steiner argued that the East, especially India, and the West "should come together on terms of mutual understanding and sympathy." And so it was decided that after the big community production of the classical Greek play *Prometheus Bound*, Walter would go to India.

When the play was over, the focus was on Walter's departure. Marion wanted to get him a copy of the *Bhagavad Gita*, the sacred Hindu scripture she had been studying. The text had provided inspiration to many Indians including political activist Mahatma Gandhi. It argued for the renunciation of desire and attachment to material possessions as the stepping stone to spiritual awakening. Marion was well-versed in its writings. There were several translations of the work, the best of which, she argued, was that of Dhan Gopal Mukerji, which had been published a few years before.

Walter became increasingly excited about the possibility of practicing architecture in a new country where his skills might actually be wanted. When someone asked him if he was going to follow Indian architecture, Marion was amused when he replied, "I am going to lead it."

Marion was proud that her husband had been invited to India:

> It is seldom that a European goes to India at the invitation of an Indian, not just as a social guest, but to assist in solving their present problems.[8]

Marion organized a big farewell celebration at Castlecrag. It was a curry party, complete with an actor dressed up as a snake charmer and his would-be snake, a vacuum cleaner. Walter gave Marion a blue Chinese rug with a dragon in the middle as a farewell gift.

One afternoon before he left, they decided to take some photos of Deirdre to show her father, Ron Craig. There were many different photos taken, including some of Walter, Ula and Deirdre, by then an 18-month-old toddler, in the garden. Some of the photos looked like the three of them were one happy family. Certainly Walter looked a lot happier in those photos than any of the ones which had been taken in recent years of him and Marion. In one photo, Walter is lying on a couch, Ula is standing behind him with Deirdre, trying to get her daughter to pull his hair. Walter is grinning happily. Marion herself may have taken the photos in their garden.[9]

By this time, Marion had a tragic secret she was keeping from Walter. She was keeping up a brave face during his final days at home. She had heard news of the sudden death of her dear friend Anna Wilmarth, the woman who had provided the money to allow Marion to pursue her dream of being an architect with a degree at MIT in Boston. Wilmarth had married the politically ambitious Harold Ickes in 1911, the same year the Griffins were married. Ickes became US Secretary of Interior in 1933 and was helping President Roosevelt implement his New Deal, a plan to help America out of the Depression. Anna had died in a car accident in New Mexico where she had been studying the culture of the Native Indians. Marion decided not to let the terrible news spoil her husband's farewell party.

Forty

A New Land

With Walter finally on the boat for India, Marion had time to think about life. She wrote to him on the ship, sending a copy of the *Bhagavad Gita* and telling him of Anna Ickes' death. Her belief in reincarnation gave her some consolation about the loss of her friend. Maybe, she wrote to Walter, there was some reason for Anna's early departure from this earth. Maybe she was destined to return to the earth in spirit at some point later on. She explained her feelings to Walter:

> Since we can no longer hold the completely unscientific concept of things happening by chance, I feel that perhaps it was more important that she should be back here toward the close of the century than that she should remain here now.[1]

Her belief gave her some comfort. A peace came over Marion and something had changed. "A great stillness seems to have fallen on Australia," she wrote in a letter to Walter. "I think I have won that thing called a quiet soul."

As usual, when they were apart, Marion and Walter furiously wrote letters to each other, detailing all the events in their separate lives. With Walter away, Marion looked after the estate. She saw that the branches of one of the gum trees were in danger of growing over the telephone wires, so she climbed the tree and cut down the branches. It reminded her of her old days at Hubbard Woods when she would climb the big tree next to the family house.

Walter's journey took him around the southern coast of Australia before heading north to the island of Ceylon and then to India. He wrote to Marion of his visit to Perth, telling her how he had walked through the wildflowers and met with a supporter who was arranging for him to meet up with the premier of Western Australia on his return journey. He signed the letter "your worser half." He also enclosed a copy of a letter written to Harold Ickes, sympathizing on the death of his wife. For two people who had gone through a lot in their marriage, it was an interesting reflection of Walter's true feelings for his wife:

> Only in thinking of what my own wife means to me, the Marion Mahony of whom Anna Wilmarth had been such a friend and benefactor, can I appreciate how tragic this loss is to you.[2]

With Walter away, Marion and Ula become even closer. They were excited that their menfolk were both going to meet up in India and kept up a busy correspondence with them. Ula would hurry up the hill from her home in The Barbette to the Griffins' home near Edinburgh Road, to drop off her letter to Walter or Craig so that it could be sent in the post with Marion's own letter to her husband.

Marion eagerly followed Walter's progress, letter by letter, as he told of his journey to a new world. Walter was excited by Ceylon, another British colony like Australia had been, which he felt was far better equipped with hospitals, schools, and other social services than Australia. He traveled by train into the hills to the ancient capital of Kandy. He admired the artificial lake which had been an outstanding feature of the old capital. Walter's attempts to have central water basins built in Canberra, as the centerpiece of the city, had been dismissed as being too grand and far too expensive for Australia, but here was the evidence before him of a royal capital highlighted by an artificial lake. The vision only served to reconfirm to him the correctness of his vision for Canberra, and the narrow-mindedness of Australian officials who could not, or would not, see what he was trying to do. The prospect of being given another chance in a new country was becoming even more exciting.

Meanwhile, Marion made a presentation to her Anthroposophical friends for the Michaelmas Festival. The Griffins had brought a copy of the Wasmuth portfolio of Wright's designs to Australia with them, and Marion used it to show some of the work she had done before she came to Australia. She also went to the movies and saw a film called *Escape Me Never*. Marion urged Walter to see it in India if he could. "It is the story of a genius and his gypsy wife!" she wrote, no doubt feeling some resonance with the Griffins' own relationship.

In his letters to Ula, Craig wrote how he had traveled to Bombay to meet Walter's ship. Waiting at the dock was an eager crowd of Indians excited to see the arrival of the Australian cricket team coming to the subcontinent to play, captained by veteran cricketer Jack Ryder.[3] Craig noted wryly that he was just there to meet a team of one—Walter. Walter and Craig walked the city together, talking day and night before beginning a journey across the country to Lucknow.

Marion eagerly kept up with the letters about their trip, happy about Walter's new enthusiasm for India. Craig was eager for his friend to see some of the great sights along the way. They stopped off at the city of Gwalior where they saw its vast Hindu fortress and palace on the hill. Then they were off to Agra to see the Taj Mahal, a grand building designed by a Muslim architect for his wife. Seeing it in the early morning, Walter marveled at its "sparkling crystalline Italian marble" and the "delicious graded shadows of its vast rounded concave and convex niches and domes," which, he told Marion, "present a perennially youthful spirit to the soul." As they traveled, Craig told Walter about the rising tide of nationalism in India.

The Congress Party was the focus of the political activism. It was founded in 1885 with the blessing of the British Viceroy at the time, to encourage an organization of the elite, educated Indians who could interact with their English rulers. But as the British administration continued to oppose independence, the party became more radical. The rising political leader was Gandhi, who had been trained as a lawyer in England and spent time in South Africa where he became an activist for the rights of Indians in the country.

Gandhi and his supporters developed a plan for Indian Home Rule. What started out as a peaceful protest movement became more militant as the British clung onto their last great colony. In Agra, Walter and Craig went to afternoon tea, at the home of one of the "patriots" who had spent 10 years in jail for his support of independence for India. Walter learned firsthand of the struggle of the Indian people against their British masters. As they approached New Delhi, Craig wondered what Walter would think of the Indian capital. Delhi's origins went back at least 3,000 years. After Britain's King George V was crowned as emperor of India, in December 1911, it was announced the capital would be moving from Calcutta to Delhi, which the British felt would be better located to administer the country. The Viceroy of India, the most senior British representative in the country, had watched the competition to design a new capital city in Australia which began in the same year. It was decided that a grand new section of Delhi, south of the old city, would be created to mark its new role as the capital.

In 1912, British architects Herbert Baker and Edwin Lutyens were appointed as joint architects of the new city, although Lutyens was the main architect. It was the same year that Walter's design for Canberra had been awarded "first premium." Over the next six winters, Lutyens traveled to Delhi, laying out the new capital. He was well-known as an architect in Britain and, unlike Walter in Australia, well-connected in society. His wife, Lady Emily Bulwar Lytton, was the daughter of the first Earl of Lytton, who had also been a Viceroy of India.

Lutyens' grand vision for Delhi was finally finished around 1929. In sharp contrast to the continual stinginess Walter faced in trying to develop Canberra, the British colonial rulers had spared no expense in building New Delhi, eager to reinforce the message that their rule was there to stay in India.

On arriving in the Indian capital, Walter realized that New Delhi was only the latest city to be imposed on the site. He told Marion that, "New Delhi is the newest of cities. New Delhi, which might better be called X Delhi for it is the 10th new capital city of India in this same locality in as many centuries—two Hindu, six Muslim, two British." He noted the Roman character of the buildings and "roadways with great lawn parkways and handsome avenues of trees of selected types of considerable variety, almost perfectly flat but planned with many monumental terminal vistas."[4]

Walter visited the centerpiece of the new capital, the massive Viceroy's Palace, on a hill. It had a large copper dome and extensive gardens and opened out onto a wide avenue, called the Kingsway. He was unimpressed with Lutyens' New Delhi. Despite the dome and Lutyens' attempts to incorporate some Mughal themes into the Viceroy's Palace, Walter felt the design was still largely a classical European concept. But he was enthusiastic about the ancient architecture of India. "The landscape is studded with domes of ancient temples and tombs among the terraces and castle walls, in all stages of decrepitude," he reported to Marion. He was intrigued by the fact that the city was "surrounded by the ruins of the previous capitals, which must have been more magnificent, and certainly more imaginative and romantic ... the more ancient, the more architecturally satisfying."[5]

Marion Mahony Griffin. Circa 1935. Eric Nicholls collection. National Library of Australia.

Play in Haven Amphitheatre. Castlecrag. Circa 1934. Eric Nicholls collection. National Library of Australia.

Forty-one

Lucknow

While Marion continued with her busy life at Castlecrag, Walter and Craig traveled by train to Lucknow, 300 miles southeast of Delhi, arriving on Monday morning, November 11, 1935. They were met at the station by an eager Mr. Alagappan. Soon after he arrived, Walter described his feelings in a letter to his wife. "I already feel more at home with these people than I was for many years in Australia."[1] The only thing he didn't like, he said, was the presence of British soldiers.

Lucknow, he was to learn, had its own rich history. During the 18th century, the Nawabs, or rulers of the province of Awadh, broke from the weakening Mughal Empire, centered in Delhi, and established Lucknow as their capital. They made their mark on the city with extravagant architectural gestures such as the Bara Imambara, the Chhota Imambara, and the Rumi Darwaza. In 1856 the British East India Company annexed the province. Indian anger at the move provoked a rebellion by the local troops in 1857, which came to be known as the Sepoy Rebellion. In Lucknow, the Europeans sheltered from the angry Indian troops inside an area called The Residency. The Siege of Lucknow went on for six months before British troops could relieve it, with more than 2,000 people inside The Residency dying of injuries and disease. The British reestablished their control by cutting down some sections of the city and replacing them with large wide roads and parks. Now its role was being further bolstered by its new role as the UP state capital, which was generating a wave of new buildings in the city.

Walter had arrived in another new capital city. He moved into a cottage near the train station and worked on the plans for the library.

There were no trams or buses in the city, so he arranged for a *tonga wallah* (a driver with a horse-drawn cart) to pick him up every morning and take him home at night. He worked in rooms at the university, which was north of the Gumti River. Walter walked around the city, absorbing its unique mixture of architecture. He described one view of the city, from a mosque, as a "perfect Arabian Nights' dream of white domes and minarets." He was one of only a handful of Westerners in the city. There were some British soldiers and some American missionaries. There was only one other practicing architect, a young Muslim who had a degree in town planning from Glasgow University.

Soon after he arrived, Walter was given a copy of a design for the university, which had been prepared by Edwin Lutyens in the early 1920s. Lutyens had been well paid for his design, but it had not gone ahead. Having already seen his handiwork in New Delhi, Walter was disdainful of Lutyens' plan and saw the English architect as part of the British colonial establishment. The apparently precious design, he said scornfully, could have been produced in two-and-a-half days in his office in Sydney. He pointed out that Lutyens had only been in Lucknow during the cool weather, so his designs had no shades for the sun, and he had not taken into account the regular flooding of the Gumti River.

Marion kept up her work at Castlecrag. She planted a cyprus tree in the front of the shop and received a visit from Henry Pynor and his wife and daughter. Pynor was the young architect who had worked for the Griffins in Melbourne and oversaw the construction of the Cooley House in Louisiana. Before Walter left, there had been some speculation of a recovery in the local economy in New South Wales, but Marion reported that this had petered out. Marion and Ula both eagerly read their letters from India and tried to imagine the exotic journeys being taken by their menfolk. But there was great sadness. One of the Castlecrag children, six-year-old Charles Morton, died from a ruptured bowel. One night soon after, Marion had a terrible dream about dark forces gathering around the world.

> I saw a great burden of blackness fall on a group of human beings and they went down under it like ninepins. And then a cry went up over the

death of children as if that was more than could be endured, perhaps the heaviest burden one could have to bear.²

Marion wondered if she was seeing into the future. Her prediction was uncanny. It was a few years before a second world war would break out with its horrific consequences. Dark forces were indeed gathering in the world.

Soon after he arrived in Lucknow, Walter was treated to a view of British colonialism at its highest level. The city prepared itself for the official visit of the Viceroy, an event that took place only once every five years. The term of the current Viceroy, Lord Willingdon, was set to finish in April the next year, and he was making one last trip to the city. Walter was no fan of British colonialism, and the visit only served to reinforce his anger about the injustices of the system. He noted the "thousands of pounds invested in temporary street arches and illuminations by the politicians and the Raja landlords," while the average yearly wage of an ordinary Indian was only one pound sterling. When the Viceroy arrived, there was a "lavish display of decorations, illuminations and fireworks on the part of the subsidiary rulers" but, he noted, "no cheering on the part of the populace."³

Walter had a meeting with the committee set up by the university to oversee the establishment of a new library. It was chaired by Professor of Physics, Dr. Wali Mohammad, who described himself as the "honorary librarian." Walter's plans for the library were unanimously adopted. But the work on the library was frustratingly slow, with Dr. Wali insisting on approving every detail of the project.

The arrival of such a prestigious international architect attracted much attention by others in the city. Soon, Walter was being approached by leading members of the university and other important people to consult on their own houses and other buildings. His reputation spread beyond the city. The treasurer of Benares University approached him about designing some low-cost housing on its campus, 170 miles southeast of Lucknow.

Walter was so taken by his new life that he wondered if he might not have been an Indian in an earlier life. Writing home to Marion, his thoughts went back to Louis Sullivan, the architect who had inspired him so many years ago.

> As to my next incarnation, I cannot think of anything better in this poor old world, than the job I am now on. Louis Sullivan found his stimulus in Saracenic architecture and may have reincarnated from a Moorish experience to give it adequate expressions. My physical appearance does not suggest much of the Indian, but I have a hunch that much of my architectural predilections must have come from Indian experience. This does not mean that the environment here provides satisfaction, so much as that it provides stimulus and motifs for satisfactory imagination.[4]

Ron Craig was delighted to become friends with the man both he and Ula regarded as a genius, and Walter was becoming fond of Craig's wife, Komalam, and their young son, Arjun. Walter and Craig talked about renting houses near each other, somewhere close to the university. With few Westerners in the city, and fewer with Indian wives, Craig relished having someone from Australia who knew his complex family situation. And it did him no harm, either, that his famous friend was also fast becoming an attraction in the city.

Craig continued to try to find more work for Walter. He arranged for him to see the editor of the *Pioneer Press*, Desmond Young, about designing a new building for the newspaper in Lucknow. It was now two and a half years since Young had moved the paper from the former capital of Allahabad into temporary premises in Lucknow. Now Young and the paper's owners wanted to have a building of their own. It was a project which would be worth as much as the Lucknow University library. Walter and Craig were invited to Young's house for a Sunday lunch.

Craig was unable to make it, but Walter went along and he and Young got on famously. The newspaper editor lived in a large rambling house with servants in a military area called the Cantonment. The two had a leisurely lunch together. There was other potential work. Mr. Alagappan talked to Walter about seeing some potential clients in Calcutta on his way home to Australia. Walter began thinking of setting up a permanent office in Lucknow. He wrote to Marion about "the possibility of creating a demand for our work if we were to establish a permanent office of European character for an Indian clientele." But, he added, "That would mean living here on the part of one or other of us."[5] He continued to explore the city, riding a bicycle through the narrow lanes of the old town. He was fascinated by its diverse architecture and its rich history, reporting it all in detail in his letters to Marion.

At Castlecrag, Marion and Ula were busy with their plans for Christmas. But it was overshadowed by some terrible news. Marion's concerns about dark forces gathering were right. On December 17, Ron Craig's mother, who lived in Sydney, received a cable telling her that her son had died.

Walter filled in the details with letters to both Marion and Ula. Days after his pleasant Sunday lunch with Young, he heard that Craig was seriously ill. He had been taken to the King George hospital with an inflammation of the liver and gall bladder. Visiting him in hospital, Walter was shocked to see Craig's red face and bloodshot eyes. He watched as his friend moved in and out of consciousness, his pain eased only by morphine injections. Later on, Walter had received a call from Mr. Alagappan. Ron Craig had died. The Indian contractor had visited Craig in the hospital to find him delirious and apparently blinded. He cried out for someone to turn on the lights so he could see his son, despite the fact that there were two glaring lights over his bed. A few days later, Walter and Craig's grieving widow and others were burying him at the Christian Cemetery not far from the university. Walter saw the devastated woman and her son off on the train home to her family in Madras. Walter's letter to Ula extended his sympathies "for your loss of a far longer standing friendship." His letter to Marion followed up on her own fears of dark forces gathering in the world.

> Three deaths in only a few months. First Anna Ickes, then Charles Morton and now Ronald Craig. What a harvest this great reaper is gathering from the fields we are in. There must be something stirring on the other side just now and these fields are productive. The death of Ronald Craig cuts to the quick.[6]

Marion, too, was devastated at the news of Craig's death. Writing to Walter on Christmas Eve she said, "What shocking, dreadful word has come to us from India, the death of Ronald Craig. Truly December was in our circle, the terrible month the astrologers have been telling us it would be."[7]

She also expressed her support of Walter's suggestion of setting up a more permanent practice in India. "As to your suggestion ... of the possibility of establishing a permanent office in India, my advice would be to do it if there was a straw of a possibility of a practice there."[8] But she had no intention of going there herself. Furthermore, if Walter did set up an office there, she was quite content that he spend most of his life there, only occasionally returning to her in Australia. "You could be back here for a month or two each year, and I am satisfied to remain here if it is necessary," she wrote, adding, "This would remain your residence."

Writing on Christmas Eve, Marion was clearly not missing her husband. Or, if she was, she was not going to show it. There was another play to be staged and lectures on Anthroposophy to attend. And Walter's father George was arriving for another visit which had been planned before Walter's trip to India.

Walter found his new relationship with Desmond Young a very useful one. The two were some of the few forward thinking Westerners in the city. Young put Walter in touch with the chairman of the *Pioneer Press* board, the Maharajah of Jahangirabad, one of the most powerful and well-connected local landowners in the region. A Sunni Muslim, he was president of the British India Association and a prominent member of the Agriculturalist Party, a moderate party that represented local landlords.[9] He invited Walter to visit his home in Jahangirabad, 30 miles north of Lucknow. He wanted him to design a house, called a *zenana*, for the women of the family. The Raja arranged to send a car to drive Walter and Mr. Alagappan to his home to discuss the project. Walter enjoyed being transported to another world. "We enjoyed a sumptuous afternoon tea with our host and his retinue of courtiers and assistants," he reported to Marion.[10] Of course, there were no women present. They lived behind closed doors in courts such as the *zenana*, which Walter was being commissioned to design.

The Raja, as Walter quickly saw, had the potential to be a very attractive client. As he reported back to Marion, "As with the Moguls themselves, the chief sport of this landlord is pulling down, rebuilding, and extending his palace buildings and gardens." The landscape architect was impressed by the Raja's extensive gardens. They were "long wide terraces with 60 acres intensively developed and cared for, including rosary, orangery, rockery, sunken garden, fern house, lake, and broad lawns punctuated and surrounded with groups and groves of trees and numerous flower borders."[11]

As he gazed over the garden, Walter, the man who had always wanted to be a landscape architect, was very happy. There was simply no comparison to make with his prospects in Australia, a country gripped by an economic Depression, where his main business was designing incinerators for municipal councils. Walter sketched his plans for the Raja's *zenana*. When he saw the drawings, the young Raja was delighted.

"How beautiful," he said. "This is something entirely new." The Raja turned to Mr. Alagappan and asked, "Can you build it?" Mr. Alagappan said he could, and Walter had his first new commission in India.

Walter spent time in Jahangirabad, advising the Raja on extensions to his palace. The Raja praised Walter to Mr. Alagappan, who was only too happy to pass on the compliment. Walter reported excitedly to his wife, "What I say goes with him, and I am his white-haired boy up to the present."[12]

The Raja was well-respected and influential. A good word from him, Young advised Walter, would carry a lot of weight in getting business with other clients. And so it did. The Raja put him in contact with his younger friend, the second largest landlord in the region, the young 22-year-old Raja of Mahmudabad. The young Raja's father had died a few years before, leaving his son in charge of one of the richest estates in the region. The Raja had been partly educated in England and was a passionate book collector. He wanted to build a library for his collection and was willing to spend a large sum of money on the project. Walter and the young Raja became fast friends. "Libraries are my particular speciality now," an excited Walter proudly wrote back to his wife.[13]

Meanwhile, back at Castlecrag, Walter's father George had arrived. His son was not there but Griffin senior was happy to escape the cold

Chicago winter and to rejoin the relaxed community in Australia that his son and his wife had established. When Ron Craig died, Ula offered to host Craig's widow, Komalam, and her son, Arjun, at her home at Castlecrag so the Indian woman could further her studies at the University of Sydney. Ula had wanted a second child, but clearly her relationship with her husband Edgar, by now very much on a "just good friends" basis, was not going to produce one. Looking after Deirdre's half-brother would at least give Ula another child to care for. George Griffin appeared to understand Ula's special situation—the fact that her daughter was not her husband's—and made a wry joke with her about it.

As Ula wrote to Walter with some amusement:

> Mrs. Griffin told him about my wanting the Craig boy. His comment wittingly and flatteringly suggested that there were other ways of solving the problem of an only child than bringing up another woman's.[14]

Marion, Ula, and George Griffin discussed the absent Walter. Had Walter stayed in America, his father said, he would have been "the first architect" in New York. Marion chimed in. "As he is the first architect in the world," she added. After 25 years of marriage, she was still full of admiration for her husband, but she had no intention of interrupting her busy life at Castlecrag to be with him.

By early 1936, Walter became increasingly frustrated at the lack of decision-making on the library project for the university. He found Dr. Wali a "pest" for his procrastination and was annoyed to find that work on the building was put on hold as Wali was to go to Europe for three months over the summer. But, as happened with his work on Canberra, which had drawn him to Australia more than 20 years before, once Walter arrived in the new country, his presence generated other work.

Walter wanted Marion to join him in India. He had lost a dear friend with the death of Ron Craig, and he could also do with some help at the drafting board. The presence in the town of a famous international architect attracted increasing attention, and he was now being approached for more interesting private commissions. Had Marion been with him on the trip, he wrote, "there would have been no escape for you from going back to drafting." Here, finally, was a chance for Walter to fulfill his dream of creating a new architecture in a new country trying to emerge from the shackles of its British masters.

Desmond Young introduced Walter to political leaders in the province who planned an exposition in Lucknow in December. It was to be an agricultural and industrial exhibition on a 60-acre site on the banks of the Gumti River. They were looking for someone to lay out the grounds and design the main buildings. It would be a more modest affair than Daniel Burnham's 1893 White City in Chicago, but it would be an important showcase for Lucknow. The city fathers were eager to see it go well. Walter was keen to be involved in the project, but he knew it would be a challenge with no architectural staff of his own in the city.

With the prospect of getting work on the industrial exposition, Walter stepped up his requests for Marion to join him in India. But she kept suggesting that other people should go there. His Sydney partner, Eric Nicholls, did not want to go. In March, Walter wrote to Marion that he was "going like a scalded cat" with work.

Marion wrote back, saying she was "so pleased" that Walter wanted her to come over, but she said it would be better that Colin Day, a young man in Griffin's office in Sydney, should come to help him. Of course, she added, "someday I would love to come over" before continuing on with her latest reports about the gatherings at Castlecrag. She was busy with her art classes for the local children, going to lectures on Anthroposophy, and planning for a production of the medieval morality play, *Everyman*, in the Haven Theatre.

Marion's reluctance to join her husband in India was observed with consternation by some of the Castlecrag residents. As Wanda noted:

> When Mr. Griffin wrote in 1936 requesting that Marion join him, we all wondered why she did not simply pack up and go. Once, she would not have hesitated. Was she really so deeply involved with anthroposophy, the theater, her children's groups and her friends? Yes, apparently. But how had that come about? It would seem that the temporary rift between them had widened her own space, extending her territory. She had been forced to look at Walter and herself as independent beings. He had asserted his claim to a separate identity, with needs of his own. She

had to see herself as a separate person, no matter how much she loved him. She could no longer be taken for granted. She could not rush to his assistance without weighing the cost to herself. It was as if she was saying: "I, too, am." She had been hurt.[15]

Desmond Young was planning to go home to Britain over the summer months as his wife was not well. He offered Walter the use of his house for the six months they were away. Walter jumped at the offer of living in their rambling home, particularly since he had been invited to draw up the plans for the industrial Exposition, but he was growing increasingly concerned at the workload it would involve.

After the successful staging of *Everyman* in April, Marion had time to think about her future. Finally, she was unable to resist her husband and maybe her own desire to be with him again in another new adventure. She wrote to Walter that she would come to India and booked a passage on a ship to Calcutta. But the mails between India and Australia were painfully slow. Marion hoped she was doing the right thing and was eager for some response from Walter before she boarded the ship. Did he still want her to come? Why didn't he send a cable in response to her letter? The day before she was to leave, Marion had not heard back from her husband, so she wrote him another letter. She had no idea if he had received her last letter telling him she would be coming, and was hoping, by the time she arrived in Calcutta, she would get some word from him.

Having made her decision, Marion was excited about going to India. Walter had passed on Desmond Young's concerns about subjecting his wife to the heat of a Lucknow summer if she were to come to India. But now she had decided to go, Marion hastened to assure him that she would not be worried about the heat. "The hot summer means nothing to me," she wrote.[16]

As the departure date approached, Marion was in a rush to get everything done. She put her last letter to Walter in the mail. An hour later, a cable arrived from her husband. She opened it up, wondering about her husband's reaction.

It contained one word only. "Thankful."[17]

The two lovers were about to be reunited again.

Forty-Two

Like an Indian, Mrs. Griffin Follows Her Man

The last days before she left for India were a blur of excitement for Marion. Ula gave Marion a tapestry bag to take with her. She even offered to lend Marion some of her summer clothes for the trip. And, to the surprise of them both, they fitted.

Marion arranged for Ula, Deirdre, and Edgar to move into the Griffins' home in The Parapet, and Eric Nicholls and his wife moved into Ula's house down in The Barbette. The rent would give Ula and her family some much needed income. Ula would take over Marion's role in selling, or trying to sell, land at Castlecrag. The day before Marion was due to leave, 20 women from a social club were coming for a visit to Castlecrag.

She often played host to visits from strangers eager to see their architectural and social experiment at Castlecrag, but this time she was too busy. Ula offered to look after them so Marion could pack. As she wrote to Walter, "We still have to thank the angels for Mrs. Maddocks."[1]

Finally, Marion was at the docks on Sydney Harbour ready to leave. She was traveling on the *SS Comorin*, owned by the Peninsular and Oriental Steam Navigation Company of London. It was a "jolly bunch," as Marion later described it, which came to the docks to see her off. There was Ula, Deirdre, and three other Castlecrag babies and others from their community. They gave her bunches of flowers and fruit and a toy koala, which Marion called a teddy bear. Ida Leeson gave her a letter of introduction as the head of the Mitchell Library, the state library of New South Wales. Walter was working on the design for the university library in Lucknow and another for a Maharajah. In a foreign country, one never knew when these letters might come in handy. Lute Drummond gave Marion an astronomy book so she could study the stars over the southern skies on the journey to India. Six years before, Marion had been on those same docks, boarding a ship for America to leave her husband. Now she traveled to India in much happier circumstances to meet him, headed for yet another adventure together in an unknown land. Marion hadn't expected the reporter to be on the docks. A photographer had taken her picture and the reporter had asked a few questions amid the chaos and the hugs and kisses of her farewells.

The next day's *Daily Telegraph* told the story:

> Mrs. Walter Burley Griffin, wife of the designer of the Federal Capital City ... is to join her husband at Calcutta, where he is engaged in designing and building Maharajah's palaces and libraries. ... Then followed orders for plans for a large picture theater at Lucknow, and a number of banks and other buildings. ... The Maharajah of a native province on the northwest frontier has ordered plans for a capital city prepared, and the work was entrusted to Mr. Griffin. The magnitude of this task is such that further assistance was needed, and Mrs. Griffin, who is also a fully qualified architect, decided to join her husband.[2]

Next to the story was a picture of Marion. Her hair, dark with lines of gray now showing, was tied back behind her head. She wore a high-necked dress. The black-and-white photo shows a woman in her 60s looking into the distance. She has clear, wise eyes, and her mouth is set with a certain determination. There is a lot on her mind. In her diary later she recalled this part of her life under the heading "Like an Indian, Mrs. Griffin Follows Her Man." Did she think, as she sailed away from Sydney, of the poem her father had written about the young Indian brave going off in search of the spirit of his own love?

When Marion was on her way, a relieved Walter wrote to Ula, telling her how much he was looking forward to his wife's arrival. "Another six months alone on my part would be too much," he wrote. "The two of us together will make it quite different."[3]

When Marion's boat finally docked in the crowded port of Calcutta in India, Walter was not there. A lesser woman might have been angry that, having come so far on her own to such a foreign country, her husband was not there to greet her. But Marion was no ordinary woman. Walter had gotten word to her that he was too busy to come, but she would be met by Mr. Alagappan. She would have to make the long train journey to Lucknow by herself.

Later that day, Mr. Alagappan put her in the Lucknow carriage of the East Indian Railroad. As she sat on the train, Marion took in her new surroundings. The trip took her through the great Ganges Delta, across an endless flatland of northern India. She looked around her, admiring the carefully made terraces "with little earth dykes everywhere." She was in awe of the painstaking care which had been taken to preserve the water and the earth itself. Just before nightfall, she saw pyramid shaped hills and mountains, rising out of the plain. The next morning, when she woke up, the train was making its way across the plains of the Gumti River. It was around noon when the train slowly pulled into Lucknow station.

Walter picked her up by car and took her to Desmond Young's house where he was now living. There were wild peacocks in the garden and monkeys living on the estate. The Youngs had already left for England, so the Griffins had the house to themselves.

An hour after she arrived at the house, Marion started working on the plans for the Exposition. At 6:00 a.m. the next morning, a draftsman arrived to help them. They had six months to get everything ready for the opening on December 5. Like the World's Columbian Fair in Chicago, it was expected to attract visitors from all over India, and it would be attended by the country's leader, in this case the Viceroy. The initial estimates were that there could be more than a hundred buildings on the site. There were plans for 1,000 booths in the show and already the organizers had received 5,000 applications. Marion was happy to be back at work. The old partnership of Griffin and Griffin was back in business. Marion set her sights high. "We are hopefully going on making the most beautiful exposition yet," she wrote.[4]

Walter had already set out his idea for the Exposition. He divided the site into different sections, focusing on agriculture, industry, and culture. Inspired by Daniel Burnham's White City, Walter decided that the buildings would be colored with tinted whitewash. The task ahead was to draw up detailed plans for each of the major buildings. As Marion recalled, it involved doing a:

> ... design a day to be turned out, sketches completed and rendered for exposition and publication to be sent all over India, and working drawings ... and endless details for the structures and forms all new, it was a task one wouldn't care to undertake more than once in a lifetime.[5]

The work took up two rooms of the Youngs' house. The government had given Walter 10 boys from the local technical school to help with the drafting. But they were very inexperienced and it fell to Marion to not only manage them but teach them how to do their work.

Years after stepping back from their combined architectural practice, Marion resumed her role as head of Walter's drafting team with gusto. The Youngs' house came with 12 servants including butlers, cooks, sweepers, a night watchman, and a laundryman. Instead of having to worry about the cooking, cleaning, and other household chores as she did at home, she was able to throw herself into her work.

She hovered over the young Indian boys like a teacher. As she recalled:

> These young fellows in their teens came into what might be called the kindergarten of architecture. None had ever used a T-square. I spent most of my time driving and scolding them. They called me "Mother" and I had a real affection for them.[6]

They were, she said, "beautiful physically, charming and appreciative in manner, earnest, devoted and hardworking and eager and enthusiastic at the opportunity."

In all, there would be some 60 major buildings in the Exposition. The Griffins painstakingly designed many of the buildings, including several rotundas, arcades, an art gallery, and a restaurant. There would be two striking structures for the fair—a 100-foot-high postal tower, which could be seen from all over the site, and an electric gate, which marked the entrance to the fair from the amusement park side. The pillars of the gate would be surrounded by bands of light, narrowing from the bottom to the top, each of different colors.

It was 25 years since Walter and Marion had worked together day and night to design the plans for Canberra in a cold winter in Chicago. Now Marion was throwing herself into a new challenge with her husband, thousands of miles away in India.

When Marion arrived at the end of May, the weather was hot and about to get even hotter. It was the time of year when the British expatriates and the other elite of India moved up into the hill stations or went "home" to England. But this did not worry Marion. One day, soon after she arrived, she put on a flame-colored sundress that Ula had given her. Walter was happy and described his wife as a "pretty goil."

Marion became as enchanted with the city as her husband. One evening, Walter took her out walking in the area near their house. "We went out into the brilliant moonlight and wandered across open fields and past low-lying, flat-roofed charming residences."[7] Walter had battled for years to get his designs for flat-roofed houses accepted in Australia. Here in Lucknow, almost all the roofs were flat. Marion joked that she felt like she might be walking through Castlecrag in 30 years' time. Or Castlecrag as Walter might have wanted it to be.

Walter knew exactly where he wanted to take his wife. Soon they came upon a stunning, large, rambling building by the river. It was *La Martiniere*. He told Marion its history. It was designed and built by a French Major General, Claude Martin, who had come to India as a penniless soldier in the late 1700s. He served in the French forces before joining the East India Company's army. He worked for the Nawab of Awadh, making a substantial fortune from his dual roles as a soldier and businessman. He built a palatial home for himself by the river, an odd mixture of designs with Gothic gargoyles and Corinthian columns. It reminded Walter of the grand French palaces of Versailles or Fontainebleau. Martin died in 1800, before it was finished, but left money and instructions in his will to make sure that it became a school. It was now an elite boys' school whose students had included Kim, the boy hero of Rudyard Kipling's story of the same name.

Marion was delighted to come upon such an intriguing architectural structure, almost hidden away from view. It was, she said:

> ... a palace for a king of kings, compared with which the palaces of Europe look like thirty cents. A magic scene, an astounding imaginative combination of the Grand Prix of the Beaux Arts and Italian splendor, an enormous building and fascinating from every angle.[8]

India was weaving its spell on her, too. Lucknow was a city of many surprises, its varied, exotic architecture reflecting its colorful history. Built by a foreigner, *La Martiniere*'s very existence only confirmed the opportunities for enterprising newcomers to the city.

Forty-three

The Exposition

All sorts of people began coming to the Youngs' house to see Walter. From 7:00 a.m. until 10:00 p.m., anyone was likely to drop in, as Walter's reputation in the town spread. But some also noticed the presence of his architect wife. One client pointed out, to Marion's great pride, that whenever he visited the house he always found her at the drafting board. Another client[1], Dr. Bhatia, owned land near the university. The doctor approached Walter to design a house for him, but Walter told him he was too busy working on the university library project. But the doctor was a man who was not used to being told no.

"Well," Dr. Bhatia told him firmly, "you'll just have to do it in your lunchtime."

With Marion by his side handling all the drafting work and managing the office as she had done in America and Australia, Walter could take on many more new projects. Marion and Walter lived in *The House and Studio of Two Architects*, something they had once dreamed of so many years before. Marion's old enthusiasm for work came flooding back again. She was freed up from the many distractions of life in Castlecrag and the demands of housework with so many servants at her disposal. Her husband needed her help, and she threw herself into the task again.

"We are convinced that the only way to conduct business in India is in your own home," she wrote to her friends in Castlecrag. "Any time of day or night is right for business. ... It is amazing what hours one can put in drafting without being worn out by it."[2]

And so Marion and Walter began one of the most intense periods of their professional lives. They knew it was a golden opportunity to finally get the recognition they felt Walter deserved for his work. As she had done in the past, Marion was more than happy for her husband to succeed and for her part to remain almost unnoticed. Maybe here was at last a chance to create a new architecture in a new land. There seemed to be endless opportunities opening up for them in this rich and complex country. With Marion at the drawing board, managing the office and home front, Walter was free to do what he did well—talk to prospective clients and come up with bold new plans for them. He was no longer dealing with cash-strapped Australians who could not get finance or battling with the local council or petty bureaucrats; he was dealing with Maharajahs with grand palaces and estates. The Griffins could achieve so much more when they worked together as a team. Walter needed Marion and she rose to the task, putting her magic in design and drawing to work, in what would become one of the most energetic, intense, and productive periods of their personal and professional lives.

Working on the Exposition had its dramas. It was a big project and the Griffins were determined to do it well, but things did not go smoothly. Designing the buildings was a plum job, and Walter's appointment generated some resentment. One person working on the project, Mr. Hussain, a Muslim who was half-Indian and half-Anglo-Saxon, wanted to push Walter aside and take over the job himself. Hussain began changing his designs, and Walter would have to see the committee overseeing the project to defend his ideas.

Walter compared his situation with the forces he had faced so many years ago in trying to establish Canberra.

> The story of Canberra and my efforts there, through local jealousy, has been repeated in miniature with this exposition. Again my coming into the undertaking has interfered with ambitions for a knighthood. For two months, the director was bamboozled into making four successive starts until he realized that the precious time was slipping away.[3]

But Walter had Marion, with her formidable drawing skills, on his side. As she had done with the drawings for Canberra, Marion was determined to produce elevations of her husband's plans that would impress the harshest of critics. They also produced drawings of Walter's designs to show future clients. As the exhibition buildings would be only temporary, it was important that Walter's works be recorded for their personal portfolio.

Walter's gratitude to his wife was evident in his letters home:

> Marion is back at the drawing board, effectively too, and apparently enjoying tossing off decorative panels of the elevations which have the effect of stopping argument. ... What I would have done without her at this juncture I don't know. ... Marion has been doing much brilliant work filling the breach with gay decorative sketches that overawed and conquered the enemy. For the time being, this fort is ours including the Exposition grounds.[4]

The diagrams had overtones of the cross-sectional drawings Marion had done of the plans for Canberra 25 years before. They were done on linen with a cream background. The buildings were drawn in black ink and highlighted by a band of burnished gold, which passed along behind the buildings. Marion highlighted the buildings with her dots and dashes of white paint that gave them a shimmering effect just as she had done with her drawings of the Australian capital.

Walter continued to express his admiration for his wife in his letters. In August, he wrote home:

> Marion is working like a slave and she is the only effective help I have had for this Exposition. We should be further ahead if we had not experimented with a dozen scratch draftsmen whom [Marion] spends much time in teaching and doing their work over again.[5]

Hussain's interventions increased until Walter threatened to resign from the project. The committee backed down, and he was given full control of the project, allowing the Griffins to continue with their work. His rival sidelined, Walter found himself up against another challenge—the weather. The Gumti River flooded regularly, but this year the monsoons came in July, a lot earlier than usual. The next month the Gumti was flooded again. Construction work on the low-lying areas of the fair was delayed and thousands of buildings in the city collapsed.

Walter was getting referrals for more business outside of Lucknow. He went to Agra for a meeting with a businessman to discuss the plans for a development of a subdivision near the city. Marion felt a twinge of jealousy that she would be staying at home to work on the drawings for the Exposition, knowing she was missing out on seeing the Taj Mahal. But there would, she thought, be plenty of time for that later.

Marion was delighted with her new living arrangements. She wrote to Molly Nicholls:

> You should see us at our meals being served by two butlers. At breakfast, for instance, the one brings in two plates and sets them before us, then stands at attention in the door of the butler's pantry while the other brings in two eggs on toast. No. 1 majestically pours lime juice in our two glasses or brings coffee, the other brings a tiny stand with two pieces of toast. No. 1 presently followed with melons or mangoes or such. ... How's that for a woman who has always refused to have a servant in the house?[6]

While they worked hard, Marion and Walter managed to escape the house for some fun. Going to the movies had always been one of their favorite forms of relaxation. One evening, when the river was in flood, Walter and Marion were walking into town to see a movie. They came to a point in the road that was covered by water. Marion had on some new cream shoes and did not want to get them wet. Walter decided he would carry his wife across the water on his back. But just then, they saw a footman who was running ahead of a grand carriage, checking to see if it was safe to pass through the water. Approaching them in the carriage was the Maharajah of Jahangirabad with a group of people including the state governor.

Walter insisted on waiting until the Raja, the state governor, and their party passed through the water. When they were out of sight, Marion jumped on Walter's back, her arms around his neck, and he carried her through the water, her cream shoes preserved. Safely across the water, they both laughed, wondering what the Raja and the governor would have made of the sight had they seen it. They could have been two young lovers, but they were a long-time married couple, who were rediscovering each other, back in love again, just having some fun.

In September, Walter went to Mahmudabad to visit the young Raja about his proposed library. The idealistic American, who so espoused democracy and democratic architecture, was finding it very easy to do business with the wealthiest of the locals. Walter was given one of the best bedrooms in the house with a view of the main driveway and the gardens. In the evening, the Raja broadcast Indian music to the village and Walter watched the scene from the balcony. The Raja showed Walter his collection of 100,000 books and his telescope. Walter looked into it and saw the rings of Saturn and the moons of Jupiter. Walter chose the site for the library and the best place for a mosque, which the Raja also wanted to build on the property. The Raja's two brothers also wanted Walter to build a swimming pool for them from the local ponds. The Raja also took him to a palace nearby in Belahara. It had been founded by one of his ancestors and was in need of repair. Maybe he could help with that.

Then Walter was taken on a hunt on the back of an elephant, their procession followed by four footmen and four horsemen. His host bagged a snake, a pigeon, and two other small birds while the peacocks kept out of range in the distance. Walter was offered lots of fine food by his hosts on the last evening but he did not feel too well. He thought he must have eaten too much rich Indian food.

Business was flooding in. There was the work on the bank building in Jhansi, a town southeast of Lucknow, while another Raja wanted help to develop some 10,000 acres of land at the foot of the Himalayas. There was more work to be had at the university including designing a garden for the library and the student union building. Walter and Marion were happier than they had been for many years.

"The fairies brought us here," Marion wrote to a friend.[7]

The months passed and the Youngs would soon be back in Lucknow. The Griffins needed to find a new place to live in a city filling up with people coming in ahead of the Exposition. Finally they found rooms in a new house in an area called Sultan Gang, opposite a grand mansion called Butler Palace built for the former governor, Sir Harcourt Butler. The Griffins' section had access to the roof terrace which had a view of the trees and the turrets of Butler Palace. Lucknow was being spruced up. The city was being given a whitewash ahead of the Exposition.

With Desmond Young back in town, Walter was eager to get going on the design of the *Pioneer Press* building. He designed a long building across the site and Marion did the drawings. On November 24, 1936, Walter and Marion celebrated Walter's 60th birthday by going to the movies.

But there was increasing tension as the Exposition was scheduled to open two weeks later on December 5. The floods had substantially delayed construction and there had not been enough money to erect all the grand buildings that the Griffins had designed.

The Exposition duly opened on time, even though Walter and Marion were disappointed that it was not as grand as they had originally planned. But the opening did have another positive spin-off for the Griffins. The Viceroy, Britain's most senior representative in the country, had come to town for the event. While he was there, he laid the foundation stone for the *Pioneer*'s new building, which Walter had designed. The Griffins organized for a silver miniature of the printing press to be cast and presented to him for the occasion. Walter wrote to his father, "I am comfortable here and find endless source of interest in the environment of an ancient civilization."[8]

Walter was looking forward to the New Year, his wife at his side, their relationship rekindled, their partnership revived, and headed for even greater heights in India, this rich, exotic country which was welcoming them both.

Forty-four

His Eyes Never Left Mine

Walter's enthusiasm for India was infectious. Marion's senses were reawakened as she was drawn into the rich chaos of the city. She reported her feelings in her letters:

> The atmosphere is one of a people completely alive with all capacities functioning, deep interests and great enthusiasms and confidence. No vestige of the fears which dominate the life of the European peoples and shatter their soul forces. In material ways it looks like India would be accomplishing in 50 years what it has taken America 150 years to accomplish.[1]

Marion redid some of the drawings on work that Walter had already done, just as she had done when she first arrived in Walter's office in Steinway Hall, when she was first in love with him. She was always enthusiastic about his designs, but she knew she could produce a drawing, a piece of art, which would show them in a far better light. She did an elevation of the Lucknow University library. It was done on a light brown background with a blue band of color behind the building to highlight its structure. She also did a drawing of Walter's plan for an addition to municipal offices in the city of Ahmadabad. It was a three-tiered structure with triangular shapes looking like the pipes of an organ. Her elegant drawing had a hint of art deco about it. Done in black ink against the brown background, it had a black band behind the drawing, with white dots again showing how the building could catch the light.

As she drew it, Marion remembered her friend Lute and her passion for developing an opera company in Sydney. Chicago had its Auditorium Building, wouldn't it be wonderful if Sydney could also have a grand opera house? Although it was for the offices of a local government, in the copy that the Griffins kept for themselves Marion put a different caption underneath which read, "Opera House for Sydney." And what a grand opera house it would have been.[2]

Walter began work on another project. The citizens of Lucknow were collecting money for a monument of King George V, who had died several months before Marion arrived in India. It was to be set in the middle of a park near the post office. A local man was commissioned to do a sculpture of the king, and Walter was asked to design a setting around it. He decided to put the statue on a platform with a staircase leading up to it, covered with a pyramid shape. Walter sketched it out, and Marion then produced the final drawing. It was set against a rich yellow background with a pale blue sky. The building was drawn in black ink and highlighted with white painted dots, reflecting the sunlight. Below it, on the same drawing, was a bird's-eye view of the pyramid from above, with Marion's touches of white highlighting the structure and flower beds softening the building's angular shape.

The Raja of Mahmudabad was eager to get moving on the design for his library. Walter designed a building of staggered cubes over three levels, a little like the design for the municipal offices of Ahmadabad. In February, Walter showed him the drawings and the young Raja was delighted. Other work flooded in. There was a house for a judge in Lucknow and homes for several university professors, a building for a paper mill in Lucknow, a palace for the Prince of Nepal, near Varanasi, as well as the *Pioneer Press* building.

"It was a happy and busy office," Walter wrote, "and we learned how completely false is the usual American conception of India."[3] Marion wrote, "After a lifetime of self-sacrifice, Walter seemed to be just on the point of gathering the fruits."[4]

But Marion was worried about Walter. The stomach pains he had been experiencing for some time were getting worse. In early February, Walter went to visit the city of Cawnpore to finalize the accounts for the Exposition. The meeting continued until after the last train back to Lucknow, so he spent three hours walking around the town in the evening. He began having severe stomach cramps. He was used to long walks, but this time something was wrong.

When he got back to Lucknow, things got worse and he was taken by ambulance to the King George hospital, the hospital where Ronald Craig had been admitted just over a year before. He had surgery for a ruptured gall bladder. The Griffins realized it must have resulted from injuries he had had in the fall in Castlecrag a few years before when Walter was fighting the fire.

What a pity, Marion felt, that Ula, who had worked as a nurse, could not have been there to help him. Walter woke up at about 5:00 a.m. and appeared to have no pain. When Marion arrived to see him, he gave her a sketch he had done for a bookrack for a carpenter to make so he could read in bed when he got home. When Marion left the hospital, she was unable to get a *tonga* so she walked the five miles home along the river and spent the rest of the day working on a perspective for the Raja's library.

But when she went back to see him the next day, she found Walter in excruciating agony, white as a sheet, in a cold sweat. Infection had probably set in after the operation. He never believed there could be such pain, he told Marion. She went home but that evening she received a call from the hospital to come back. She arrived just before midnight to find Walter almost unconscious, lying with his eyes half-closed. An hour later, he woke up and began talking, only half-rationally, about his work. Marion tried to keep him quiet. A Church of England chaplain came, and Marion prayed with him by Walter's bed.

> As the end drew near, I talked to him, telling him what a wonderful life I had had with him, how he was beloved by everybody and suddenly he turned—as if with a great effort and looked straight into my eyes, his own wide, round and startled as if it had never once occurred to him that he could die. His eyes never left mine till he drew his last breath and I closed them.[5]

Marion walked the five miles home along the riverbank for the last time. The Griffins' great love affair had come to an end, all too soon.

Perspective of Pioneer Press Building, Lucknow, India. 1936. Drawing by Marion Mahony Griffin. New-York Historical Society. Magic of America collection, BV Griffin, Marion Mahony, section 4.

Front elevation of perspective for municipal offices in Ahmadabad, India, which the Griffins suggested could also be used as the design for an Opera House for Sydney. Drawing by Marion Mahony Griffin. 1936. Eric Nicholls collection. National Library of Australia.

Forty-five

Going Home

It was in the cool of the morning when Marion arrived home to be met at the gate by their Indian gardener. He looked at her and she raised her hands.

"He's gone," she said. The gardener turned and fled.

Walter was buried in the Christian cemetery, near his friend Ron Craig. Marion turned to Anthroposophy to try to make sense of Walter's death. She wrote to her friends in Australia:

> By whatever means the crossing of the boundary came about it was brought about because Mr. Griffin himself had decided that that step should be taken. He will return when he is ready for the next task.[1]

She remembered the time, a few months before, when she had urged Walter to go to the bank to make sure her name was on the account. If something happened to him, she said, she would need access to the money. They did put her name on the account, but Walter brushed aside the thought of something happening to him. His death, he said, was "a long way off."

"He didn't want to go," she wrote to her friends. "Things were pouring in here and he was very happy."

Marion was devastated, but she kept on working. One morning, one of her assistants came to see her and told her about a dream that he had the night before. He had met Walter on the road walking along the riverbank. He was very happy and wanted him to deliver a message to Marion. "Be sure to remember. You must lead an active life."

Marion took it as a sign that he wanted her to stay in India and continue their work. She worked on the plans for the *Pioneer Press* building, the Raja's library, and the drawing of the canopy for the statue of King George V. She wrote to Eric Nicholls and asked him to come to India to work with her, but he did not want to leave Australia.

She approached the trustees of the university for payment for the work Walter had done on the library, but they refused her. She had several other offers of work, including a position with an architectural firm, but after a few months on her own in India, she decided to head back to Australia. She returned home to Castlecrag where everyone was desolate. Louise Lightfoot came to see Marion, finding her lying on a couch, her eyes closed. Lightfoot later recalled the scene:

> After a while she opened [her eyes] and recognized me.
> "I was trying to contact Waltie's spirit," were the first words she said.
> Old scores were forgotten and we talked freely.
> I asked, "Do you ever do any drafting these days?"
> She replied, "I never want to hold a pencil again."[2]

Marion moved into the Mower House, or Casa Bonita, as she called it, with its rooftop at street level. With its great views of the harbor and its space on the roof for parties, it was one of her favorite houses in Castlecrag. But with Walter gone, the finances of their estate became even more difficult. Eric Nicholls convinced her to agree to relax the convenants Walter had set down for any development on the estate. It made the land easier to sell, but it would mean the new houses did not have the same character he had been trying to preserve.

The plays at Castlecrag continued, including a production of Goethe's *Faust* with Lute, but Marion's heart was not in it. Without Walter there, life was not the same. It was time to go back to her family in America.

But she wanted to make one last visit to see Canberra, the city she and her husband had created. A journalist friend who lived in Castlecrag, Walter Trinick, offered to take her there. They decided to go "incognito" so there would be no fuss about her visit. They drove around the city and called into a shop. Trinick asked the shop assistant if people living in Canberra liked the city and if they knew who designed it. Marion recalled the scene:

> The youth flared.
> "There is not anyone in Canberra who does not know that Mr. Burley Griffin designed Canberra. They feel that through his great inspiration, the soul of Australia is being developed."
> That was a nice farewell for me, his wife, and I realized that the old bitter fight was over. Canberra was born undeformed and healthy and would grow on and do her work.[3]

Marion had one last wish. She wanted to see the view from the summit of Mount Ainslie, the view she had imagined so intensely on a cold Chicago winter almost 30 years before. They drove up the winding hill to the top of the mountain. She looked down at the city that she and her husband had designed and saw a:

> ... young city and all its suburbs laid out on the ground before them, beautiful scenery and the background of mountains, streets constructed, splendid tree plantings evergreen and blooming, with street lights in all, Parliament House and other government buildings, several residential centers fairly occupied, residences, shops, theaters.[4]

But she knew it was still unfinished.

> The one thing lacking to make a truly grandiose scene is that the waters of the Molonglo had not yet been dammed to form the permanent reflecting basin. The plan, as one looks down from the heights, will not really be comprehensible till this is done.[5]

She left Sydney with a heavy heart but she would take home all that she had learned from her time in Australia and India to the country of her birth which she still loved.

> I left Castlecrag, truly a bit of Paradise on Earth, to take on the next adventure ... to put my shoulder to the wheel of molding the destiny of my country.[6]

In October 1938, a sad group of friends farewelled Marion at the dock, weeping. She left many of their possessions in Australia, including their architectural drawings, in the care of Eric Nicholls. She went to stay with her sister, Genie, in the house in Rogers Park.

Almost 25 years before, Marion had left America and an architectural community in Chicago that had some appreciation of her skills. She had created a new life for herself in Australia in Castlecrag, full of good spirit and friendship, but now she was back home, a 67-year-old widow little known to many beyond her immediate family.

In 1939, she went back to MIT in Boston for a class reunion. A photograph was taken of the 21 people there. Marion was one of only two women. Exactly why Marion always insisted on her face being side-on to the camera in photographs has never been explained. While everyone else looked at the camera, Marion stood side-on, as usual, engaged in an intense conversation with a tall man in the center.

Dwight Perkins had a son, Lawrence, who had also become a successful architect. In 1940, Lawrence organized for Marion to speak to the Chicago Chapter of the American Institute of Architects at the Cliff Dwellers Club. But when she spoke, it was not so much about architecture and her experiences in Australia but her passion for Anthroposophy. Her audience came away mystified and unimpressed.

Without the balancing force of Walter and his work, Marion's obsession with Anthroposophy intensified. Her niece, Clarmyra, was also living in the Mahony's house in Rogers Park. Her husband had died and she had moved back with her three children, to live with her mother. Marion became involved in their care. She wanted to continue with her work, but the family's finances were tight and she found herself spending much time looking after the children. Had her wealthy friend Anna Wilmarth still been alive, things may have been different. There were few people in Chicago who remembered Marion anymore. In 1941 Dwight Perkins died in New Mexico on his way to his summer home in California. Relations had soured with Barry Byrne and their dear friend William Purcell had retired to southern California. Frank Lloyd Wright's career was undergoing a revival but Marion's view of him was bordering on hatred.

Marion had been right about dark forces gathering in the world. War broke out again in Europe, ending any immediate prospect of her returning to Australia. Marion resumed her friendship with Lola Lloyd, a member of the Lloyd family of Winnetka, long-time friends of the Mahonys. A few years younger than Marion, Lloyd had been born in Texas to the wealthy Maverick family but had moved to the area north of Chicago after her marriage. She was a strong supporter of the campaign to get women the vote in America and a staunch opponent of America's involvement in the Great War. She became a political activist, dedicating herself to promoting peace and helping to organize Henry Ford's Peace Ship, in 1915, an unsuccessful bid to end the war.

After the war, she stepped up her involvement in the National Women's Party to push for women's suffrage, which finally came into force in 1920 after the passing of the 19th amendment to the US Constitution. It was almost 20 years after the Australian Parliament had passed a law allowing women to vote in federal elections. Lloyd was passionate about working to promote world peace. When Marion returned to Chicago, she had just set up the International Campaign for World Government.

But the world was being drawn into another terrible war in Europe. Marion had opposed America's involvement in the Great War and supported the idea of setting up an international organization working for peace and global unity. Lloyd, who held similar views, was involved in a Council of World Fellowship, which owned land in Conway, New Hampshire, where it planned to establish a center. Lloyd approached Marion to help design the World Fellowship Center. Marion visited Conway in August 1942 and drew up a plan for the site. Determined to keep the property as natural as possible, she designed the estate to fit around the contours of the land with circular roadways as the Griffins had designed for Castlecrag. She signed her plans, Marion M. Griffin, Architect, Landscape Architect.[7]

One of the women working on the project wrote to Lloyd enthusiastically describing Marion's visit.

> Mrs. Griffin's great creative vision, resourcefulness, practical experience and manifestly deep and genuine interest have been abundantly

> evidenced. Thank you most sincerely for your wise, resourceful statesmanship in proposing her work here at this ... early stage—and for your gracious generosity in making it possible for her to help us.

Later that year, Marion was invited to go to the Lloyd family's ranch in Boerne, Texas, which was being managed by Marion's brother Gerald and his wife. Having thought about setting up a center in Conway, and seen Marion's plans, Lloyd could see the potential of developing a Castlecrag type estate on her family's property in Texas. Marion visited the ranch and in January 1943 drew up plans for the town of Hill Crystals and its suburb, Rosary Crystals. The plan for the estate, which would have more than 100 houses, included some of the ideas the Griffins had included in their plans for Canberra and Castlecrag, including an open-air theater. Determined to preserve as much of the natural environment as possible, Marion proposed terraced landscaping and houses with flat roofs so each house on the estate could have a view. Lloyd was excited about Marion's plan, writing a letter to her brother describing it as a "humdinger." Sadly neither of the projects which Lloyd had initiated took place. Lloyd died of cancer in July 1944, and Marion lost another supporter and a potential source of income.

By this time, the war in Europe had been underway for several years. Realizing that she probably would not be returning to Australia, Marion decided to donate the Haven Theatre to Willoughby Council. She wanted it preserved forever. In 1945 the 74-year-old Marion submitted plans for the Better Chicago Contest for the *Chicago Herald-American* and another design for the Chicagoland Prize Home Competition in the *Chicago Tribune*.

She also embarked on a much more ambitious project. Angry at Frank Lloyd Wright's rising success and still devastated at Walter's loss, she was determined to let the world know of her husband's brilliance and his contribution to world architecture. Walter was little known in the country of his birth, yet he had such great vision and high ideals. She would write a book about her husband's work in America, Australia, and India.

She spent more than a decade putting together a manuscript of more than 1,000 pages—a compilation of letters, photographs, and documents from their past as well as her current-day views. It was a work of sheer love for her husband, but one which also helped to record their unique life together. Maybe with some inspiration from the stories of the *Bhagavad Gita,* she depicted his life as a series of battles: the Individual Battle (his early life and career in the United States); the Federal Battle (the story of Walter's battles with Australian politicians and bureaucrats); the Municipal Battle (his battle with the local council over his plans to build Castlecrag); and the Empirial Battle or An American Architect's Year in India.

It was a massive task which took in 1,400 pages of typed text and some 650 photographs, illustrations, and architectural drawings. Some of it was made up of letters to and from the Griffins, some was the extensive work she had done writing the long descriptions of Australian flora for the *Forest Portraits.* It included rambling recollections by Marion which took in her mystical views, her passion for America as the great home of democracy and more recent events such as the "smashing of the atom." Running through the text was an unashamed glorification of her husband Walter as he fought his great battles. It was a huge challenge, particularly given her age, but Marion was determined that her work, which she called *Magic of America,* would record Walter's true place in history.

The work done, she was desperate to have it published. She appealed to their old friend, architect William Purcell, for help and advice. She was very clear on her goal. She didn't want to produce a boring architectural document but a story of Walter's life that would appeal to a broad public. She wrote to her friends in Australia, asking for help to raise funds for its publication. Librarian Ida Leeson appealed to King O'Malley to help, but he refused. With the help of some friends, Marion arranged for one copy to be given to the New-York Historical Society and another to the Burnham Library at the Art Institute of Chicago.

In 1949, Marion's sister Georgine died, leaving her to help Clarmyra, a teacher, bring up her three children. Marion's passion was strong, but as she got older, her memory continued to fail her. Scholars of the early work of Frank Lloyd Wright began to seek her out for her recollections. Visiting her in 1952 for his book *The Chicago School of Architecture*, Mark

Peisch found the 81-year-old "living in rather ramshackle surroundings" and suffering memory loss, although he found her quite happy.[8]

With the help of Eric Nicholls, some of the Griffins' work that had been left in Australia was given to the Burnham Library at the Art Institute of Chicago. Marion gave some of her *Forest Portraits* and other work to Northwestern University, north of Chicago near Rogers Park where she lived. Other work was donated to the Avery Architectural Library at Columbia University. Some of her *Forest Portraits* went to the Perkins family but a considerable volume of their work was still in Australia with the Nicholls family.

It was sometime in the 1950s when Louise Lightfoot, who had set up a successful dance company in Australia, passed through Chicago with some friends. She was determined to find Marion. She knew her niece, Clarmyra, had the surname Smith. She phoned around until she found what she hoped was the right address. She arrived at the door and knocked, just as she had done as a young girl 30 years earlier, when she arrived at Castlecrag from Melbourne, not quite sure what she would find. She recalled the occasion:

> Marion gave the same old welcome.
> "Come right in!"
> She looked so old but was quite gay. [She was] wearing a faded helio dressing gown and gray silk stockings trailing down her legs. There were sounds of children crying a little in the next room. Marion called out,
> "No crying, my darlings! Only happiness in this house!"[9]

Marion looked after the children of her niece who taught during the day. Lightfoot asked her how she was. "Fine and dandy! They can't kill me. I'm a vegetarian."

Lightfoot asked her about her fine artwork, her brilliant Japanese-style silk drawings. She had watched Marion draw with amazement and had seen her *Forest Portraits* as they hung in their home in Castlecrag. Where were these treasures now? Where was the rest of the work the Griffins had done together?

"I don't know," Marion replied. "I can't remember what I did one minute ago."

Then she added: "Waltie was mean. He went away and left me too soon."

Saddened, Lightfoot and her friends left. Their aging friend was but a shadow of her former self. She was still busy looking after young children, still determined to be happy, but still missing her dear Walter.

On August 10, 1961, Marion Mahony, artist, architect, loyal wife, passionate environmentalist, proud daughter of America, finally passed away, at the age of 90. She died penniless and almost unknown, thousands of miles away from her beloved husband. Her death certificate misspelled her name, described her occupation as a teacher, estimated her age to be around 80 and declared that she was "never married." She was cremated and her ashes interred at Graceland Cemetery in Chicago. How little was known about her in her home city. The news of her death prompted Lightfoot to remember how they had once had a cultural group discussion in Castlecrag entitled, "Does the Ego Persist and Whither Goes It?"

"Marion may know," she wrote later. "I imagine those two spirits, united like drops of water in the cosmic ocean where egos persist."[10]

Maybe she was right.

Tasmanian Eucalypts Leptospermum Shrubs. Forest Portrait No 12. Late 1918–early 1919. Courtesy Peter B. and Joanne S. Griffin.

Epilogue

Marion's Legacy

Any assessment of Marion's life and achievements is made difficult by the fact that her work is scattered around the globe. Some of her brilliant *Forest Portraits* are in private hands in the United States, owned by the descendants of her cousin Dwight Perkins, who played such a critical role in her early career. Some are in the Block Museum at Northwestern University north of Chicago. Other work, including her drawings of Griffins' plans for buildings in India, are at the Avery Architectural Library at Columbia University in New York. The Ryerson & Burnham Library at the Art Institute of Chicago also has some of the Griffins' work. The Art Institute also features a stained glass window made by Marion for her brother's house in Elkhart, Indiana.

In Australia, the National Library of Australia in Canberra has acquired a substantial amount of the work that Marion left in Australia with Eric Nicholls. The National Archives of Australia is the proud custodian of Marion's brilliant drawings of the Griffin plan for Canberra, which have been miraculously preserved and restored. Normally stored in the archives, they were on rare public display throughout 2013, when the city of Canberra celebrated its 100th anniversary. And Marion's brilliant mural of *Fairies Feeding the Herons* is still on the wall of what is now the G.B. Armstrong School of International Studies, north of Chicago near Rogers Park, again miraculously preserved. Other work may also be in private hands.

While Walter Burley Griffin will always be remembered as the architect who designed the Australian capital, interest in Marion's role and her artistic and architectural achievements grows today.

Grant Carpenter Manson was one of the first to seek Marion out for her reflections of Frank Lloyd Wright in 1940. After several conversations with her, he was struck by her role in Wright's studio. In his book *Frank Lloyd Wright to 1910, The First Golden Age,* published in 1958, about the key staff in Wright's Oak Park studio, Manson wrote, "Marion Mahony is certainly the key figure. If The Studio had been organized on more conventional lines, she would have held the rank of 'head designer.'"[1]

Manson points out that Marion worked with Wright for more than 13 years, the longest of any of his associates in his early years. Taking a close look at her work in the studio, he says:

> She was not only a skilled designer but a gifted draftswoman; many of the fine pen perspectives turned out by The Studio were hers, as well as most of the finished drawings for the Wasmuth monograph, and she may have designed some of the decorative murals of the Prairie Houses, such as that in the living room of the Coonley house.[2]

Charles E. White, who worked in Wright's studio for several years when Marion was there, described her in his letters to friends and family as "one of the finest in this country of this class of rendering."[3] Barry Byrne, who was also approached for his views on Marion, described her as a "spectacularly brilliant person."[4]

Architectural historian Mark Peisch also became curious about Marion's role in Wright's office and in her partnership with Walter when he began researching his book, *The Chicago School of Architecture,* in the 1950s. He spoke to Marion in her later years, when her memory was sadly fading. He was able to elicit a valuable comment from Roy Lippincott about Marion's drawing techniques and her work on the plan for Canberra. He also quotes an unnamed British critic to suggest that it was Marion's drawings of Walter's plans for the Australian capital that may have been what "charmed" the judges. Clearly impressed by Marion's role in the partnership, Peisch observed that:

> In many ways their [the Griffins'] marriage was a complete merging of personalities and ideals, an artistic union so complete that to distinguish or separate their careers after this date becomes impossible.[5]

Interviewed in 1996 for a documentary for America's Public Broadcast Service, Peisch also noted her animosity toward Wright.

> First of all she didn't want to mention Wright's name which was significant. ... She very very obviously felt she had been treated badly by Wright. Didn't trust him. ... One suspected she might have been romantically involved with him and that he had somehow spurned her, but there is no proof of that.[6]

He saw Marion as the "intellectual equal" of Wright. Asked about Marion and Walter, he replied:

> It was difficult to distinguish between them. They seemed to be a wonderful, sympathetic unit. They were in total harmony with each other. ... She was not subservient to her husband but was absolutely genuine in her devotion to him. At times, in Australia, he was under terrible pressure from the political forces that opposed his plan ... the Griffins didn't have time to argue; they were defending themselves, and they were helping each other, supporting each other.[7]

Interviewed for the PBS documentary, Lawrence Perkins, the son of Dwight, described her as "a vital nervy, colorful individual who had to struggle for that kind of training, which was most unexpected of any supposedly fragile female." He noted that:

> She was very much in love with Walter all her life. She was desperately afraid she would diminish his reputation. The fact of the matter is, she was right. She would have. So she retired from the practice of architecture in Australia and made tree portraits as an overt denial that she was doing his architecture for his firm. ... She cared about the guy [Walter]. And she wasn't wound up in her own fame at all. She wasn't chasing fame.[8]

In 1966, Prairie School scholar H. Allen Brooks attempted to analyze the origins of the drawings in the Wasmuth portfolio of Wright's work, which had been published in Germany in 1911 and was instrumental in establishing his reputation on a broader stage. After careful analysis, he reported that:

> Of the delineators, Marion Mahony was unquestionably the most prolific. Judged in terms of the Wasmuth drawings, she contributed nearly half of those which appear attributable. There appear to be some seventy-two plates with architectural perspectives and, of these, at least twenty seem to be primarily by her hand.[9]

In the same year, young academic David Van Zanten published one of the first scholarly attempts to assess Marion in her own right, as opposed to the loyal helpmate of Frank Lloyd Wright and then Walter Burley Griffin. Published in *The Prairie School Review*, "The Early Work of Marion Mahony Griffin" was not particularly flattering but it did begin to draw attention to her role.

With the wisdom of further scholarship, he upgraded his view of her. In a paper prepared in 2005, he declared: "I would argue that Marion Mahony Griffin was the third great progressive designer of turn-of-the-century Chicago after Louis Sullivan and Frank Lloyd Wright."[10]

There has been much debate over the influences of Wright and Walter in Marion's design for the three houses in Millikin Place, Decatur, Illinois, with many wanting to downplay her role in these houses. But it does appear that two of the three houses in Millikin Place—the houses for Robert and Adolph Mueller—were Marion's designs. The Adolph Mueller House, the last of the three to be designed for Millikin Place, and the Amberg House have strong similarities and are easily her two architectural masterpieces, with their strong flowing designs and colored glass on the outside and overhead in the living rooms giving them a unique atmosphere.

Another great frustration is that Marion's design for the Henry Ford House in Rouge River, Michigan, was never built. Anyone who looks at Marion's wide design for a flowing house to be built in natural hewn stone, with its long band of colored glass windows, set into the landscape, and the actual building now called Fair Lane, a gray-faux Gothic house, can only wonder what might have been. Had both the Griffins remained in America they would have carved out a very successful architectural practice together and found themselves ranked in history with other Prairie School architects.

It cannot be disputed that Marion Mahony changed the course of Australian history with her drive to get her husband to enter the competition to design the Australian capital and her brilliant renderings of his plans. Without her energy and support, Walter would not have made the commitment to put in such a substantial and well thought out plan. Exactly what influence she had on the plan itself is more interesting. Marion was a sounding board for Wright's ideas when she was in his studio and then for Walter.

Five years older than her husband and educated at the best university for architecture in the country at the time, Marion was a very experienced architect when they married. It is impossible to believe that she sat by with a pen, waiting to draw the ideas that her less experienced husband came up with. Scholar after scholar agrees that her magnificent depiction of Walter's ideas won the judges' vote. As Lawrence Perkins points out, Walter's design for the Australian capital only just beat one done by Finnish architect Eliel Saarinen who went on to become a most influential international architect.

> The fact remains that she made the drawings that won the competition over the second prize competitor, Eliel Saarinen, which, in my opinion, was a very much better design but not nearly as well packaged. Rightly or wrongly, I believe that she indeed did win the Canberra competition for it [Walter's plan].[11]

But what of the plan itself? The idea of using the highest hill in the landscape as a capitol, a place of the people which would be above the houses of parliament, has strong resonances with Rome. In Washington, DC, Capitol Hill is the location of the houses of Congress. But in the Rome that Marion saw when she visited with her brother in the 1890s, the Capitol was a public space, designed by Michelangelo, with the meeting place for the politicians down below. This was Griffin's vision for Canberra. Appearing before a Royal Commission in Australia in the 1920s, Walter noted that Rome also had its capitol.

At the time the couple worked on the plan for the competition for Canberra, Walter had never left America. It is not hard to believe that Marion's vision of Rome would have inspired Walter to make this critical decision about the layout of Canberra. Interestingly, one person who was inspired by the Griffin plan was Italian architect Romaldo Giurgola. As a young student in Rome, he saw Griffin's plans for Canberra— Marion's drawings—on the walls of his university. When he moved to America, his fascination with the Griffin plan continued. In the 1970s, the government of Australia finally decided to build a new parliament house. Instead of Walter's plan to locate the houses of parliament set into the hill, leaving the hilltop itself as a place for the people, it was decided to locate it on what the Australians called Capital Hill. As Walter had correctly predicted in the 1920s, once the government had decided to build a "temporary" parliament house, just in front of the area he wanted for the permanent houses of parliament, it would never be taken down. This meant the permanent structure was placed on top of the hill and the Griffins idea of a Roman style capitol was ignored.

But one man didn't forget it. When the government decided to hold a competition for the building, they approached the New York based Giurgola to be a judge. He opted to be an entrant and his design won. His striking, unusual design for the Australian Parliament tried to encapsulate the Griffins' ideas by having a grassy area over the top of the building where the public could walk and overlook the city. Tighter security has made it more difficult to get to the grassy top above the parliament but for those who want to make the effort it is still accessible.

In the final years of Marion's life, events were taking place in Australia to help grant one of her dearest wishes. The strong-willed Australian Prime Minister of the day, Robert Menzies, was determined that Canberra would finally get its lake. But, even for him, it was not easy. When he became prime minister in 1949, Canberra was a village with a disorganized collection of buildings with sheep paddocks in the middle. Menzies initially regarded the city as a national embarrassment but then became a champion for its development.

In 1959, a decision was made that the river would be dammed and a central lake constructed in Canberra, but there was still opposition about the cost of the project. When Menzies went on holiday, some officials from the Treasury managed to convince ministers not to provide the money for the lake. But when he came back, he overturned their decision. Bridges were built across the river and a dam was built and, in 1964, three years after Marion's death, the lake which was such a crucial centerpiece to the Griffin plan, was finally built. Menzies rejected suggestions that the lake be named after him and insisted that it be called Lake Burley Griffin. Marion would have been proud.

The community of Castlecrag developed into an unusual enclave attracting people such as political activist and Marxist scholar Guido Baracchi and his partner, playwright and author Betty Rowland. The relaxation of Walter's covenants meant that much of the new building on the estate was not in keeping with his style as he would have liked, but it did allow continual development. Had Marion remained in Australia, she may have been able to benefit from their work in creating an ideal suburb but, sadly, her decision to go back to America meant she died in near poverty.

About 15 houses were built to Griffin's designs in Castlecrag, most of which are still standing. There is evidence of another 30 of his designs that were never built. But while Walter designed the houses, it was Marion's spirit and energy, her love of people and the Australian countryside, which forged a unique community atmosphere.

The suburb now hosts a school that teaches in accordance with the views of Rudolf Steiner. Marion's Haven Theatre remains a public space and often hosts outdoor plays. Castlecrag has since become an upmarket suburb with many striking architect-designed houses, but it still retains a unique history and a character like no other in Australia. The Griffins and their friends planted some two thousand trees in the area, turning a barren estate into a showcase for native Australian gum trees and plants. Marion's study of Australian trees also needs to be acknowledged. Her *Forest Portraits* drawings and their detailed and passionate descriptions in *Magic of America* need to be added to her eight painstakingly produced, color-coded notebooks about Australian plants now in the National Library, her speeches urging Australians to appreciate their natural trees and landscape and her work on the gardens of Newman College and other projects. Together they are a body of work in its own right, an appreciation and a study of the Australian natural landscape and flora.

In 1997 Marion's ashes were re-interred and marked with a plaque at Chicago's Graceland Cemetery, giving her some recognition in the burial ground of many of its other leading architects. She lies thousands of miles away from her beloved Walter, but she is not far from the resting place of her dear cousin Dwight Perkins and other Chicago architecture greats, including Daniel Burnham and Louis Sullivan.

Looking back, one thing is very clear. The Griffins were a most unusual couple, well ahead of their time in Australia. Both found themselves in opposition to many authority figures of the day, but many of their ideas have later proved to be correct. Australians have since learned to love their natural landscape, although maybe not with quite the passion of Walter and Marion. The concept of preserving native trees has finally seeped into the Australian consciousness. The idea of flat-roofed houses and houses with gardens on their roof and laced around the buildings has become fashionable around the world.

Two of Marion's Castlecrag "babies" later married. Ivor Morton married Ula Maddocks' daughter Deirdre and together they built their own home out of mud brick in bushland in the Blue Mountains near Sydney. The Mortons' house embodied the spirit of the Griffins. It was a flat-roofed house with a garden on top and was built around a gum tree, overlooking a rock ledge surrounded by native trees. Showing the house, Deirdre looked out at the trees and said, "Marion's Angophoras."[12]

One passionate student of Marion was an architect from California called Janice Pregliasco, who wrote an essay called *The Life and Work of Marion Mahony Griffin* in 1995.

> Marion Mahony Griffin was the greatest architectural artist of her generation, which included men such as Wright, Charles Rennie Macintosh, Sir Edwin Lutyens, and Adolf Loos, and perhaps in American history. She was recognized as such by colleagues. ... The range and effect of her spaces are extraordinary, from the airiness of the Mueller House master bedroom, the architectural division of the Amberg House living and dining rooms, and the sublime transcendence of the Newman College rotunda to the crystalline wonder of the Capitol

Theatre and the dynamism of the Lucknow University Student Union. These are masterful spaces ranking with the greatest achievements of the Prairie School.[13]

Pregliasco also wrote a book about Marion with the same title but it was never published.

In 2005, the Block Museum at Northwestern University held an exhibition of Marion's stunning *Forest Portraits,* some of which are owned by the museum and others are in the hands of the Perkins family. The museum produced a superb book called *Drawing the Form of Nature.* It showed the beauty of her *Forest Portraits* and included her detailed and powerful observations of the Australian flora she drew which have been preserved in the *Magic of America* documents. In 2011, Van Zanten produced a book of edited papers from a symposium held with the exhibition called *Marion Mahony Reconsidered,* the first published book devoted to studying Marion's life.

Marion's achievements as a woman in what was very much a man's world have been discussed but not in great detail. She was not one to trumpet her own work or complain about the difficulties she might have faced as a woman in architecture. Interestingly, her friend, Australian author, activist, and feminist, Miles Franklin, who was living in Chicago when the Griffins got together, saw firsthand the challenges facing women in the profession in America at the time. Franklin recorded some of the realities of the time in an article in *Life and Labor* in February 1914 about an architect called Elisabeth Martini. While it discussed the problems Martini faced as a woman architect, the article is illustrated with some of Marion's buildings including her All Souls Church in Evanston and one of the Mueller houses in Decatur.

In 2007, one of Marion's dearest wishes came true. Her long manuscript which she called the *Magic of America* was put online by the Art Institute of Chicago. Finally, her great work was published and accessible to anyone.

The passionate and sometimes erratic work is meant to be a tribute to the work of her late husband, but by allowing broader scholarship of her work, it has also drawn more attention to Marion's own role and achievements.

In 2008, Marion's achievements were included in a book by Sarah Allaback on *The First American Women Architects*, which notes:

> Marion Mahony Griffin stands alone among early women architects as the only one of her gender included in the canonical architectural histories. Although she has been considered worthy of biographical accounts since the 1960s, Griffin is most often described as an artist or delineator of exceptional ability. ... Although early scholarship on Marion Mahony emphasized her role as an artist and collaborator, more recent work has described her as an architect whose gender kept her from being recognized as a major figure of the Prairie School.[14]

Marion's achievements do not fall into any neat box, and her life defies any simple label. She was both an architect and an artist. Some seek to downplay her role, declaring that she was not an architect. Clearly she was both an architect and an artist although there are only a few buildings which can be attributed solely to her. Her best two, the Amberg House in Grand Rapids, Michigan, and the Adolph Mueller House in Decatur, Illinois, provide stunning examples of the style she might have developed had she been able to become an architect in her own right. She was also a botanist and an idealist, an astute social observer, a loyal wife, and a woman very much ahead of her time.

There is also the mystery of her actions as she got older. On some of the plans for houses, she blacked out the names of some of the architects, including Walter's name. Why she did it is a mystery. Maybe she was, at last, trying to assert her role as a designer. Another mystery is what happened to the silk drawings for Canberra, which she did at the same time as they were working on the plans they sent to Australia. It is clear that the Griffins kept the drawings themselves but they were sent to Lyon in France for an exhibition and disappeared in the chaos of World War I. Walter wrote to France several times to get them back but was never able to find them. It is a great tragedy that these historical drawings appear to have been lost for all time.

Walter and Marion had a grand love affair spanning three continents. Their love and intellectual closeness is revealed in their constant letters to each other throughout their lives. Their most intense periods working together as both husband and wife, and architect and architect, produced the design for the Australian capital, houses in Mason City, Iowa, he Café Australia and Newman College in Melbourne, the creation of not just a suburb but a community at Castlecrag in Sydney, and one burst of intense work in India where Marion and Walter were together for one last time, the strains in their marriage put behind them. Had Walter lived longer, many of the works they produced together in India would have been built, but at least Marion's drawings remain as witness to that period.

By 2013, as Canberra celebrated its 100th anniversary, there was increasing interest in Marion and her role. Not only were the original plans for the Canberra competition put on display for the whole year, it was decided that Marion's great vision for the city, the lookout which showed the *View from the Summit of Mount Ainslie*, a view which has remarkable resonance with Marion's drawing of 1911, should be named after her.

In November 2013, there was a ceremony at the top of Mount Ainslie. The Chief Minister of the Australian Capital Territory, Katy Gallagher, said:

> This significant site will now formally honour the architect, wife and professional collaborator of Walter Burley Griffin. Often all the credit for the design of Canberra is given to Walter Burley Griffin, however his wife, Marion Mahony Griffin, also had a significant and influential role in designing the Canberra we know and love today. Marion's input into Walter's grand design was both crucial and seamlessly integrated. It is astonishing that her watercolors accompanying their entry capture the Australian landscape so faithfully when neither Walter nor Marion had ever been to Australia.

And on a cold Saturday in May 2015, following a long campaign by the Rogers Park/West Ridge Historical Society, local Alderman Joe Moore, and the Australian Consulate-General in Chicago, a local beach and park near where she spent her last days was renamed the Marion Mahony Beach Park.

Marion Mahony Griffin remains an elusive spirit. Her great work, *Magic of America*, was a reflection of her great love for her own country, its unique form of democracy, and a tribute to her late husband. But it also revealed much about Marion herself.

Marion Mahony made magic. Like watching a magician, you can never be sure exactly what she did or how she did it. She poured her heart out in the hundreds of pages she wrote and tried to get published, yet, in many ways, her true spirit remains elusive. Her artwork and her architectural delineation are breathtaking, with touches of sheer brilliance.

She was driven by passion and energy, idealism, a restless creativity, and a strong view of the importance of community and the human spirit. But she deliberately understated her own role in the work of Wright and then Walter, making an appreciation of her true contribution frustratingly difficult. If Marion's work could ever be brought together in one place, it would be easy to see her unique role in history and appreciate her artistic skills. But that is an almost impossible dream.

Truly appreciating Marion Mahony takes some imagination, carefully putting together the pieces of a jigsaw puzzle that she has left for us to discover, scattered in different places around the world. The picture will never quite be finished, but if you look closely enough, you will glimpse enough of her spirit to appreciate her magic.

Plaque marking Marion's ashes in wall at Graceland Cemetery, Chicago. Photograph by Vin Plant. 2013.

Endnotes

Abbreviations

AAL   Avery Architectural & Fine Arts Library, Columbia University, New York

ADB   Australian Dictionary of Biography

MOA   The Magic of America (MOA I The Empirial Battle, MOA II The Federal Battle, MOA III The Municipal Battle, MOA IV The Individual Battle)

NAA   National Archives of Australia

NLA   National Library of Australia

Chapter 1: The Telegram

1. "*Your design awarded*: MOA II, 1c.
2. "*Ah, then*: MOA II, 435.
3. "*Thanks for notifications*: "Competitive Designs for Federal Capital City – Adjudication." National Archives of Australia: A110, FC1912/4133.
4. "*Make no little plans*: Burnham's address to the 1910 London Town Planning Conference and similar expressions in earlier speeches.

Chapter 2: The Fire

1. Joseph Kirkland quoted in Donald L. Miller, *City of the Century*, 153. Chapter 6, "My Lost City," describes the fire in detail.
2. "*The only two logical positions*: MOA IV, 130a. The Individual Battle section of *The Magic of America* has the richest detail on Marion's upbringing.
3. "*The loveliest spot*: MOA IV, 130a.
4. "*Our home was at the head*: MOA 1V, 131.

Chapter 3: Roaming Free

1. "*wild hickory nuts*: MOA IV, 131.
2. "*battering and foaming*: MOA IV, 131.
3. "*a poet, a journalist*: MOA IV, 130a.
4. "*the reputation of being*: MOA IV, 137.
5. "The Legend of the Canyon." MOA IV, 81.

Chapter 4: Back to the City

1. *In the summer of*: MOA IV, 133.
2. *"What a strange combination*: MOA IV, 90.
3. *"great prairies*: MOA IV, 90.
4. *The town of Tremont*: For a more detailed account of the early development of Tremont and Lincoln's links with the town, see Guy C. Fraker's *Lincoln's Ladder to the Presidency*, 69–75, 197.
5. *"It feels as if it were filled with gold*: MOA IV, 136.
6. *Marion's fight with Gerald*: MOA IV, 249.
7. *"My soul was filled*: MOA IV, 134.
8. *"I guess I never was a conformist*: MOA IV, 20-2.

Chapter 5: The Architect

1. *He was sent out to work*: Details of Dwight Perkins' life from unpublished family manuscript, "Perkins of Chicago."
2. *"In 1800 ... a new generation*: Miller, *City of the Century*, 178.
3. *Dwight believed*: "Perkins of Chicago," 27.
4. Anna Wilmarth finances Marion's education: MOA IV, 152.

Chapter 6: The House and Studio of a Painter

1. *"I don't see*: MOA IV, 155.
2. *Marion scored well*: For more details of Marion's time at MIT, see James Weirick, "Marion Mahony at MIT," in *Transition*, Winter 1988, 49–54.
3. *"The handsomest man*: MOA IV, 153.
4. *Despite the fact*: For more on Sophia Hayden's work on the 1893 World's Columbian Exposition and her meeting with Daniel Burnham, see Larson, 142–3.
5. *"blowing their heads off"*: MOA IV, 276.
6. *She was fond of*: MOA IV, 276.
7. *There was a courtyard*: For more information about Marion's time at MIT, including a copy of Marion's *House and Studio of a Painter*, see David Van Zanten, ed., *Marion Mahony Reconsidered*, 26–29.
8. *Journalist Richard Harding Davis*: "The Last Days of the Fair," in *Harper's Weekly* 37, October 21, 1893, 1002. Quoted in Miller, 488.
9. *"I felt right proud*: *1894 Class Book*, Massachusetts Institute of Technology, 1898.
10. *"One year in the office*: MOA IV, 110.

Chapter 7: Enter Frank

1. *She worked for several months*: 1894 Class Book, Massachusetts Institute of Technology, 1898.
2. *"Superintendent of the Office Force"*: Ibid.
3. *"In entering my second office*: MOA IV, 306.
4. *In the summer of 1896*: Marion briefly recalled her visit to Europe in MOA 1, 35. Professor David Van Zanten provided the details of her return to America.
5. *"I had met Robert Spencer*: Frank Lloyd Wright, *An Autobiography*, 155.

Chapter 8: Oak Park

1. *How much Marion's own thesis*: James Weirick, Professor of Landscape Architecture at the University of New South Wales, argues that Marion's MIT thesis may have provided inspiration for the design of the Wright studio in Oak Park. See James Weirick, "Marion Mahony at MIT," *Transition*, No 25, Winter 1988, 48–54.
2. *Marion developed an unusual relationship*: Brooks, 79 (Brooks' interview with Barry Byrne, March 24, 1965).
3. *"a thin, angular, shallow person*: Brooks, 79.
4. *"Her mordant humor attracted me*: Brooks, 79 and Byrne, 4.
5. *Her conversations with Wright*: Mark Peisch recollections in PBS documentary, *Walter Burley Griffin: In His Own Right*, aired in 1999, www.pbs.org/wbgriffin/interv.htm.
6. *Wright used his conversations*: Pregliasco, 166.
7. *Sculptor Richard Bock*: Autobiography, unpublished, 1946, Chapter 10, 9. As noted by Pregliasco, 166.
8. *Louis Sullivan speech:* "The Young Man in Architecture," 1900, in *Louis Sullivan: The Public Papers*, 141.

Chapter 9: Our Little University

1. *"Why have you brought us*: MOA IV, 165.
2. *"Did you notice*: MOA IV, 166.
3. *"This was my first job*: MMG letter to Mrs. Herbert Brough, June 30, 1938. MOA papers, Art Institute of Chicago.
4. *"doing designs for furniture*: Van Zanten, "The Early Work of Marion Mahony Griffin," 40, and Brooks, 80.
5. *"It is hard to describe*: MOA IV, 117.
6. *"His brilliant and attractive personality*: Wright, John Lloyd, 35.
7. *As Byrne recalled later*: Byrne, review of *The Drawings of Frank Lloyd Wright* by Arthur Drexler, *Journal of the Society of Architectural Historians* 12. 2 (May 1963), 108–9.

8. *Wright would often hold competitions*: Van Zanten, "The Early Work of Marion Mahony Griffin," 10.
9. *She designed T-shaped houses*: Pregliasco, 167.
10. *Marion was the most enthusiastic actress*: MOA IV, 250.
11. *"Anna said she would hurry to cross the continent*: MOA III, 68.

CHAPTER 10: JAPANESE WOODCUTS

1. *"influence of Japanese prints*: See MOA IV, Frontispiece Caption, 20–2, 106, 215, 263. For an excellent essay on the influence of Japanese prints on the work of Marion Mahony and Frank Lloyd Wright see: Ellen E. Roberts, "Ukiyo-e in Chicago: Frank Lloyd Wright, Marion Mahony Griffin and the Prairie School," *Art in Print*, July–August 2013, 3–10.
2. *Wright became an evangelist*: Secrest, 146–7.
3. *"It was my misfortune*: Frank Lloyd Wright, *An Autobiography*, 140.
4. *"the most radical departure from traditional church architecture ever attempted."*: *Oak Leaves*, February 24, 1906.
5. *"Marion Mahony has been doing great work*: "Letters, 1903–1906 by Charles E. White, Jr, from the Studio of Frank Lloyd Wright," *Journal of Architectural Education*, Fall 1971.
6. *"The style of these drawings of Miss Mahony's*: Byrne in book review of Arthur Drexler's *The Drawings of Frank Lloyd Wright*, *Journal of the Society of Architectural Historians*, 22 (May 1963), 109.
7. *While Marion copied Japanese prints*: Gill, 188.
8. *Marion also did some architectural work*: Charles E. White letters.
9. *"Though it was a hot day*: MOA IV, 261.
10. *The same year, she also*: Weirick, "Motifs and Motives in the Lifework of Marion Mahony," in *Marion Mahony Reconsidered*, 103.
11. *Like his ancestors*: Wright, John Lloyd, 43.
12. *Marion was good friends with*: Maud Summers, *The Summers Readers,* Frank D. Beattys and Company, New York, 1908.

CHAPTER 11: SCANDAL

1. *In February 1909, Wright traveled*: James Weirick argues that Marion did not go to the Como Orchards site and did her brilliant bird's-eye perspective from her conversations with Wright and her imagination. See *Marion Mahony Reconsidered*, 101–102.
2. House for Ingwald Moe: See www.chameyer.net/669vanburen.html.
3. *While Marion may not have realized*: Brooks, "Frank Lloyd Wright and the Wasmuth Drawings," 20.
4. *"Wright's inability*: Manson, 213.
5. *Wright took Marion aside*: MOA IV, 20–2.

6. *Finally, he found someone*: For a detailed discussion of Wright's deal with von Holst, see Paul Kruty and Paul E. Sprague, *Marion Mahony and Millikin Place*, 12.
7. *"I engaged Miss Mahoney [sic]*: Hermann von Holst to Grant Manson, 16 February 1940, Manson Collection, Oak Park Public Library, Oak Park, Illinois.
8. *She continued working*: Paul Kruty, "Melding Architecture to Landscape in North-Central Iowa," in *Rock Crest/Rock Glen. Mason City, Iowa. The American Masterwork of Marion M. and Walter B. Griffin*, 42.
9. *"Leave families*: *Chicago Tribune*, November 7, 1909.
10. *"two abandoned homes"*: Secrest, 203.
11. *In November 1909, it* [Oak Park] *was abuzz*: *Oak Leaves*, November 13, 1909.
12. *Three years before*: Secrest, 203.
13. *"One night he took"*: Lloyd Wright, John, 53.
14. *Dwight told people*: "Perkins of Chicago."
15. *Chicago had a big population*: Susan E. Hirsch and Robert I. Goler, *A City Comes of Age. Chicago in the 1890s*, Chicago Historical Society, 1990, 27.
16. *"When the absent architect*: MOA IV, 20–2.

CHAPTER 12: OUT ON HER OWN

1. *Von Holst's agreement*: Kruty and Sprague, *Marion Mahony and Millikin Place*, 16.
2. *Drummond was making*: Kruty, McCoy, Sprague and Weirick, 42.
3. *"I was ... assigned to"*: Roy Lippincott to David Van Zanten, September 24, 1965. In "The Early Work of Marion Mahony Griffin," *The Prairie School Review*, second quarter, 1966.
4. *"A friend in the office*: MOA IV, 157.
5. *"Unforgettable was the expression"*: MOA IV, 278.
6. *Marion used the natural*: MOA IV, 126.
7. *The other project*: For a detailed discussion of the houses in Millikin Place see Kruty and Sprague, *Marion Mahony and Millikin Place*.
8. *The Millikin Place investors*: Kruty and Sprague, *Marion Mahony and Millikin Place*, 24.
9. *Marion commissioned George Niedecken*: There is some difference of opinion over the design of the furniture for the Irving house. In *The Magic of America*, Marion includes a photograph of the living room captioned: "Furniture, Carpets, Draperies, Radiator Screens and Glass, MMG & von Holst/Mural by Niedecken." However, some scholars of Niedecken claim he was responsible for the furniture in the Irving House. It is clear that Marion had oversight of the construction of the Irving House and brought

in Niedecken to help, but her caption in *Magic* makes it very clear that she recalled much of the interior, except for the mural, was done by her team in von Holst's office.
10. *The living room*: The author is most grateful to a former owner of the house, Marschall Smith, for not only giving her a tour of this house in July 2013, but also allowing her time to sit quietly in the magnificent living room and absorb its atmosphere. It is not hard to believe that Marion was falling in love with Walter when she designed this house.
11. *To the outside world*: Kruty and Sprague, *Marion Mahony and Millikin Place*, 20.
12. *He had studied*: MOA IV, 3.
13. *The Moe House in Gary, Indiana*: See www.chameyer.net/669vanburen.html.

Chapter 13: The Serpent's Wisdom

1. *"during my early life*: MOA IV, 329.
2. *wisdom of a serpent*: MOA IV, 274.
3. *The one thing she knew*: MOA IV, 274.
4. *Once she was planning*: MOA IV, 274.
5. *"tow-headed, blue eyed*: MOA IV, 87.
6. *It was, as she told people later*: MOA IV, 278.
7. *"So many times, they paddled*: MOA IV, 279.
8. *Walter "immediately saw worlds*: MOA IV, 275.
9. *By this time*: MOA IV, 275.
10. *"A stretch of shallows*: MOA IV, 280.
11. *One weekend they found themselves*: MOA IV, 280.
12. *"Militarism breeds beasts*: MOA IV, 281.
13. *"Two people on a cold night*: MOA IV, 289.
14. *"Socrates was, in every domain*: MOA IV, 274.
15. *"We can't go here*: MOA IV, 283.
16. *"They watched veil after veil*: MOA IV, 283.
17. *"Why don't I join*: MOA IV, 283.
18. *Marion drew the house*: There are two drawings of the Marshall House. One is in the Mary and Leigh Block Museum of Art at Northwestern University, Illinois, and the other is in the Nicholls collection at the National Library of Australia. The one in the Nicholls collection contains Marion's monogram and Walter's signature, but the one in America has both blocked out, something which Marion did on her return to Chicago for reasons she never explained.
19. *"And now, on coming into his office*: MOA IV, 286.
20. *"became deeply centered*: MOA IV, 329.

Chapter 14: Madness When It Struck

1. *"I was swept off my feet*: MOA IV, 157.
2. *Wright was furious about the allegations*: Draft of a letter from Wright to Griffin dated June 16, 1910, in Wright Archives, Fiche id G001 B10. In *Marion Mahony and Millikin Place*, 25, Paul Kruty argues that the letter Wright was responding to was most likely sent by Marion.
3. *Ricker had been*: See Peisch, 7–16.
4. *"It was I who won the plan*: MMG letter to William Purcell, August 7, 1947. William Gray Purcell papers, University of Minnesota.
5. *"The drawings*: Preamble to Frank Lloyd Wright, *Drawings and Plans of Frank Lloyd Wright. The Early Period (1893–1909)*.
6. *Later that year he wrote*: Secrest, 232.
7. *"Forgive my heat*: October 1911, Wright archives. As quoted in Secrest, 232.

Chapter 15: Proposals

1. *Walter's sister, Gertrude*: Gertrude Sater talking with Helmut Behrens, November 7–8, 1953. Elmhurst Historical Museum.
2. *"Come along now*: Harrison, 25.
3. *On Thursday June 29, 1911*: Marriage certificate of Marion Mahony and Walter Burley Griffin.
4. *"We eloped. It was wonderful"*: Marion Mahony letter to Mark Peisch. Peisch papers, AAL.
5. *"When I went into his office*: MOA I, 11.
6. *Marion wanted to add*: For a discussion on Marion's work on the Ricker House, see Kruty and Strong, 30–34.
7. *While in Grinnell*: Letter from Benjamin J. Ricker to Walter in 1911. Peisch papers, AAL.
8. *"Oh, look at the myriads of gastropods*: MOA IV, 292.
9. *Before them was a municipal*: MOA IV, 292.
10. *the sand was "as hot*: MOA IV, 293.
11. *"For the love of Mike*: MOA IV, 294.
12. *"Perhaps I am the swiftest*: MOA IV, 294.

Chapter 16: Fetching Up the Genii

1. *"always rubbing a lamp*: Mark Twain, *Life on the Mississippi*.
2. *"Never, they felt, had there been*: Miles Franklin article in *The Bulletin*, March 5, 1937, 2.
3. *"Marion was always experimenting*: Roy Lippincott letter to Mark Peisch, November 28, 1954. Peisch papers, AAL.

4. *Walter got a long wooden box*: For a description of what was available to competitors, including the Coulter paintings, see Paul Reid, *Canberra Following Griffin*.
5. *"If you project a line*: MOA IV, 327.
6. *"City planning*: MOA II, 436.
7. *the "last word of all the longest-lived*: Walter Burley Griffin, "Canberra: The Federal City Site and Its Architectural Possibilities," *Building*, Dec 12, 1913, 68.
8. *"When I first worked with Marion*: Peisch, 111.
9. *"After nine weeks of driving work*: MOA II, 435.

CHAPTER 17: NEWS FROM AUSTRALIA

1. *"The drawings are beautiful*: "The Federal Capital for the Commonwealth of Australia," *Town Planning Review* II, October 1912, 167.
2. *Not long after*: The visit by Miles Franklin and Alice Henry to the Griffins' office on June 4, 1912, is detailed in their joint article, "Walter Burley Griffin. Winner of the Federal Capital Prize," in the Sydney *Daily Telegraph*, July 3, 1912.
3. *Franklin, they found out*: For more information about Miles Franklin and her time in Chicago, see Jill Roe, *Stella Miles Franklin. A Biography*. Note Franklin was most commonly referred to as Miles Franklin.
4. *The Griffins discovered they had*: Ibid., 151.
5. *"We two Australians*: Franklin and Henry, *Daily Telegraph*, July 3, 1912.
6. *"It is not often*: *Construction News*, Chicago, June 1, 1912.
7. *"remarkable for its completeness*: Harriett Monroe, *Chicago Tribune*, September 22, 1912.

CHAPTER 18: MASON CITY

1. *Another major project was afoot*: For a detailed account of how Frank Lloyd Wright and the Griffins came to be working in Mason City, see "Rock Crest/Rock Glen: Prairie School Planning in Iowa," by Mason City historian and Griffin home owner Robert E. McCoy in *The Prairie School Review* 5, no. 3, 1968, 5–39. For more detail on the history of Mason City and the Griffins' work there, see: Kruty, McCoy, Sprague and Weirick, *Rock Crest/Rock Glen. Mason City, Iowa. The American Masterwork of Marion M. and Walter B. Griffin*.
2. *The best person for him*: MOA IV, 296.
3. *He signed up*: *Mason City Times*, July 20, 1912.
4. *She drew a magnificent*: In her article in *Art in Print*, Ellen E. Roberts includes a photo of a color woodblock owned by Wright called *Bamboo*

Fence at Kume Village by Japanese artist Katsushika Hokusai. There is a striking resemblance between the depiction of Kume Village and Marion's drawing of her ideal community around Willow Creek, Mason City. Marion's drawing was reproduced in the *Western Architect*, August 1913.
5. *The Griffins decided*: MOA IV, 307.
6. *Years later*: Robert E. McCoy interview with Barry Byrne, Evanston, January 22, 1966, in McCoy, 29.
7. *Marion designed a table*: McCoy interview with Melson House owner, Mrs. A.A. Adams, June 14, 1966, in McCoy, 29.
8. *When it was finally built*: MOA IV, 306–7.
9. *"He was going to have to charge*: MOA IV, 299.

CHAPTER 19: THE WORLD TURNED UPSIDE DOWN

1. *In November 1912*: Paul Reid, *Canberra Following Griffin*, 104. Also mentioned in *Royal Commission on Federal Capital Administration*, Minutes of Evidence, column 998.
2. *Walter wrote to Murdoch*: *Royal Commission on Federal Capital Administration*, Minutes of Evidence, column 998.
3. *After Wright left for Europe*: There are various references to the involvement of Wright and von Holst's offices in Henry Ford's commission for Fair Lane. See Ford R. Bryan, *Clara. Mrs. Henry Ford*, 146–147; Ronald O. Patterson, *The Mystery Behind Wrightian Influence in the Ford Fairlane Home*, May 20, 1973, in Benson Ford Research Center, Dearborn, Michigan; Grant Carpenter Manson, *Frank Lloyd Wright to 1910*, 213; Terry Smith, *Making the Modern. Industry, Art and Design in America*, University of Chicago Press, 1993.
4. *Marion and von Holst*: MOA IV, 386. Marion visits the Ford site. It appears that relations with Henry Ford were amicable at this stage. Von Holst and his wife also visited the site on December 8, 1913, according to the recollections of Mrs. Mary Louise Gregory Brand in an interview in February 1955, now in the Benson Ford Research Center.
5. *Was he passing some island in the Pacific?*: MOA IV, 386.
6. *A representative from the city*: MOA IV, 386.
7. *"My thought is with you*: MOA IV, 386.
8. *Walter wrote back to her*: "The Federal Capital. First Prize Designer in Melbourne. Enthusiastic Approval of Site," *The Age*, August 26, 1913.
9. *"I have decided*: MOA IV, 387.
10. *"His wife is an architect, too*: Henry Hyde Champion. *The Book Lover–A Literary Review* 16, no. 173, September 1913, 99.

11. *"All the works were executed on silk*: "Along the Bye-Paths: Exhibition of Mrs. Griffin's Work," *Journal of the Proceedings of the Royal Victorian Institute of Architects* 11, no. 4, September 1913, 200.
12. *"Walter, me darlint*: MOA IV, 388.

Chapter 20: Leaving Home

1. *It was a grand evening*: The evening as reported in *Construction News*, Chicago, February 14, 1914. Note this article confirms that Marion and Walter retained the satin drawings of their entry for the Canberra competition.
2. *Marion and Walter got the train*: For a detailed account of the Griffins' trip to Europe in 1914, see David Van Zanten, "The Griffins in Europe," 24–35.
3. *By now*: For one account of the deterioration in relations with Henry Ford over Fair Lane, see Ford R. Bryan, *Clara*, 146–147.

Chapter 21: The Arrival

1. *Twenty years before*: Mark Twain, *Following the Equator*, 1897. As republished in *The Wayward Tourist*, Melbourne University Press, 2006, 6.
2. *"If people will back me*: Sydney *Daily Telegraph*, May 13, 1914.
3. *Florence Taylor was tall*: For an excellent biography of Florence Taylor, see Freestone and Hanna, *Florence Taylor's Hats*.
4. *"We hail Frank*: George A. Taylor, "The Architecture of Tomorrow," *Building*, April 11, 1914.
5. *"The Federal prize*: *Building*, May 12, 1914.

Chapter 22: Storm Clouds

1. *"On clear days*: MOA II, 26.
2. *Taylor was less than impressed*: Freestone and Hanna, 51.
3. *The Griffins got a letter*: Ibid., 145–6.
4. *Elgh had left*: For more details on the life of George Elgh, see Christopher Vernon, "Out from the Shadows: George Elgh, the Griffins and Frank Lloyd Wright."
5. *"I hope you told:* MOA II, 67.

Chapter 23: The Dogs of War

1. *Marion was very fond*: MOA II, 316.
2. *"There is a very strong*: MOA II, 22.
3. *The Griffins found*: MOA II, 47.
4. *"A big husky officer*: MOA II, 253.
5. *"utterly European in its ideas*: MOA 11, 22–24.

6. *"There is bitter class feeling*: MOA II, 22.
7. *"He didn't come over here*: MOA II, 23.
8. *"Australian Federal politicians*: MOA II, 18.
9. *"We are hopeful*: MOA II, 19–20.
10. *"I am afraid*: MOA II, 20.
11. *In March 1915*: Details of Marion's fight with Florence over the women's section of the Town Planning Association are reconstructed from Marion's correspondence in MOA II, and in Freestone and Hanna, 147–149.
12. *"I passed around*: MOA II, 60.
13. *"The first year in Australia*: MOA II, 51.
14. *"As a man did*: "Buildings, Plans and Tenders, Women as Architects," Sydney *Daily Telegraph*, October 12, 1915.
15. *"Fortunately my job*: MOA II, 24.
16. *"Now you mustn't think*: MOA II, 23.
17. *O'Malley had actually been born*: For more on King O'Malley, see Arthur R. Hoyle, *King O'Malley. "The American Bounder,"* and Dorothy Catts, *King O'Malley. Man and Statesman*.
18. *O'Malley and his wife, Amy*: Hoyle, *King O'Malley*, 143, notes O'Malley and his wife Amy invited the Griffins to a dinner soon after their arrival in Australia "which laid the foundation of an unlikely but long enduring friendship."

Chapter 24: Newman College

1. *Irish-born priest*: ADB, online edition. For more information about Mannix, see Frank Murphy, *Daniel Mannix. Archbishop of Melbourne*, Advocate Press, Melbourne, 1948, and James Griffin, *Daniel Mannix. Beyond the Myths*, Garratt Publishing, Mulgrave, Victoria, 2012.
2. *Walter sketched out his idea*: MOA II, 240.
3. *Donovan went out of his way*: For more details of Donovan's letters over Newman College, see Donovan papers, Newman College Archives.
4. *"Dr. Mannix was a power*: MOA II, 240.
5. *A meeting of the college building committee*: Marion recalls the evening's celebrations in MOA II, 27e.
6. *"If anything*: MOA II, 27d.

Chapter 25: The Most Beautiful Café in the World

1. *"He was not Anglo Saxon*: MOA II, 92.
2. *"When I went over to her studio*: MOA II, 90.
3. *Toward the end*: MOA II, 92.
4. *"Except for the purpose*: MOA II, 26–27a.

5. "*agonizing days and months*: MOA II, 92.
6. "*very useful slave*: MOA II, 186.
7. "*[Wright] blames his pupils*: Freestone and Hanna, 51–52.
8. "*ghastly affair where Australian boys*: MOA II, 257.
9. "*We spent a lot of time trying to*: MOA IV, 168.
10. *The opening was a grand affair*: "Café Australia Opened. Enterprise Admired," Melbourne *Herald*, October 26, 1916.
11. "*In the midst of the dull tints*: MOA II, 80.
12. "*One could perhaps say*: MOA II, 85-2.
13. "*My speciality is*: Henrietta C. Walker, "Woman, the Architect," *The Lone Hand* 7, no. 1, December 1916, 43.

CHAPTER 26: THE CASE OF MR. REEVES

1. "*at present I am doing mostly listing of*: MOA II, 27a. Marion's color-coded books on Australian plants are part of the Nicholls collection at the National Library of Australia in Canberra.
2. "*So planned as to create the impression*: MOA II, 32.
3. "*delineated mass plantings of Australian flora*: Christopher Vernon, "Newman College Landscape Plan," in Turnbull, Jeff and Navaretti, Peter Y., eds., 135.
4. *commissioned Marion*: For details of the dispute and the judgment, see James Weirick, "Motifs and Motives in the Lifework of Marion Mahony," in *Marion Mahony Reconsidered*, 110.
5. *In November, she went into*: The plan is contained in a document dated November 10, 1916, lodged with the federal Copyright Office now on file in the National Archives of Australia in Canberra.
6. "*How absurd it is*: MOA II, 224e.
7. "*The Plaintiff knew*: "Legal," *NSW Contract Reporter* 21, no. 26, June 27, 1917, 104.
8. "*The courts of this community*: MOA II, 203a.
9. "*I am not bothering my head*: MOA II, 203a.
10. *The Lippincotts, she wrote home, "have just finished*: MOA II, 203a.
11. "*We are planting the shrubbery there, too*: MOA II, 203a.
12. "*The last day we ran away*: MOA II, 203a.

CHAPTER 27: AN ANCIENT LAND

1. *She was invited*: Marion addressed the society on March 5, 1918. Reported in "Women Horticulturalists' Association of Victoria," in the *Australasian*, March 23, 1918.
2. "*I feel that the Archangel who painted*: MOA III, 106.

3. *Marion and Bertha*: Information on Marion's trip is contained in her diaries in MOA (including MOA III, 83). Also see Vernon, " 'The Silence of the Mountains and the Music of the Sea,'" 22–40.
4. *"Fine trees*: Marion's postcard to Walter. Vernon, " 'The Silence of the Mountains and the Music of the Sea,' " 39.
5. *"You have no idea*: Ibid., 39.
6. *"vegetation originated in*: MOA III, 86.
7. *As she sketched the tree*: MOA III, 183. Marion's comments about the Tasmanian gum tree. The painting referred to is in the Block Museum at Northwestern University. For more information about Marion's *Forest Portraits*, see *Marion Mahony Griffin. Drawing the Form of Nature*, edited by Debora Wood.
8. *"color runs riot*: MOA III, 183.
9. *"decorating the edge of a precipice*: MOA III, 10.
10. *"Tree ferns!*: MOA III, 144.
11. *"We had been discussing*: MOA III, 455.
12. *She had developed:* For details on Marion's painting and printing techniques, see Debora Wood, ed., *Drawing the Form of Nature*, vii-xii.

Chapter 28: A Home of Their Own?

1. *"compelled under protest*: Walter's letter to Walter Bingle, resigning, Dec. 23, 1920. "Correspondence with Mr. Walter Burley Griffin in regard to the position on the Federal Capital Advisory Committee," NAA: A199, FC21/76.
2. *"the cheapest, most perfect*: MOA II, 342.
3. *"The one moment of pure romance*: MOA II, 338.
4. *"It nestled far back*: MOA II, 351.
5. *"Well, let them pull it down*: MOA II, 349.
6. *"Garbed in restful blue*: MOA II, 188.

Chapter 29: No Fences, No Boundaries

1. *Walter was determined*: The author is most grateful to Castlecrag historian and Griffin home owner Bob McKillop for his information on the development of the suburb. For more information on the development of Castlecrag, see Meredith Walker, Adrienne Kabos and James Weirick, *Building for Nature. Walter Burley Griffin and Castlecrag*, and Alasdair McGregor, *Grand Obsessions*, 379–397.
2. *"Castlecrag to be built*: C.C.D. Brammall, "He Built the Australian Bush into His Homes," 1947. Eric M. Nicholls papers, NLA MS9957.
3. *In January 1924*: Jill Roe, *My Congenials*, 167.

Chapter 30: A Crystal Cave

1. *Marion took on the massive task*: Mark L. Peisch, in *The Chicago School of Architecture*, 130, notes: "The interior decoration [of the Capitol Theatre] was somewhat bizarre and probably was the work of Marion Mahony Griffin who was frequently responsible for the interior décor and furniture design for Griffin's buildings." Peisch's book was written after correspondence with Barry Byrne, Roy Lippincott, William Purcell, Eric Nicholls and Marion Mahony.
2. *The design and the approval process*: Roy Lippincott letter to Mark Peisch, November 28, 1954. Peisch papers, AAL.
3. *It may have been*: Architects Registration Board of Victoria, Marion Mahony Griffin registration form, June 29, 1923, as cited by James Weirick, "Motifs and Motives in the Lifework of Marion Mahony," 116, 162n77.

Chapter 31: Changes

1. *"There had been a strange conflict*: MOA III, 118.
2. *"It certainly was no pleasure*: MOA III, 118.
3. *It was agreed*: Writing in 1925, Charles John Cerutty, a senior federal public servant, who bought a half share in GSDA in November 1922, stated that "Mrs. Griffin took temporary charge of sales from March 2, 1924 to June 30, 1924." Papers at University of Melbourne accessed by Bob McKillop. The comment implies that it had been specifically agreed that Marion would go to Castlecrag to take charge of the sales process before she went, but as it was written in 1925, after the event, it does not confirm how long she originally planned to stay there.
4. *There was a boathouse*: MOA III, 120.
5. *One Saturday, after the opening*: James Weirick, "Spirituality and Symbolism in the Work of the Griffins," in Anne Watson, ed., *Beyond Architecture. Marion Mahony and Walter Burley Griffin. America. Australia. India*, 79.
6. *It may have been*: Walter mentioned Wright's use of concrete blocks in a paper in 1927. As Wright's first such house was built in Pasadena in 1923, it could have been during their visit back to America in 1924–25 or soon after that they learned of these houses. For a discussion on this issue, see Donald Leslie Johnson, *The Architecture of Walter Burley Griffin*, Macmillan, 1977.
7. *"I can't say that the development*: WBG to Purcell, January 7, 1925. Purcell papers, University of Minnesota.

Chapter 32: A Community Develops

1. *The Griffins had hired*: See Louise Lightfoot paper. Also see Walker, Kabos, and Weirick, *Building for Nature*, 32.

2. *Selling Pholiota*: MOA III, 202.
3. *But O'Malley felt*: Hoyle, *King O'Malley*, 174–7.
4. *"It appears to me*: Papers of C.J. Cerutty, 1925, University of Melbourne. By courtesy of Bob McKillop.

CHAPTER 33: NEW FRIENDS

1. *One day, a lawyer friend*: James Weirick, "Spirituality and Symbolism in the Work of the Griffins," in *Beyond Architecture*, 79.
2. *"This morning I went*: J.J. van der Leeuw, letter to J.N. van der Ley, August 4, 1926, as quoted by Weirick, Ibid.
3. *"Before then, I had been saying*: MOA IV, 169.
4. *"It was rather like*: Norna Kollerstrom Morton, *Hands Full of Life. Reflections and Anecdotes*, Butterfly Books, 1993, 168. Given to the author by Norna's son, Ivor Morton.
5. *"They were walking along*: Spathopoulos, 28.
6. *"another burst of genius*: MOA III, 134.
7. *From then on*: Walker, Kabos and Weirick, *Building for Nature*, 26.
8. *"A bridge across a bit of a chasm*: MOA III, 309.

CHAPTER 34: DRAWING NATURE

1. *"Anyone needing privacy*: Lightfoot, 3.
2. *"Marion's style was to*: Lightfoot, 6.
3. *"She was a remarkable woman*: Lightfoot, 1.
4. *"It was the flapper era*: Spathopoulos, 29.
5. *"I had my hair cut*: MOA III, 134.
6. *"My own knack of costuming*: MOA III, 134.
7. *"I was most interested*: Lightfoot, 3.
8. *"Marion could have been called*: Lightfoot, 6.
9. *"The combination of the natural loveliness*: MOA III, 134.
10. *"There were canoe trips*: Lightfoot, 5.
11. *"Viewed from the harbor*: MOA III, 109.
12. *"Botanists tell us*: MOA III, 86.
13. *"The trunk of the Angophora*: MOA III, 86.
14. *"strained to the point*: MOA III, 345.
15. *"There was always a minor strain*: MOA III, 345.
16. *"The Wattles are the Golden Rod trees*: MOA III, 298.
17. *"The poor man*: Letter from Franklin, August 20, 1928, in Jill Roe, *My Congenials*, 199.

Chapter 35: 1929

1. *Meanwhile, in Castlecrag*: The Fishwick House. Walker, Kabos, and Weirick, *Building for Nature*, 62–63.
2. *"Castlecrag has concentrated*: MM letter to Miles Franklin. Miles Franklin papers, Mitchell Library, Sydney. Reproduced by Walker, Kabos, and Weirick in *Building for Nature*, 34.
3. *Bernard Hesling, a young Englishman*: Hesling, 165.
4. *"People said Marion*: Lightfoot, 6.
5. *"Marion—fifteen years older*: Hesling, 167.
6. *"A decision to move*: Martin, 82.

Chapter 36: The Split

1. *"titles are usually given*: MOA III, 239.
2. *"who feel greater and greater bitterness*: MOA III, 239.
3. *"opened up the real way*: MOA IV, 169.
4. *Writing in her book*: Spathopoulos, 275.
5. *"Because Marion is not infrequently*: Ibid., 271.
6. *"In 1930 at the end*: MOA IV, 159.
7. *"The many years were packed full*: MOA IV, 157.
8. *"curious conflict of interests*: MOA IV, 157.
9. *"his mind was always*: Spathopoulos, 275.

Chapter 37: Fairies and Herons

1. *"One boy said to Miss Reynolds*: MOA IV, 232.
2. *"I explained to them*: MOA IV, 234.
3. *"The Fig is a sort of rubber plant*: MOA III, 52.
4. *"In love, when one really loves*: MOA IV, 159.
5. *"Anything that can be proved*: MOA IV, 157.
6. *"Steiner says without the molding force*: MOA IV, 160.
7. *"Your truly human letter*: MOA IV, 162.
8. *"I jolly well would have deserved*: MOA IV, 162.
9. *"Thanks for the distinction*: MOA IV, 162.
10. *"During Mrs. G.'s absence*: Spathopoulos, 292.

Chapter 38: A New Life

1. *Now in her late 30s*: Information about Ula Maddocks from author conversations with her daughter, Deirdre Morton, 2010, 2011.
2. *"The process of re-adjusting*: Spathopoulos, 297.
3. *"Walter's affair had broken*: Ibid., 275.
4. *"The Valley was astir*: MOA III, 430.

5. *They started with*: Spathopoulos, 321–322.
6. *"The choruses took up their groupings*: MOA III, 440.

Chapter 39: An Invitation from India

1. *"the tiniest dwelling*: Spathopoulos, 298.
2. *"cascading down the cliff*: Comment of James Birrell, quoted in Turnbull and Navaretti, 332.
3. *"beautiful, majestic, as unique as any*: MOA III, 89-2.
4. *"We both saw angel forces*: MOA I, 11. Marion's comments imply that there may have been some Anthroposophical inspiration for the project, but it is not known if she had any involvement in its design.
5. *When he arrived in Lucknow*: For more information on the history of Lucknow, see Rosie Llewellyn-Jones, *A Fatal Friendship. The Nawabs, the British and the City of Lucknow*, Oxford University Press, 1985, and *Lucknow. Memories of a City*, edited by Violette Graff, Oxford University Press, 1997, particularly the section on "Making Lucknow the Capital," 214–219.
6. *"looks and feels quite Indian*: MOA I, 9.
7. *"Plans accepted*: MOA I, 9.
8. *"It is seldom that a European*: MOA I, 10.
9. *One afternoon before he left*: The photos of Walter, Deirdre, and Ula Maddocks are in the National Library of Australia in the Nicholls collection. There is no date on them but given that Deirdre was walking by then and looks around 18 months old, they may have been part of a photo session taken just before Walter left for India.

Chapter 40: A New Land

1. *"Since we can no longer*: MOA I, 12.
2. *"Only in thinking of what my wife means to me*: MOA I, 20.
3. *Waiting at the dock*: This was not the Australian "first" cricket team that was playing in South Africa. Ryder's team was an unofficial team of veterans.
4. *"New Delhi is the newest of cities*: MOA I, 33.
5. *"The landscape is studded*: MOA I, 33.

Chapter 41: Lucknow

1. *"I already feel more at home*: MOA I, 32.
2. *"I saw a great burden*: MOA I, 36.
3. *"thousands of pounds*: MOA I, 40.
4. *"As to my next incarnation*: MOA I, 43.
5. *"the possibility of creating*: MOA I, 46.
6. *"Three deaths in only*: MOA I, 49.

7. *"What shocking, dreadful word*: MOA I, 53.
8. *"As to your suggestion*: MOA I, 53.
9. *A Sunni Muslim*: Lionel Carter, ed., *United Provinces Politics 1936–1937*, Manohar Publishers, New Delhi, 2008, 64.
10. *"We enjoyed a sumptuous afternoon tea*: MOA I, 66.
11. *"As with the Moguls*: MOA I, 65.
12. *"What I say goes*: MOA I, 69.
13. *"Libraries are my particular speciality now*: MOA I, 58.
14. *"Mrs. Griffin told him*: MOA I, 70. This cryptic reference makes it clear that George Griffin knew that Ula Maddocks was not able to have a child by her husband Edgar.
15. *"When Mr. Griffin wrote*: Spathopoulos, 329.
16. *"The hot summer means nothing to me*: MOA I, 116a.
17. *It contained one word only*: MOA I, 116b.

Chapter 42: Like an Indian, Mrs. Griffin Follows Her Man

1. *"We still have to thank*: MOA I, 117.
2. *"Mrs. Walter Burley Griffin*: Sydney Daily Telegraph, April 30, 1936.
3. *"Another six months alone*: MOA I, 119.
4. *"We are hopefully*: MOA I, 146.
5. *"design a day to be turned out*: MOA I, 140.
6. *"These young fellows*: MOA I, 138.
7. *"We went out into the brilliant moonlight*: MOA I, 121.
8. *"a palace for a king of kings*: MOA I, 121.

Chapter 43: The Exposition

1. *Another client, Dr. Bhatia*: Conversation with Dr. Bhatia's son in Lucknow, January 2011.
2. *"We are convinced that*: MOA I, 128.
3. *"The story of Canberra*: MOA I, 130.
4. *"Marion is back at the drawing board*: MOA I, 131, 134.
5. *"Marion is working like a slave*: MOA I, 149.
6. *"You should see us*: MOA I, 122.
7. *"The fairies brought us here*: MOA I, 169.
8. *"I am comfortable here*: MOA I, 57.

Chapter 44: His Eyes Never Left Mine

1. *"The atmosphere is one of people*: MOA I, 137.
2. *Marion redid some of the drawings*: Marion's drawings from the Griffins' time in India are now in the Avery Architectural Library, Columbia University,

New York. Many are reproduced by Kruty and Sprague in *Two American Architects in India*.
3. *"It was a happy and busy office*: MOA I, 196.
4. *"After a lifetime of self-sacrifice*: MOA I, 202.
5. *"As the end drew near*: MOA I, 199.

CHAPTER 45: GOING HOME
1. *"By whatever means the crossing*: MOA I, 8.
2. *"After a while she opened*: Lightfoot, 8.
3. *"The youth flared*: MOA II, 431.
4. saw a *"young city*: MOA II, 431.
5. *"The one thing lacking*: MOA II, 431.
6. *"I left Castlecrag, truly a bit of Paradise*: MOA I, 208.
7. *Marion resumed her friendship with Lola Lloyd*: For more detail on Marion's activities on her return to Chicago, see: Anna Rubbo, "Marion Mahony's Return to the United States," in *Marion Mahony Reconsidered*, edited by David Van Zanten, 122–145.
8. *Visiting her in 1952*: Peisch letter to Eric Nicholls. January 15, 1954. Peisch papers, AAL.
9. *"Marion gave the same old welcome*: Lightfoot, 8.
10. *"Marion may know*: Lightfoot, 8.

EPILOGUE
1. *"Marion Mahony is certainly the key figure*: Manson, 217.
2. *"She was not only*: Manson, 217.
3. *"one of the finest*: White, 110.
4. *"spectacularly brilliant person*: Byrne correspondence with Peisch, March 22, 1960. Peisch papers, AAL.
5. *"In many ways their*: Peisch, 59.
6. *"First of all, she didn't want to mention*: Peisch, "Walter Burley Griffin: In His Own Right," PBS documentary, 1999.
7. *"It was difficult to distinguish*: Peisch, Ibid.
8. *"She was very much in love*: Perkins, PBS documentary.
9. *"Of the delineators*: Brooks, PBS documentary.
10. *"I would argue*: Van Zanten, in *Marion Mahony Griffin. Drawing The Form of Nature*, 2.
11. *"The fact remains*: Lawrence Perkins, PBS documentary.
12. *"Marion's Angophoras."*: Interview with the author, December 2011.
13. *"Marion Mahony Griffin was the greatest*: Pregliasco, 181.
14. *"Marion Mahony Griffin stands alone*: Allaback, 89.

Bibliography

Allaback, Sarah. *The First American Women Architects.* University of Illinois Press, Urbana and Chicago. 2008.

Brooks, H. Allen. *The Prairie School. Frank Lloyd Wright and His Midwest Contemporaries.* W.W. Norton & Company, New York. 2006.

Brooks, H. Allen. "Frank Lloyd Wright and the Wasmuth Drawings," *Art Bulletin* 48, 2, June 1966.

Bryan, Ford R. *Clara, Mrs. Henry Ford.* Ford Books, Dearborn, Michigan. 2001.

Byrne, Barry. "The Chicago Movement." Paper delivered to Illinois Society of Architects, November 28, 1939. Manuscript in Ricker Architectural Library, University of Illinois.

Catts, Dorothy, *King O'Malley. Man and Statesman.* Publicity Press, Sydney. 1938.

Champion, Henry Hyde. *The Book Lover—A Literary Review* 16, no. 173, September 1913.

Drexler, Arthur. *The Drawings of Frank Lloyd Wright.* Horizon Press, New York. 1962.

Fraker, Guy C. *Lincoln's Ladder to the Presidency. The Eighth Judicial Circuit.* Southern Illinois University Press, Carbondale. 2012.

Freestone, Robert, and Hanna, Bronwyn. *Florence Taylor's Hats.* Halstead Press, Ultimo, NSW. 2007.

Gill, Brendan. *Many Masks. A Life of Frank Lloyd Wright.* Da Capo Press, New York. 1998.

Graff, Violette, ed. *Lucknow. Memories of a City.* Oxford University Press, Delhi. 1997.

Griffin, Marion Mahony. *The Magic of America. Electronic Edition.* The Art Institute of Chicago and The New-York Historical Society. 29 October 2008. http://www.artic.edu/magicofamerica/index.html.

Harrison, Peter. *Walter Burley Griffin. Landscape Architect.* National Library of Australia, Canberra. 1995.

Hesling, Bernard. *Stir Up This Stew*. Ure Smith, Sydney. 1966.

Hirsch, Susan E., and Goler, Robert I. *A City Comes of Age. Chicago in the 1890s*. Chicago Historical Society, Chicago. 1990.

Kruty, Paul, McCoy, Robert E., Sprague, Paul E., and Weirick, James. *Rock Crest/Rock Glen. Mason City, Iowa. The American Masterwork of Marion M. and Walter B. Griffin*. Walter Burley Griffin Society of America, St. Louis. 2014.

Kruty, Paul and Sprague, Paul E. *Marion Mahony and Millikin Place*. The Walter Burley Griffin Society of America, St. Louis. 2007.

Kruty, Paul and Sprague, Paul E. *Two American Architects in India. Walter B. Griffin and Marion M. Griffin. 1935–1937*. University of Illinois School of Architecture, Urbana-Champaign. 1997.

Kruty, Paul and Strong, Daniel. *Walter Burley Griffin and Marion Mahony Griffin in Grinnell*. Faulconer Gallery, Grinnell College, 2011.

Larson, Erik, *The Devil in the White City*. Vintage Books, New York. 2003.

Lightfoot, Louise. "With the Burley Griffins." 10 pages of notes written in 1975 in correspondence with Donald Leslie Johnson. In Donald Leslie Johnson papers. NLA MS7817.

Llewellyn-Jones, Rosie. *A Fatal Friendship. The Nawabs, the British and the City of Lucknow*. Oxford University Press, Delhi. 1985.

Manson, Grant Carpenter. *Frank Lloyd Wright to 1910. The First Golden Age*. John Wiley & Sons, Inc., New York. 1958.

Martin, Sylvia. *Ida Leeson: A Life. Not a Blue-stocking Lady*. Allen & Unwin, Sydney. 2006.

McCoy, Robert. "Rock Crest/Rock Glen: Prairie School Planning in Iowa," *The Prairie School Review*, vol.5, third quarter, 1968. 5–39.

McGregor, Alasdair. *Grand Obsessions. The Life and Work of Walter Burley Griffin and Marion Mahony Griffin*. Lantern, Penguin Group, Camberwell. 2009.

Miller, Donald L. *City of the Century*. Simon & Schuster Paperbacks, New York. 1996.

PBS. *Walter Burley Griffin: In His Own Right*. Documentary aired in 1999. www.pbs.org/wbgriffin.

Peisch, Mark L. *The Chicago School of Architecture. Early followers of Sullivan and Wright*. Random House, New York. 1964.

Perkins, Eleanor Ellis. "Perkins of Chicago." Unpublished manuscript.

Pregliasco, Janice. "The Life and Work of Marion Mahony Griffin," *The Art Institute of Chicago Museum Studies* 21, no. 2, 1995.

Reid, Paul. *Canberra Following Griffin. A Design History of Australia's National Capital.* National Archives of Australia, Canberra. 2002.

Ridley, Jane. *The Architect and His Wife. A Life of Edwin Lutyens.* Chatto & Windus, London. 2002.

Roberts, Ellen E. "Ukiyo-e in Chicago: Frank Lloyd Wright, Marion Mahony Griffin and the Prairie School," *Art in Print*, July–August 2013.

Roe, Jill. *Stella Miles Franklin. A Biography.* Fourth Estate, London. 2008.

Roe, Jill, ed. *My Congenials. Miles Franklin and Friends in Letters.* Angus & Robertson, Pymble, NSW. 2010.

Roe, Jill. "The Magical World of Marion Mahony Griffin," in *Minorities. Cultural Diversity in Sydney.* Edited by G. Fitzgerald and G. Wotherspoon. State Library of NSW Press, Sydney. 1995.

Secrest, Meryle. *Frank Lloyd Wright. A Biography.* The University of Chicago Press, Chicago. 1998.

Spathopoulos, Wanda. *The Crag, Castlecrag 1924–1938.* Brandl & Schlesinger, Blackheath, NSW. 2007.

Summers, Maud. *The Summers Readers.* Frank D. Beattys and Company, New York. 1908.

Turnbull, Jeffrey John. "The Architecture of Newman College." PhD thesis. University of Melbourne, 2004.

Turnbull, Jeffrey John, and Navaretti, Peter, eds. *The Griffins in Australia and India.* Melbourne University Press, Melbourne. 1998.

Van Zanten, David. "The Early Work of Marion Mahony Griffin," *The Prairie School Review,* vol. 3, second quarter, 1966, 5–24.

Van Zanten, David. "The Griffins in Europe," in *Drawing the Future, Chicago Architecture on the International Stage, 1900–1925.* Edited by David Van Zanten. Northwestern University Press, Evanston, Illinois. 2013.

Van Zanten, David. "Marion Mahony Griffin," in *Marion Mahony Griffin. Drawing the Form of Nature.* Edited by Debora Wood. Mary and Leigh Block Museum of Art and Northwestern University Press. Evanston. 2005.

Van Zanten, David, ed. *Marion Mahony Reconsidered*. University of Chicago Press, Chicago. 2011.

Vernon, Christopher. "Out from the Shadows: George Elgh, the Griffins and Frank Lloyd Wright," *Fabrications: The Journal of the Society of Architectural Historians, Australia and New Zealand*, vol. 23, no. 1, 2013. 122–126.

Vernon, Christopher. " 'The Silence of the Mountains and the Music of the Sea': The Landscape Artistry of Marion Mahony Griffin," in *Marion Mahony Griffin. Drawing in the Form of Nature*. Edited by Debora Wood. Mary and Leigh Block Museum of Art and Northwestern University Press, Evanston. 2005. 22–25.

Walker, Meredith, Kabos, Adrienne, and Weirick, James. *Building for Nature. Walter Burley Griffin and Castlecrag*. Walter Burley Griffin Society, Inc., Sydney. 1994.

Watson, Anne, ed. *Beyond Architecture. Marion Mahony and Walter Burley Griffin. America. Australia. India*. Powerhouse Publishing, Sydney. 1998.

Weirick, James. "Marion Mahony at MIT," *Transition*, no. 25, winter 1988. 48–54.

Weirick, James. "Motifs and Motives in the Lifework of Marion Mahony," in *Marion Mahony Reconsidered*. Edited by David Van Zanten. University of Chicago Press, Chicago. 2011. 95–120.

White, Charles E. Jr. "Letters from the Studio of F.L.Wright, 1903–1906," *Journal of Architectural Education* 25, fall 1971.

Wood, Debora, ed. *Marion Mahony Griffin. Drawing the Form of Nature*. Mary and Leigh Block Museum of Art and Northwestern University Press, Evanston. 2005.

Wright, Frank Lloyd. *An Autobiography*. Horizon Press, New York. 1977.

Wright, Frank Lloyd. *Drawings and Plans of Frank Lloyd Wright. The Early Period (1893–1909)*. Dover Publications, New York. 1983.

Wright, John Lloyd. *My Father, Frank Lloyd Wright*. Dover Publications, New York. 1992.

Young, Desmond. *Try Anything Twice*. Hamish Hamilton, London. 1963.

Acknowledgments

Writing this book has been an amazing journey of many years which has taken me from Canberra, Castlecrag, Melbourne and Heidelberg to Chicago and the American Midwest, to New York, and on a memorable visit to Delhi and Lucknow in India.

It has involved meeting a generous and inspiring group of people—from academics and scholars, to Griffin home owners and enthusiasts, to researchers and devoted librarians and two wonderful "children of Castlecrag."

The book draws on the extensive work done by diligent Griffin scholars and authors. Paul Kruty in the US has researched and published extensively on the work of the Griffins. His book on Millikin Place and others, such as Mason City and India, are invaluable sources of detail and discussion about Marion's role.

It was a privilege to meet, and have many discussions with, one of the first scholars to take Marion seriously—Professor David Van Zanten from Northwestern University in Evanston, Illinois. Van Zanten began studying Marion as a young man in his 20s and had spoken with people who knew her, including Barry Byrne. He helped me organize my first viewing of Marion's drawings in the National Archives in Canberra and was also generous with sharing his observations, including those on Marion's clever use of white paint in her drawings for the Canberra competition. He also helped organize a tour of Marion's mural in the G.B. Armstrong School north of Chicago. The headmaster, Otis Dunson III, allowed us a generous amount of time to take in the work. It is a miracle it has survived and more needs to be done to help the school preserve Marion's magic mural. Van Zanten has also helped further appreciation of Marion by expertly editing another important book, *Marion Mahony Reconsidered*, from the papers at a conference at Northwestern.

I longed to meet American architect and writer Janet Pregliasco who wrote a book about Marion which was never published. But I was never able to track her down. I was able to have several rich discussions by email with Elizabeth Birmingham, at North Dakota State University, who has her own feminist critique of how Marion has been treated in the recounting of history.

In America, it has also been a joy and privilege to meet Peter Griffin, Walter's grandnephew, who has done a wonderful job founding and keeping the Griffin Society alive. Few of us will forget the society's 2014 visit to Mason City and the tour of Griffin homes. Staying in Wright designed Park Hotel in Mason City was a real treat. In Mason City one cannot but be amazed at the energy and passion of long-time Griffin home owner and local historian Bob McCoy. He spent half a day showing me and my husband around the Griffin homes, and has done much to preserve the city's unique architectural history. We were also delighted to meet the owners of the Melson House, Roger and Peggy Bang. Seeing an original Marion drawing of the Melson House in the Melson House, was one of those "take your breath away" moments.

In Decatur, the wonderful Brigitta Kapp kindly arranged for us to see the houses in Millikin Place. Marschall Smith was most kind in letting us see his newly acquired Adolph Mueller House, one of Marion's masterpieces, and show us around the city. In Grand Rapids, long-time home owners of Marion's Amberg House, Tom and Anne Logan, were kind to show us their house while they were in the process of moving out.

In Chicago we are most fond of Griffin home owners Ron Duplack and Tannys Langdon, architect and Griffin Society board member. They opened up their homes to us in Chicago and Galena, and arranged several delightful meals. We have had several long animated discussions in which Tannys and I remained the official "designated drinkers." It has also been great to meet other US Griffin Society members, including Griffin home owner Rich Berry, George Shutack and Will Hasbrouck. In New York, the wonderful Judith and Ray McGuire have been generous hosts and suppliers of late night rosé.

It was also a privilege to meet with two of Dwight Perkins' most successful and talented grandsons, Dwight H. Perkins, distinguished economist and China expert at Harvard University, and Bradford Perkins, New York based architect and founder of the international architectural firm, Perkins Eastman. Bradford Perkins was very generous in giving me a copy of his family history which helped to provide insights into the life and times of Marion's grandparents and their links with Abraham Lincoln, and the story of Dwight Perkins and his own mother, Marion. Their amazing grandfather would have been most proud of them.

Debora Wood was also most helpful in arranging viewing of Marion's work at the Block Museum at Northwestern University. In New York Janet Parks at the Avery Library at Columbia University was most helpful. Thanks to the Ryerson & Burnham Library at the Art Institute of Chicago for permission to use the quotations from *The Magic of America* and Chicago researcher and history fan Elizabeth Patterson for her help.

In Australia, the Walter Burley Griffin Society does a wonderful job, headed by James Weirick who has an encyclopedic knowledge of Griffin. He is a passionate speaker and a prolific writer, with an expertise in the Griffins won from decades of research. His work has done much to keep the study of the Griffins alive. The society's executives also include its wonderful secretary, Kerry McKillop, a Griffin home owner. Husband Bob McKillop is a keen historian of the area and open with his local knowledge. Adrienne and John Kabos are two Griffin home owners who have also worked tirelessly to preserve the Griffin legacy. In a bizarre twist of fate, our own house in Sydney was designed by architect Caroline Pidcock, who went on to be awarded the Marion Mahony Griffin prize by the Australian Institute of Architects in 2011, and to marry another long-time Griffin expert and Griffin Society patron, John McInerney.

My husband and I spent many happy lunches in the Blue Mountains, a few hours west of Sydney, with Deirdre and Ivor Morton in their hand built, mud brick home, as they shared their memories of Castlecrag. Both are most delightful "children" of Castlecrag who embody many of the Griffins' ideals. It was not an easy journey for Deirdre whose mother, Ula, so fiercely adored both Griffins and whose own life has a complicated history. Being prepared to discuss and research her mother's story has helped dispel some myths, and provide an important explanation for the Griffins' links to India.

MAKING MAGIC: THE MARION MAHONY GRIFFIN STORY

I spent some time talking with early Castlecrag resident Wanda Spathopoulos, and her book, *The Crag*, is a most valuable source about the times when the Griffins were living there. Alasdair McGregor's book on the Griffins, *Grand Obsessions*, is also an important record, particularly for highlighting Marion's clashes with Florence Taylor and the high cost for both Marion and Walter from their fallout with the Taylors.

In Canberra, Glenda Lynch was a fast and efficient researcher of the files at the National Library. In America, Lorraine Fico-White of Magnifico Manuscripts was very helpful in providing an American insight into my writing—and provided many helpful structural suggestions and a US style copy edit. Others to thank include Anne Watson, Griffin enthusiast, and Heidelberg architect Max Chester, and Melbourne Open House.

At *The Australian* newspaper, thanks to the editor-in-chief, Chris Mitchell, editor, Clive Mathieson, and former business editor, Geoff Elliott, for allowing me time off to research the book.

My daughter Anna was a great companion and researcher into Griffin's time in India. My sister Jeanette and her family came with us for moral support. In India, we used Lucknow travel agent Tornos which was most familiar with the Griffin story and an expert on Lucknow itself. They arranged a visit to Lucknow University, Griffin's grave, La Martiniere, The Residency and the one remaining Griffin designed house. Lucknow is not on the beaten tourist path and having a local guide was invaluable.

Lastly, my husband Vin has been on my American journey since our arrival in an almost deserted Dulles Airport in 1981. The welcome we had expected at the airport did not materialize and a slightly exasperated porter had to explain the value of the American coins I needed for the payphone. It was a six year stint in Washington and New York which changed and enriched our lives, including obtaining three US university degrees between us. It laid the foundation for a lifelong passion to learn more about America and its rich history and its energetic creative people, as well as its links with Australia. He has helped me and provided much needed moral support at every step of the way. To detail it all would require another book. This book is a thank you to all the people we have met on our journey, one which is still very much a work in progress.

Illawarra Palms. New South Wales. Forest Portrait No. 2
Circa 1925. Courtesy of Peter B. and Joanne S. Griffin.

Index

A

Addams, Jane 26, 38, 39, 104, 117, 146, 149
All Souls Church (Evanston) 42, 48, 57, 75, 307
Amberg House (Grand Rapids) 75, 79, 302, 306, 308, 335
Anthroposophy 234, 235, 236, 237, 239, 241, 250, 251, 268, 271, 289, 292
Archibald, William Oliver 141, 144, 148, 152
Armstrong School (Chicago) 245, 246, 299, 334
Avery Architectural Library (Columbia University) 296, 299, 329

B

Bailey, Liberty Hyde 80, 167, 222
Baracchi, Guido 185, 305
Baskerville, Margaret 160, 161, 197
Blake, James Vila 47, 48, 49, 53
Blythe House (Mason City) 123
Bock, Richard 35, 42, 45, 50, 61, 88, 160, 313
Burnham, Daniel Hudson 8, 29, 30, 31, 37, 97, 106, 108, 150, 271, 276, 295, 296, 299, 306, 311, 312, 336
Byrne, Barry 44, 51, 52, 60, 123, 133, 143, 148, 169, 292, 300, 313, 314, 319, 324, 329, 330, 334

C

Café Australia 162, 165, 166, 174, 177, 180, 194, 195, 197, 202, 309, 322
Capitol Theatre 193, 194, 196, 198, 199, 201, 202, 306, 324
Cheney, Martha (Mamah) Borthwick 53, 60, 65, 66, 69, 70, 71, 143, 238
Chicago
  establishment 9
  Great Fire 10–11
  World's Columbian Fair 29, 30, 102, 275, 312
Clamp, John Burcham 137, 147
Cook, Joseph 126, 140
Cooley House (Monroe, Louisiana) 264
Craig, Ronald 247, 248, 254, 255, 256, 258, 259, 260, 263, 266, 267, 268, 270, 287, 289

D

Dana House (Springfield) 50, 53, 76, 79, 160
Donovan, Thomas 153, 155, 156
Drummond, Ruth Janet (Lute) 250, 254, 274, 286, 290
Drummond, William 51, 66, 68, 69, 77, 88

E

Elgh, George 143, 154, 195

F

Fairies Feeding the Herons (mural), (Chicago) 240, 245, 246, 299
First World War
  anti-Americanism 145
  breakout 141
  Marion's comments 145, 146
Fishwick, Thomas 228, 229, 243, 253
Ford, Henry 67, 126, 130, 134, 293, 302
Forest Portraits 2, 175, 179, 195, 207, 224, 295, 296, 297, 299, 305, 307
Franklin, Stella Miles 116, 117, 128, 148, 165, 192, 225, 229, 307

G

Greater Sydney Development Association (GSDA) 189, 191, 192, 201, 207, 208, 222, 225, 231, 232
Griffin, George 237, 270
Griffin, Walter Burley

Café Australia 159, 160–162, 165–166
Capitol Theatre 194–196
childhood 92
death 287
fights with Australian bureaucrats 140, 144, 148, 182
founding Castlecrag 188–191, 192, 200–201, 206
friendship with King O'Malley 118, 151, 152, 188, 189
incinerators 227, 243, 253, 254
inspiration by Louis Sullivan 45, 203, 266
interest in Anthroposophy 243, 251
marriage to Marion 95–96
Newman College (Melbourne) 153–157, 171
work in India 255, 263–271, 275–278, 279–284, 285–287
work in Mason City 121–124
work on design of Australian capital 103–114, 115, 166
work with Wright 45, 52, 56, 57, 93
Gumnuts Cottage (Frankston, Victoria) 181, 183

H

Haven Theatre (Castlecrag) 250, 271, 294, 305
Hayden, Sophia 28, 29, 151, 172
Heidelberg (Victoria) 171, 183, 185, 221, 334, 337
Henry, Alice 116, 117, 165
Herbert, Grace 239
Herbert, Wanda 215, 216, 219, 236, 238, 245, 249
Hiroshige, Utagawa 38, 56, 59, 60
Holman, Ada 149, 150, 157
Hookey, Mabel 175, 178
Hughes, William Morris (Billy) 152, 163, 164, 169, 182
Hull House (Chicago) 26, 38, 39, 44, 104, 117

I

Ickes, Harold 256, 257, 258, 267
Incinerators 227, 243, 253, 254

K

Kanevsky, Nisson Leonard 227, 243
K.C. de Rhodes House (Indiana) 66, 93
Kelly, W.H. 126, 140, 141

L

Leeson, Ida 230, 231, 251, 273, 295
Lightfoot, Louise 206, 207, 218, 219, 220, 221, 222, 224, 230, 237, 238, 290, 296, 297
Lincoln, Abraham 2, 14, 19, 20, 28, 35, 178, 336
Lippincott, Roy 73, 105, 111, 131, 157, 183, 195, 300
Lloyd, Lola Maverick 293
Lucas, A.J.J. 159, 162, 165, 166, 168, 180, 194, 195, 197
Lucknow 254, 255, 263, 264, 265, 337
Lutyens, Sir Edwin 212, 260, 261, 264, 306

M

MacDougall, Pakie 226, 229
Maddocks, Deirdre 248, 249, 256, 270, 273, 306, 336
Maddocks, Ula 210, 211, 212, 213, 214, 247, 248, 249, 252, 254, 256, 258, 259, 264, 266, 267, 270, 273, 274, 277, 287, 306, 336
Mahony, Clara 9, 10, 11, 13, 14, 17, 19, 20, 21, 22, 47, 67, 119, 134, 202, 216, 250
Mahony, Gerald 8, 13, 21, 36, 61, 84, 216, 294
Mahony, Jeremiah (Jere) 9, 10, 11, 13, 14, 15, 20, 21, 53
Mahony, Marion Lucy
    Amberg House, Grand Rapids 75–76
    at MIT 27–30
    birth 9
    childhood 9–11, 13–15, 17–23, 26
    death 297
    design of Australian federal capital 103–113, 166
    dispute with Richard Reeves 168, 170–171
    establishment of Castlecrag 188, 190, 191, 200–201, 206

Fairies Feeding the Herons 240–241
fight with Florence Taylor 149–150
Forest Portraits 177, 224, 296
friendship with Louise Lightfoot 206–207, 218, 290, 296
friendship with Ula Maddocks 210, 247–248, 258, 267, 273
Haven Amphitheatre 250, 251, 262, 294, 305
Henry Ford house 126, 130, 134
interest in Anthroposophy 213, 242
leaves Walter 239
love of acting, plays 28, 32, 53, 219, 220, 250–251, 271, 272, 290
marriage to Walter 95–96
Mason City 121–124
Millikin Place, Decatur 76–80
observations on Australia 145, 147–148, 235
return to the US 292
travel to India 273–275
trip to Tasmania 174–179
work on Café Australia 159–162, 165–166
work with Dwight Perkins 30–32, 33
work with Frank Lloyd Wright 33–39, 41–45, 47–53, 55–63, 65–68, 72, 93, 94
work with Hermann von Holst 68–70, 73–74, 80
Mannix, Daniel 153, 154, 155, 156, 164
Manson, Grant Carpenter 300
Mason City (Iowa) v, 66, 68, 69, 73, 77, 88, 120, 121, 124, 134, 143, 154, 169, 189, 190, 229, 309, 334, 335
Massachusetts Institute of Technology (MIT) 6, 26, 27, 28, 30, 33, 34, 36, 37, 68, 93, 151, 172, 220, 221, 256, 292
Melba, Dame Nellie 165, 166
Melson, Joshua 73, 120, 121, 122, 123, 124, 126, 132, 134, 154, 189, 190, 191, 228, 335
Menzies, Sir Robert 304, 305
Merfield, Bertha 158, 161, 174
Miller, David 140, 141
Millikin Place, houses (Decatur) 76, 77, 78, 81, 84, 99, 142, 302, 334, 335

Moon Children fountain 50
Mount Ainslie (Canberra) 4, 107, 108, 111, 112, 113, 122, 291, 309
Mower House (Castlecrag) 216, 225, 290
Mueller, Adolph and Robert Houses (Decatur) 73, 76, 77, 78, 79, 80, 81, 82, 99, 109, 142, 302, 306, 307, 308, 335

N

New Delhi 212, 260, 261, 264
Newman College (Melbourne) v, 153, 154, 156, 162, 166, 167, 171, 191, 202, 305, 306, 309
Nicholls, Eric ii, 4, 54, 102, 113, 124, 158, 186, 187, 193, 216, 227, 228, 233, 243, 252, 261, 262, 271, 273, 282, 288, 290, 292, 296, 299
Niedecken, George 50, 76, 78

O

Oak Park studio (Chicago) 42, 43, 45, 47, 49, 50, 53, 55, 59, 67, 68, 69, 71, 73, 76, 83, 91, 93, 121, 159, 300
Olmsted, Frederick Law 106, 108
O'Malley, King 118, 125, 126, 132, 140, 151, 152, 163, 169, 170, 182, 188, 189, 191, 201, 208, 295
Owen, Percy 141, 182

P

Pankhurst, Adela 165
Peisch, Mark L. 296, 300, 301, 313, 317, 318, 324, 329, 331
Perkins, Augustus 14, 18
Perkins, Dwight 13, 25, 37, 57, 292, 299, 306, 312, 335, 336
Perkins, Lawrence 301, 303, 329, 336
Perkins, Lucy Fitch 63
Perkins, Marion Heald 20
Pholiota (Heidelberg) 184, 185, 186, 187, 207, 221, 325
Purcell, William Gray 2, 129, 133, 143, 203, 204, 292, 295, 317, 324
Pynor, Henry 203, 204, 264

R

Raja of Jahangirabad 268, 269, 282
Raja of Mahmudabad 269, 283, 286
Reeves, Robert Henry vi, 167, 168, 170, 171, 322
Reverberatory Incinerator and Engineering Company (RIECo) 227

S

Saarinen, Eliel 303
Simonds, Ossian Cole 77, 92
Smith, James Alexander 125, 144, 296, 316, 319, 331, 335
Steiner, Rudolf 213, 234, 235, 236, 241, 242, 244, 250, 255, 305, 326
Steinway Hall (Chicago) 5, 31, 32, 33, 35, 36, 37, 38, 41, 42, 45, 55, 57, 68, 69, 71, 77, 85, 90, 103, 105, 142, 195, 203, 285
Sullivan, Louis 31, 33, 34, 35, 37, 38, 45, 55, 106, 133, 162, 195, 203, 266, 302, 306, 313, 331

T

Tasmania 172, 174, 175, 176, 177, 178, 179, 240
Taylor, Florence 136, 149, 150, 151, 320, 330, 337
Taylor, George 136, 149, 163, 174, 211
Theosophical Society 210, 211, 212, 214, 237
Towler, William Alfred 180, 181
Town Planning Association 149, 151, 321
Tremont (Illinois) 9, 14, 17, 19, 20, 27, 76, 214, 312
Twain, Mark 103, 135, 178, 317, 320

U

Unity Temple (Chicago) 57, 58, 59, 62, 66, 80, 154
Universal Portland Cement Company 62
University of Lucknow 255
University of Melbourne 153, 170, 206, 324, 325, 332

V

Von Holst, Hermann 68, 72, 73, 80, 315, 319
Voussoirs 122, 123, 191

W

Wade, Leslie 142, 145
Wasmuth Portfolio 66, 69, 84, 94, 111, 133, 259, 300, 301, 302, 314, 330
Willoughby Council 237, 245, 253, 294
Willoughby Incinerator 253
Wilmarth, Anna 32, 53, 256, 258, 292, 312
Wilmarth, Mary Hawes 26
World Fellowship Center (New Hampshire) 293
World's Columbian Exposition (Chicago) 29, 30, 102, 275, 312
Wright, Catherine (Kitty) Tobin 42, 43, 53, 55, 56, 65, 66, 69, 70, 72, 204, 249
Wright, Frank Lloyd 1, 2, 3, 6, 33, 40, 44, 46, 64, 69, 93, 137, 143, 210, 292, 294, 295, 300, 302, 313, 314, 317, 318, 319, 320, 330, 331, 332, 333
Wright, John 71
Wright, Maginel 88

Y

Young, Desmond 266, 268, 271, 272, 275, 284
Young, Ella Flagg 20, 21

www.ingramcontent.com/pod-product-compliance
Lightning Source LLC
Chambersburg PA
CBHW071619170426
43195CB00038B/1427